Small Time Operator

HOW TO START YOUR OWN SMALL BUSINESS, KEEP YOUR BOOKS,
PAY YOUR TAXES, & STAY OUT OF TROUBLE

A Guide and Workbook
by Bernard Kamoroff, C.P.A.

Small Time Operator discusses common types of laws and regulations affecting small businesses, including a general discussion of federal income tax laws. The information presented herein is meant to serve as a general guideline only. The information given is not intended to substitute for legal advice and cannot be considered as making it unnecessary to obtain such advice. In all situations involving local, state or federal law, obtain specific information from the appropriate government agency or from a competent person.

The word, once printed, cannot be altered. The laws, however, change all the time. Use the information in **Small Time Operator** with this in mind.

You can keep this book up to date. This edition of **Small Time Operator** is current as of the date shown below. Every January, we publish a one-page **Update Sheet for Small Time Operator**, listing changes in tax laws and other government regulations, referenced to the corresponding pages in the book. If you would like a copy of the Update Sheet, send a self-addressed, stamped No. 10 envelope and $1.00 to Bell Springs Publishing, Box 640, Laytonville, CA 95454.

Published by
BELL SPRINGS PUBLISHING
P. O. Box 640
Laytonville, California 95454

Revised Edition, 27th printing, April 1986

Printed in the United States of America

Library of Congress Catalog Number: 86-70180

ISBN: 0-917510-06-2

"Small Time Operator" is a trademark of Bell Springs Publishing.

In this world a man must either
be anvil or hammer.

—Longfellow

BE YOUR OWN BOSS

You can be your own boss. All it really requires is a good idea, some hard work, and a little knowledge. "A little knowledge" is what this book is all about. *Small Time Operator* will show you how to start and operate your own small business.

Small Time Operator is a technical manual, a step-by-step guide to help you set up the "machinery" of your business—the "business end" of your business—and keep it lubricated and well maintained. It is written in everyday English so anyone can understand it. You will not need a business education or an accounting dictionary to grasp the concepts or do the work. *Small Time Operator* is also a workbook that includes book-keeping instructions and a complete set of ledgers, especially designed for small businesses.

Many people think businessmen and businesswomen all come out of business school, kind of like Chevys coming out of a G.M. assembly plant. This just isn't true. I know many people in business who had no formal business education and little or no experience. They are people just like you and me who got tired of the nine-to-five life, tired of working for someone else, and who decided to go into business *for themselves*. They have done it, and so can you.

Business, to many inexperienced people, is a mystifying and often maligned world. You mention the word, and they start thinking about giant corporations and oil monopolies. Businessmen, business suits, big business. The words conjure up images of subways and elevators crowded with men, all dressing alike, all talking alike, all thinking alike. To most people, business means *big business*, the world of the office and the corporation.

But there is such a thing as a small business, and the difference between big business and small business is more than just size. Men and women involved in big business work for someone or some company. They are employees. They have a job and they do it (or else they get fired). A small business, one that you yourself have created and that you yourself run, is completely different. You are your own boss. You are the person who is going to make the business work if it's going to work at all.

Small Time Operator comes out of my experience during the past fifteen years as a financial advisor and tax accountant for small businesses, businesses started from scratch by inexperienced people, and from operating two of my own small businesses. I've learned from successes and I've learned from mistakes—my own and others'. Now I hope to teach you what I've learned.

Small Time Operator will show you things to do and things not to do. But like any book, it can't do more than that. You've got to go ahead and do it yourself. Bilbo Baggins said, "One should always begin at the beginning." That's where you are now. Other people—many others—now run their own small businesses. You can too.

The journey of a thousand miles begins with a single step.

—Lao Tzu

Contents

Foreword: Be Your Own Boss 7

SECTION ONE: GETTING STARTED 11

A Small Time Operator: A True Story 13

What Kind of Business? 13

Can You Do It? 14

The Market 16

Business Location 16

Before You Act 18

Financing: How Much Do You Need? 18

Stalking the Elusive Business Loan 20

   Small Business Administration 21

   Limited Partnerships 22

   Venture Capital 23

Sole Proprietorship: The Traditional One Person Business 23

Some Technicalities and Legalities 24

   Fictitious Name Statement 24

   Local Business License 25

   Other Local Permits 25

   State Occupational Licenses 26

   Sales Tax and Seller's Permits 26

   Other State Regulations 27

   Federal Identification Numbers 27

   Federal Permits and Regulations 27

Insurance 30

Initial Cash Outlays 32

Choosing a Business Name 33

SECTION TWO: BOOKKEEPING 35

Warming Up to An Unpopular Subject 37

Why Keep a Set of Books 37

Setting Up Your Books 38

Business Bank Accounts 38

An Introduction to the Single Entry System 39

Cash Accounting Vs. Accrual 40

Recording Income 40

The Income Ledger 42

Sales Returns 43

Return (Bounced) Checks 44

A Simple Credit Ledger 45

Direct Credit Sales 46

Credit Cards 47

The Expenditure Ledger 48

Petty Cash 52

Calculators and Adding Machines 53

Computers 55

Profit and Loss Analysis 56

Cash Flow 57

Inventory Control 59

SECTION THREE: GROWING UP 61

Growing Up 63

Hiring Help 65

Steps to Becoming an Employer 68

Payroll Ledgers 71

Partnerships 73

Partnership Bookkeeping 75

You, Incorporated: A Corporation Primer 78

S Corporations 80

Steps to Incorporating a Business 80

SECTION FOUR: TAXES 83

Deep in the Heart of Taxes 85

Accounting Period: Calendar Year vs. Fiscal Year 86

Tax Calendar for Businesses 87

Who Must File a Tax Return 90

Business Expenses 90

Non-Deductible Expenses 103

Investment Tax Credit 103

Self-Employment Tax 105

Retirement Deductions 107

Estimated Tax Payments 108

Operating Losses 108

The Internal Revenue Service and You   110

Federal Excise Taxes   113

State Taxes   113

Inventory (Floor) Tax   114

SECTION FIVE: APPENDIX   115

How to Balance a Bank Account   117

Balance Sheets   119

Seeking Professional Help   121

Cash Method of Accounting   121

A Special Chapter for Farmers   122

Husband & Wife Partnerships   124

Filing Your Business Records   125

Access: A Small Business Encyclopedia/Catalog/Bibliography   126

SECTION SIX: THE LEDGERS   145—188

Income Ledgers

Year-End Income Summary

Credit Ledger

Expenditure Ledgers

Year-End Expenditure Summary

Depreciation Worksheets/Equipment Ledgers

Payroll Ledger

ACKNOWLEDGEMENTS   189

INDEX   190

Section One
GETTING STARTED

Trying seems to be a start for getting things done
You get to know the right way by doing it wrong
And when you cross a bridge over shallow water
Does it always mean you're afraid to get wet
When you ought to?

—Barbara Pack

A Small Time Operator: A True Story

When I first met Joe several years ago, he was working as a switchman for Southern Pacific. He liked working on the railroad—didn't love it, but it was a job.

Joe's hobby and one of his great pleasures in life was electronics. He especially enjoyed assembling electrical gadgets from kits, repairing old radios, playing with anything that had wires and resistors. In the process of building and experimenting, Joe also acquired a good theoretical and technical knowledge of radio and electronics. It was not long before he'd built himself a few test meters and started repairing the neighbors' TV's and radios. He used to offer to fix my stereo for free, just to get the experience.

Gradually, Joe's hobby developed into a business. He moved slowly at first, a step at a time. He set up a small test bench in the spare bedroom and began taking in paying business on evenings and weekends. Joe was a good repairman, he didn't charge very much, and he gave his customers fast service. And Joe's business grew. He soon found himself with more business than he could handle in his spare time. He started working less hours for the railroad, then quit altogether and set up a small repair shop of his own.

Joe is a success, but not just because he makes his own living. Joe has shaped his life around his interests. He enjoys his work, and his customers recognize and appreciate the personal interest he takes in what he's doing. Joe "made it" because he worked hard to develop his interests and because he had the ambition to learn his trade. It *never* just

comes naturally. Prior experience? He had none. A business background? None. Money? He saved a few hundred dollars to spend on test gear and parts, not much more.

The most important lesson to learn from Joe, I feel, is that you can start out easily and simply. You don't have to make the Big Plunge, selling everything you own and going into debt. Start slowly, try it out and learn as you go. You'll get there.

Things worked well for Joe. But if they had not—if he really did not have it in him to be in business for himself, or if he just picked the wrong thing at the wrong time — he could easily have stopped anywhere along the way with little or no loss. And maybe try it again sometime.

What Kind of Business?

Joe's repair shop is an example of what is commonly called a "service" business. He *does* something for his customers and they pay him for his services. You can also support yourself by *selling* something ("sales") or by *making* something ("manufacturing"). Many businesses combine several of these aspects, such as manufacturing and sales, or sales and service.

A *service* business is the easiest to set up. It requires the smallest initial investment and the simplest bookkeeping. It is also the easiest kind of business to operate out of your own home. On the other hand, you will have to be reasonably competent at the service you render. More than any other business, service will require some experience. The owner of a service business is also more likely to be subject to state licenses and regulations (discussed in the Technicalities and Legalities chapter).

If you do something well—fixing things, painting or decorating, writing or editing, cutting hair—these are all possibilities for your own service business. And if you are good at something, you might consider teaching those skills to others. Be imaginative. Don't ignore your own resources.

A *sales* business can take many different forms: retail, wholesale, storefront, mail order, door-to-door. Your own sales business allows you to select and handle merchandise that reflects your own interests and tastes and your personal estimate of the needs of your community. Most sales businesses will require inventory—stock on hand—which means a bigger investment than a service business. You are also more likely to need a storefront to display your goods. You will have to keep inventory records. Bookkeeping is a little more complex. Sales businesses, however, offer more flexibility than service. Service people are often limited by their training and experience. With sales, as your interests change and as the fashions change, it is easy for your sales business to change with them.

Manufacturing, for most small businesses, means crafts—leather, clothing, pottery, jewelry and furniture to name a very few. Crafts offer, probably more than any other business, an opportunity for the craftsperson to do what he or she enjoys for its own pleasure, and get paid for it, too.

A crafts business, on the other hand, is probably the most risky business of all. You will need money to invest in your materials and your tools. Again, you have to be good at what you're doing. Nobody wants an ugly necklace or a chair that falls apart. And more than with a simple sales or service business, you will have more work finding a steady and reliable market for your product. But if you have imagination and talent, you might discover that what you think of as your hobby can become your source of income.

Find a need and fill it.
— Lettered on a concrete truck in Oakland, California

Mike Madsen owns Easy Rider Leather, Oakland, California: "Look around, figure out what you want to do, and then try to sum up your business in one sentence or a paragraph at the most. No more than that or you haven't done it. And then concentrate on doing just that. Realize that business is just like life in a lot of ways, and you take things step by step. You don't become a big business overnight. You build it little by little every day you walk into the building. You get started through your own will and determination and have a little fun at it.

"You can learn an awful lot by observation. Anyone in a small business should try to visit other people who are in similar businesses. When I was in Argentina I went to seven leather factories. They're very willing to show you something when you're not in direct competition, and they're kind of pleased to show off their business. But if you and I lived in the same city, you might be less willing to show your manufacturing process to a future competitor.

"Small business is the backbone of this country. Big businesses provide main line products, but it's the small business that provides all the little things that make your life interesting. I think it's also the kind of people who are in small business, those of a pioneering spirit. We built a country on pioneering spirit. That's just what being in a small business is, being a pioneer."

Can You Do It?

You don't have to be an expert in the line of business that you're thinking of going into, but you do have to be willing to learn. There are people who actually try to start a certain business because it's a "sure thing," a "guaranteed" big seller, and they know absolutely nothing about the field. Some of these people are, of course, real hustlers, selling refrigerators to Eskimos and all that. Not my favorite kind of people. But there are also a lot of honest dopes in this group. They think that a little money and some good intentions are all they need to get started. And most of them soon wind up with neither their money nor any intention of ever being in business again.

I've known a lot of people in business—some who made it, some who didn't. And while nobody has a

And Now a Warning About Fad Businesses
(Reprinted from *Rags* magazine)

Boutiques are a French invention. They're nothing more than small specialty shops, really, just like the Village Clothing Shoppe in Your Hometown, but 'boutique' is a French word and thus classier and vaguely risque. They were often located in the corners of hotels, serving tourists who wanted locally made goods without having to hassle with the language barrier.

In the trip across the Atlantic, however, the concept was changed. In the land of department stores, 100-shops-under-one-roof, the galloping homogenization of consolidation, boutiques served as an alternative. And like many alternatives to American culture, the boutique was seized on by the (you know) young. And the boutique emerged from its bourgeois cocoon and became hip.

And then it became hip to be hip, and there was no stopping it. Boutiques appeared like slugs after a spring rain. There were good boutiques and bad boutiques, plastic boutiques and natural-wood boutiques, psyche-delic boutiques and straight boutiques, smart boutiques and stupid boutiques—more boutiques, indeed, than there was room in the mind of God. It was not a pretty situation.

When times were good and everybody loved a boutique, a young designer named Susan Harris started a boutique on 6th Street in the East Village. It was called Okefenokee, and it was a success the day it opened. Susan and her store got a good reputation in the industry, and big manufacturers started trooping down to see where the action was. For the first five months of its life, Okefenokee doubled its gross income every month.

Six months later it was closed. Susan talks about why. "Right after Christmas the recession hit. Business began petering out. It just got worse and worse . . . Face it, this city is saturated with stores. Oversaturated."

The pinch is on, and the marginal boutiques—poorly run, poorly located, too new, too old, too imitative, too original—are going under. The business is alive with rumors about established names floundering and in more and more stores the most frightening words of all are appearing, neatly lettered, on the backs of cash registers. "All sales final", they say. "Everything must go."

guaranteed secret for success in business, I believe that there are a few basic characteristics that you've got to have or be willing to develop if you're going to start a business, *any* business

The first and most important characteristic, I feel, is a clear head and the ability to organize your mind and your life. The "absent-minded professor" may be a genius, but he will never keep a business together. In running a small business, you are going to have to deal with many different people, keep schedules, meet deadlines, organize paperwork, pay bills, and the list goes on. It's all part of every business. So if balancing your checkbook is too much for you, or you just burned up your car engine because you forgot the oil, maybe you're not cut out for business. The work in a small business is rarely complicated, but it has to be done and done on time. Remember, this is going to be *your* business. It's all up to you.

A second important characteristic is the ability to read carefully. Most of your business transactions

will be handled on paper, and if you don't pay attention to what you're doing, you could miss out. You may receive special orders for your product. You will be billed by your suppliers in all kind of ways, sometimes offering discounts if you are prompt in paying. You will have to fill out a lot of government forms. Government agencies can't exist without forms, and the instructions for these forms are sometimes tricky. If you mess up, these agencies having the most aggravating way of casually telling you that you're going to have to do it all over again.

A third important trait is, if not a "head for numbers," at least a lack of fear of numbers. Tax accountants get rich off of people who look at a column of six numbers and panic. It doesn't have to be that way. The math involved in running a small business is mostly simple arithmetic—addition, subtraction, some multiplication.

Is all of this too much for you? Still feel you have a good product to sell but, Oh! all this paperwork.... If you are alone in you venture, short of hiring a bookkeeper or finding a partner, there is no alternative. You're gonna have to learn to do it. Very often, however, the future business owner with no business moxie is blessed with a wife or husband who has all those fine traits and is just itchin' to be part of it all.

Mike Snead, owner of Ms. Perc Leather, San Francisco: "Our business grew incredibly fast, and word of mouth helped us a whole lot. So did the fact that we were one of a kind at a time, sociologically, when that kind of business was ripe to own. The hippie concept was brand new and it generated a lot of curiosity, and the curiosity generated sales. I don't know if that can happen now. It's no longer unique. As a matter of fact, it's pretty much the status quo, and I suspect it's going to be one of the things people will rebel against on their way to the next new thing. And whoever it is who has some concept of what's coming next will be in the same position we were in.''

The Market

Now here's one more thing to remember. No matter how good your business idea is, you still must have a market—someone who is willing to buy your product or pay for your services. Talk to your friends; they're consumers. How many of them would buy what you have to sell? Then look around your community. How many other people are doing the same thing? What would it be like to compete with them? Don't be afraid to talk with your future competition. You will learn a lot from them, not only about the business but also about your chances for success. A new business always starts at a disadvantage. Try not to duplicate services already available in your area unless you have good reason to believe that you can attract customers away from existing businesses.

Mike Simon, owner of Metric Motors, Palm Springs, California: "There are some people who want to work for themselves, and they're not going to be happy working for anybody else. And then other people don't like the responsibility. They want to go in and work their nine to five and not have to worry about it when they go home. It takes a certain kind of person to do your own business, to accept the responsibilities of it and be thinking abut it all the time. The first two years I worked, I worked seven days a week from seven o'clock in the morning until seven o'clock at night. And now I take Sundays off. But I wouldn't have it any other way. I could have made a lot more money the other way, working for somebody else, but I'm happy with the way it is. And I think later in the future it will be to my advantage. As for the guy who's working nine to five, I'll be better off than he is. Of course, he thinks he's better off than I am.''

Business Location

Your choice of location will be one of the most important decisions you will make when going into business, so consider it carefully. Most people want to locate in their own neighborhood, but is it a good

If you can't do it excellently, don't do it at all. Because if it's not excellent it won't be profitable or fun, and if you're not in business for fun or profit, what the hell are you doing here?

—Robert Townsend from *Up the Organization*

business area? How many people shop in your neighborhood? Is there adequate parking? Is there already a similar business in the area?

Before you rent a storefront, find out why it's vacant in the first place. Try to locate the former tenant and ask him why he moved. Talk to other shopkeepers in the area and learn as much as you can about the area and its shoppers. A nearby supermarket or discount store is usually a plus because it will draw a lot of people to your area. Be wary if there are several unoccupied buildings for rent. Besides being a general sign of a poor business area, vacant buildings make poor neighbors. Shoppers tend to stay away from them—and from you. Spend a full day or two observing the area. A steady stream of pedestrians passing by your door is the biggest single help a little store can get.

Before you sign a rental agreement, be sure the building is right for you. Is it large enough, or is it perhaps too large? Will it require extensive remodeling? Can you afford it? Can you get a suitable lease? Have the store examined by the local building inspector and, if you plan to serve food, by the health inspector. You don't want to learn *after* you've moved in that you must spend $300 to bring the toilet up to code.

"As far as I'm concerned, location is everything." Lara Stonebraker, Cunningham's Coffee in Oakland, California: "That can make or break a business. If you don't already have an established reputation, nobody will go looking for you in some obscure place. So you have to be where there is a lot of foot traffic, and you have to be located next to some other significant business that already has a clientele you can draw on.

"The corner is obviously the best choice, and you usually have to pay more rent for it. The middle of the block is less desirable because there isn't the visibility that a corner affords and there's not as much parking. Parking can be a great problem. I've known a lot of very fine businesses to fail because people would just get exasperated not being able to find a parking space and never go in them.

"One of the things we did at every location we looked at was spend a day just sitting around, hanging around, and watching the traffic flow, the patterns of the way people walk,

where they stopped, and how many people came in and out of different stores in order to assess the desirability of that location.

"When you negotiate your lease you want to be careful not to do it before you talk to the building inspector and the health inspector and find out what the building codes and health codes are for your particular business. We made the mistake of seeing them after we signed the lease and then discovered that we had to put in just a load of improvements that rightfully should not have been our responsibility. That was a tremendous amount of money which will just be lost. They don't check old businesses, but they check every new one. You apply for a permit; you have to get a business license, then they know what kind of business it is and they send out their people. If you're doing any kind of reconstruction inside and any electrical work, the plumber has to get a permit, the electrician has to get a permit—you can't get away from it. And they'll come around every six months to check and see that everything is up to code if you're handling food."

Joe Campbell owns Resistance Repair, a stereo repair shop in Berkeley, California. He recently moved his shop *away from* a high foot traffic area into a more remote section of town:

"In a service business, especially a technical service business, customers don't have the slightest idea how to determine even the most rudimentary things about their equipment. If it doesn't work, they don't have the means of determining what is wrong. So you get an incredible amount of people who come in and just bullshit with you about some problem which is extremely minor and usually is a hookup problem. They've just got it hooked up wrong, which means they didn't read their instruction book. But it's very hard to convince them of that, and they all want detailed explanations.

"If you're in a high foot traffic area, you get the guy who's going to the restaurant next door for lunch, and as he walks out he thinks, 'Ah, there's a stereo repair shop. I'll stop in here and ask this guy about my problem...' and he comes in and there's twenty minutes gone. And the next guy comes in and there's fifteen minutes gone. You get all the people in town who have wires that need to be soldered. You get people who come in and say, 'I need your recommendation of the fifteen best stereos you can buy, and why.' Just enormous energy sinks and time sinks. Those people do not spend money. The kind of people who spend money are the people who walk in the door with stereos under their arms, and say, 'Fix this mother, it doesn't work, and call me when it's ready.'

"My traffic was never off the street. It was from referrals from other stereo shops. I took around cards and there was such a big demand for a reasonable, good repair shop that they'd send people by. You don't need those twerks who walk in off the street. You need the people who have the confidence in you and, by reputation, know that they can dump it in your hands. Now, when somebody walks through that door they've either got a stereo under their arm or they're there to pick one up. If they're there to pick it up, that means when they leave you're going to have money in the cash register. If they're coming in the door with one, that means two weeks later you're going to have money in the cash register. Those are the only two reasons you want that front door to open."

Another Roadside Attraction

Perhaps you're thinking about moving out of the city altogether to set up a small business in the country. Many people try to open shops out there in the sticks, and a very large percentage of these rural shops fail. The reason is solely this: there are not enough people and not enough money in rural communities to support anything but the most basic businesses. The typical small town has a grocery, general store or hardware store, feed store, tavern and gas station. If the population is more than a few thousand, there may be a clothing store, a restaurant and a beauty parlor. Not much else.

A hanging plant store is not going to survive in West Pork Chop, Oklahoma. Nor will a gourmet coffee and tea shop, an art gallery or a leather crafts workshop. The business just isn't there. Service businesses—repair shops, trades—have the best chance of survival in a rural area. But even these will probably have to compete with established locals who already know everyone in town and have all the business.

If you are interested in setting up a "country store," first take a drive through some small towns and see what's there. If you do come across a shop

of the sort you have in mind, stop in and find out how they're doing, how long they've been there, and—if they'll tell you—any of their "secrets of success." When you have a particular area in mind, get to know the area and its inhabitants first before you try to set up a business. Ideally, you should live there a while, and then try to judge what product or service the people need. Nobody—least of all, country folk—is going to spend money on things they have no use for.

Before You Act

Let's say you've decided on an idea for a new business. Now comes the most important step:
  Ponder
   Think
    Relax
Let the idea simmer for a week or two and see how it feels then. Picture yourself as the owner-operator of the business you have in mind. Does it still sound like a good idea? This new business is going to take a lot of your time and energy. Above all else, it's got to feel right.

Lara Stonebraker, Cunningham's Coffee: "If you don't enjoy what you're doing, it's going to be very obvious to the customers. It will be obvious in your attitude. I find it very exciting, and I also find it a great challenge to try to make the business profitable. That's why I look at all the angles to decrease my expenses and bring in more income. I want to prove that I can do it. I don't just want a mediocre business, I want a booming business."

Financing: How Much Do You Need?

How much money you need depends a lot on the type of business you are starting and the type of person you are. If you are willing to work hard, to make a few sacrifices, to live on canned beans for a while, you can start a successful business for little or no investment.

Every service business I know started with almost no money. I started my accounting practice with a $30 adding machine and 500 business cards. My friend Joe Campbell started Resistance Repair with $300 worth of test equipment. Another friend's computer programming service was started with $10 in supplies. Self-employed carpenters, mechanics and repair people often start with their box of tools, period.

If you start a crafts business, you will need—besides your tools—raw materials to make your product. But you do not have to stock a large supply of inventory, and if you hunt around you can always find good deals on remnants and close-out materials. All of the craft business owners interviewed for this book started their businesses with less than $500 initial investment.

A retail store requires a good stock of inventory, which often costs at least a few thousand dollars. Kipple Antiques had an initial investment of $1,400. Lara Stonebraker's tiny coffee shop has a coffee and accessory inventory of over $10,000. A retail business can sometimes save on initial inventory costs by taking goods on consignment—as in a custom dress shop—or by having only samples on hand and taking orders for the goods.

Mike Simon, owner of Metric Motors (a repair shop): ''I started with basically nothing and built from that. I had a box of hand tools, and my partner had some heavy equipment, jacks and things like that, nothing very impressive. If I had to have a tool, I'd buy it and then I'd have it. I'd just keep going like that. I guess I have about $3,000 worth of equipment now. A lot of garage owners buy $20,000 worth of equipment right at the start and don't have the clientele to pay it off. I'd say starting out small would be a very smart thing to do. Find some place that's not expensive to rent, like this place. Don't put a lot of money into tools or inventory, and try to keep your costs down to a minimum until you can build your business up.

Lara Stonebraker's coffee shop (a retail store): ''The worst thing you can do is start a retail business on a shoestring. If you're under-capitalized in the beginning, your store will not be impressive when you open because it will be empty. There's nothing worse than walking into an empty store. It's just bound to fail because it embarrasses people. If you don't have your shelves just crammed with stuff, and if you don't have an attractive, prosperous looking store, you might as well forget it. And you really ought to have not only enough money to open the doors, but enough money to run the business for the first six months, because you'll be running it at a loss for sure.''

Jan Lowe, former owner of the Midnight Sewing Machine, Mendocino, California (clothing store): ''One of our biggest problems was that we started with zero capital. We had 37 cents to our name after we bought the shop. You can't really expect to start it out that way. You gotta have some kind of backing. I don't know what amount it would take, but I know 37 cents didn't make it.''

Key Dickason is the former co-owner of Xanadu Computer Service: ''We got the business on a no-cash deal. We just took over their accounts, and the only thing the prior owner wanted was that we continue the employees on. We didn't have to pay anything. We just took the equipment and the accounts and the employees.''

The fullness of time is here and now—and spring does not last forever. It is time to gather my energy and walk through the confusions and paradoxes, the opposing pulls and contradictory challenges, the desires and attachments, needs and programs and all kinds of fears and blocks, and get it on. This means getting centered on a path that is chosen for no better reason—and no worse—than that my intuition says "It feels right."

—River from *Dwellings*

Mike Snead, manager/operator of Ms. Perc Leather, San Francisco: "Starting on a shoe-string is a very viable concept. It's possible to start with nothing and build something up, but it in-volves a lot of sacrifices. It did for us."

Pat Ellington, Kipple Antiques, Berkeley, Califor-nia: "We started this business on $1,400 cash and a lot of work, a lot of energy. When my partner first approached me with the idea for the business, she asked, 'What do you think it will take—how much money?' I sat down and figured out cost sheets, budgets, projections. And the very best I could come up with for six months' operation was $15,000, which appalled her. But that was reasonable. It was as cheap as I could get it, because you've got to assume you're going to lose your shirt the first six months."

Mike Madsen, owner of Easy Rider Leather, Oakland, California: "I started by not wanting to work for someone else. It's a hard thing to define. You just have an idea, and put it together. It took $20 and an Austin Healey and a girlfriend in Santa Barbara."

Stalking the Elusive Business Loan: The Outlook for Borrowing Money

Right at the start, let me warn you not to expect sure-fire sources of loan money from this chapter of the book. It offers some guidelines, a few ideas to track down. But it also gives an honest, though not cheery, appraisal of the money situation. And the money situation is not good.

If your friends have no money to lend and the relatives are not going to help, you have two other possible sources of loan money: the "private sec-tor" (banks) and the "public sector" (Uncle Sam).

Private Sector Financing

Last year I attended a conference sponsored by the University of California on the subject of finan-cing new small business ventures. The panelists in-cluded the vice presidents of Bank of America, the second largest bank in the world, and Wells Fargo Bank, one of the largest banks in California. Both men had the same discouraging comment: loans are hard to get. The banks are less willing than ever to take chances on new and untested businesses and new and untested entrepreneurs. Bankers, it seems, forget quickly how they man-aged to get rich in the first place—by taking chances on ventures just like yours.

The door is not completely closed. Banks still make some small business loans, and a bank just may make one to you. Banks generally will lend up to 50% of the required starting capital if they can be convinced that your business has a good potential for success, that you are competent and reliable, and that you have a good plan for repayment of the loan.

Not All Banks Are Alike

Put on your Sunday Best (or borrow your brother-in-law's), screw up your courage, and visit several local banks. Mornings early in the week are the best time. "Friday afternoon financing" is rarely, if ever, available. A young and progressive bank is more likely to be interested in you and your needs than staid old First Conservative, Est. 1833. The physical appearance of the bank and the character of the bank's advertising may give you some indica-tion of its progressiveness.

Too many entrepreneurs think extra cash will solve most every problem. But good management—not money— is the key to whether a business flourishes or dies. According to one prominent business authority, "If a company has everything except good management, it may prosper awhile, but eventually it will fold. On the other hand, if a company's strongest asset is good man-agement, it will make the grade."

—from *Avoiding Management Pitfalls*, Bank of America

When you meet a banker, sell yourself. Openly discuss your plans and difficulties with him (or her). Come well prepared. Bring a personal resume, which should include your general and educational background and your prior experience. Bring a personal financial statement and a statement projecting income and expenses of your business for the first six months or year. The chapters "Profit And Loss Analysis" and "Cash Flow" in the bookkeeping section will help you to prepare this projection.

If you have done business with or obtained a loan from a particular bank, that bank is a good place to start. When a bank knows you, knows something of your willingness and capability to repay a loan, it will be more willing to give serious consideration to your ideas. If you have collateral, security to give the bank in exchange for a loan, you are yet another step closer to cash-in-hand. If you own your own home (if there is a mortgage on your home, you still "own" it) and are willing to mortgage it further, a bank may very likely loan you money on it.

But stop! Are you ready to risk your home or other valuables on your new business venture? When you borrow money for your business, you are *personally* liable to pay it back. If the business fails, you will be required to repay the loan from your personal funds. In taking out a loan, you are making a big personal commitment. Be sure you are not getting yourself in over your head.

Banks, when granting loans, will usually require you to take out property and liability insurance on your business and a personal life insurance policy naming the bank as beneficiary.

Other Possible Loan Sources

If you own a life insurance policy and have been making payments for at least a few years, you can probably borrow on the "cash value" of your policy. Most long-term life insurance policies acquire a cash value within a few years. That is, the policy is worth money to you. If you were to cash in your policy, you would receive that money—sort of a refund. As long as you keep the policy, you cannot get the money, but you can borrow as much as your cash value from the insurance company. The insurance policy remains effective during the loan. Interest rates on insurance policy loans are substantially lower than bank interest rates. Your own insurance agent can give you all the details.

The company that sells you your equipment may also "loan" you money in the form of credit. Most manufacturers have financing plans allowing you to buy your equipment on the installment basis. Commercial finance companies also offer short-term loans for purchase of equipment and inventory.

Your wholesalers or suppliers may also extend short-term credit. But if you are new to the world of business, you may have difficulty proving your credit worthiness. You will probably have to operate C.O.D. with your suppliers until you are a little better established.

Public Sector Financing:
The Small Business Administration

I blow hot and cold on government agencies and on the reliability and consistency of government policy. Too much depends on politics and the whims of whoever is in power this year.

With that little bit of a warning, you may want to investigate, and you may even get your money from, the United States Small Business Administration (SBA). The SBA has a variety of loan programs for new and expanding "small" businesses. But watch out here: by government definition, a "small" business is one with as much as $22 million in yearly sales and as many as 1,500 employees! So there are a lot of big businesses in these small business programs.

The loan program most applicable to new business ventures is one the SBA calls the 7(a) Program, also known as the Loan Guarantee Plan. Under this program, a commercial bank loans you money and the SBA guarantees up to 90% of the loan. The maximum 7(a) loan is usually $500,000 with a 7-10 year payback period. The bank sets the terms and interest rate of the loan.

The only direct SBA loans normally available to small businesses (money loaned to you directly by the SBA) are made through their 7(a)11 Program. These loans are made to "economically and socially disadvantaged" businesses—primarily blacks, Native Americans and Spanish speaking people. The 7(a)11 loan ceiling is $150,000 and you have up to 25 years to repay. The interest rate is somewhat lower than the regular 7(a) rate.

The SBA will make loans for up to 70% of your starting capital (as opposed to a 50% bank maximum). You will be expected to have some of your own capital invested in your business.

SBA loans are only available to people who have been unsuccessful in obtaining financing through the private sector. In other words, first the bank has to turn you down. Then the government may step in. To get an SBA loan, you will have to convince them that you have the ability to operate a business successfully and that the loan can be repaid from the earnings of your business.

The SBA makes or guarantees only about 32,000 loans per year, and only about 30% of the available loan funds go to new businesses. The bulk of the money is lent to existing and expanding small businesses.

SBA loans also come with strings attached. The agency has a set of operating guidelines you must follow, which limits your freedom and flexibility somewhat. The SBA will periodically audit your books, which can be both a help and a nuisance.

There are 86 SBA field offices in the country. Contact the one closest to you or write Small Business Administration, Washington, D.C. 20416.

I met with an SBA loan officer in San Francisco and presented this hypothetical situation: A young man wishes to open a small repair business. He's had experience working for someone else, and his boss gave him a good recommendation. He is industrious, clear headed and willing to work hard. The neighborhood where he wants to open his business is a good one and in need of a repair shop. He has $1,300 of his own money to invest, and he wants to borrow $3,000 more. Will the SBA loan him the money?

The officer said, "Maybe. And maybe not. I would recommend that he get the loan, but then it's up to my supervisor who must review and approve all applications."

I said, "And whether he approves or not can depend as much on the mood he's in that day as the merit of the application."

And he said, "Yep."

Pat Ellington, Kipple Antiques: "There's no point in even going to a bank and talking to them unless you can say 'Well, we've been operating now for two years, and we've established a certain track record, and we want to expand. We've got our books, our balance sheets, and we've got good references, some people do ex-

tend us credit.' I know that from my own credit experience. If you go there armed with a certain amount of paperwork, a certain kind of history, you'll have fewer problems dealing with them.

''I have mixed feelings about SBA loans. Sometimes they can be gotten easily, but it's sort of like by magic. And other times, no matter what you give them, no matter what sound business approach you give them, they're deaf to you. Officers in the SBA say how far you get there really depends on who you know. That's kind of discouraging. It's like grantsmanship. There's a whole lot to applying, and if you don't have the art, you don't get the grant.''

Investors

When a bank or an individual lends you money, you promise to repay the loan whether your business succeeds or not. You also pay a set interest rate.

When someone invests in your business, the investor earns a percent of the profits of the business. The investor shares the profits with the owner. The investor is taking a chance on the business. If the business fails, the investor loses his money. The owner of the business is not obligated to repay the investor unless the business succeeds.

What percentage of profits goes to the investor and what percentage to the owner of the business is something to be negotiated. A 50-50 split is the most common. I've known investors to accept as little as 30-35% of the profits; it's rare for an investor to get more than half. Investments can be for a specified, limited time or for the life of the business.

Two typical investment arrangements are limited partnerships and venture capital.

Limited Partnerships

Limited partners are not partners in the usual sense of the word. They are investors only. Their liability is limited to the amount of their investment. They are legally prohibited from participating in the management and operation of the business. Don't confuse a limited partner with a regular business partner who invests money in the business. Limited partnerships are very different from regular (general) partnerships. Both types of partnerships are discussed further in the Partnership chapters.

Venture Capital

Venture capitalists are a different breed of investor than limited partners. Limited partners are usually friends and relatives. Venture capitalists are usually wealthy and make their living as investors. Venture capitalists love to play with their money. They love new ideas and new products. They love to gamble, looking for the big payoff. And they invariably love to stick their noses in your business affairs. They are not restricted from management the way limited partners are. When you get financing from a venture capitalist you will be taking on a partner who not only wants a percent of the profits but may even want ownership control (51% interest) of your business.

Venture capitalists come in all guises. The majority of them are individuals and privately owned corporations. You may be able to locate one of these people through referral (talk to other business people) or in the Yellow Pages.

A new breed of venture capitalist is the Community Development Corporation (CDC), which combines public interest with private business investment. Many CDC's are non-profit, community sponsored and community operated organizations and many receive government grants. Their goal, in addition to making money on their investments, is to encourage small-scale local enterprises and to expand local job markets. To locate a CDC, contact a regional Community Action Agency, SBA office or state office of community affairs; or write the National Congress for Community Economic Development, 2025 I Street NW, Washington, D.C. 20036.

Venture capital is also available from Small Business Investment Companies (SBIC's) and Minority Enterprise Small Business Investment Companies (MESBIC's). SBIC's are licensed by the Small Business Administration but they are privately organized and privately managed firms; they set their own policies and make their own investment decisions. The SBA often makes loans to SBIC's so they can turn around and invest the money in your business. The National Association of Small Business Investment Companies (618 Washington Building, Washington, D.C. 20005) publishes a state by state directory of SBIC's; the directory also lists other venture capitalists. The Small Business Administration publishes a National Directory of SBIC's. Write the SBA, Washington, D.C., 20416.

Herbert Heaton, a well known business counselor, once described venture capital financing as "selling out before starting." Bill Friday, author of *Successful Management For One to Ten Employee Businesses* put it this way: "At best you will be taking on backseat drivers, and at worst you will get pushed to the back seat with an investor doing the driving." Caveat emptor.

Sole Proprietorship: The Traditional One Person Business

A one person business that has not incorporated is known as a "sole proprietorship." There are over 13 million small businesses in this country, and most of them are sole proprietorships. This form of business has flourished over the years because of the opportunities it offers to be boss, run the business, make the decisions and keep the profits. A sole proprietorship is the easiest form of business to start up. Despite all the regulations, it is the least regulated of all businesses.

You, the owner of the business, the sole proprietor, are your own man (or woman). You make or break your business, which may sound singularly appealing to those of you instilled with the entrepreneurial, pioneering spirit. But you also have sole responsibility as well as sole control. You and your sole proprietorship are one and the same in the eyes of the law. Any debts or obligations of the business are the personal responsibility of the owner. Damages from any lawsuits brought against the business can be exacted from the personal assets of the owner. You should be fully aware of these legal aspects of the sole proprietorship. If you get your business into legal trouble or too far into debt, not only could you lose your business, you could lose your shirt.

There is only one way to avoid the unlimited personal liability of the sole proprietor, and that is to incorporate your business. Generally speaking, the debts, obligations, and legal liability of a corporation are limited to the assets of the business and are not the personal responsibility of the owner (or owners). Corporations are discussed later in the book.

The owner of a sole proprietorship cannot hire himself as an employee. This is a point of law often misunderstood by new business people. You may withdraw from the business (i.e. pay yourself) as much or as little money as you want, but this "draw" is not a wage, you do not pay payroll taxes on it, and you cannot deduct the withdrawal as a business expense. The profit of your business, which is computed without regard to your personal draws, is your "wage" and must be included on your personal income tax return. If your business made a $10,000 profit last year, you personally owe taxes on $10,000. Even if you only withdrew $5,000 from the business, you still must pay taxes on $10,000. And if you withdrew $15,000, you still pay taxes only on $10,000. The sole proprietorship itself does not file income tax returns or pay income taxes. Owner's draw will be discussed in more detail in the bookkeeping and tax sections of the book.

When a husband and wife operate a business together, that business may be a sole proprietorship or it may be a partnership depending on several factors. The Appendix includes a chapter explaining husband-and-wife partnerships. Couples who plan to operate a business together should read this chapter before deciding how to structure their business.

Some Technicalities and Legalities

Licenses and Permits

The Lord's Prayer contains 56 words. Lincoln's Gettysburg Address has 268 words. The Declaration of Independence is 1,322 words long. Federal regulations governing the sale of cabbages are 26,911 words long.

When you open a new business, every government agency that can claim jurisdiction over you wants to get into the act. There are forms to file, permits and licenses to obtain, regulations and restrictions to understand and to heed. And, always, there are fees to pay.

Why all the government regulations? Why does water flow downhill? It's just the nature of government to regulate, license, permitize, officialize, "fees, fines and forms" you to death. Some of the laws were passed to protect the consumer public from unscrupulous or incompetent business people. Some were created solely to provide additional revenues to the government. Some...well, who knows.

Most business licenses and permits are required and administered by local governments: the city if you live within city limits; possibly the county. Some businesses must also have state and federal licenses. This chapter will describe the different types of licenses and permits typically required by states and municipalities and those currently required by the federal government. Regulations, however, vary from city to city and state to state; and they are changing and multiplying all the time, now more than ever. You should make it your responsibility to contact state and local government agencies (anonymously if you prefer) to learn the most recent requirements and restrictions.

Fictitious Name Statement (DBA)

When a business goes by any name other than the owner's real name, the business in being operated under a "fictitious name" (also known as a DBA which is short for "doing business as"). Country Comfort Carpentry, A-1 Market, Mad Creek Inn are all examples of fictitious names. People doing business under a fictitious name are required to file a Fictitious Name Statement with the county in which they do business. The county will charge a filing fee. Filing a Fictitious Name Statement prevents any other business in the county from using the same business name.

In addition to filing for the name, you will be required to publish the Fictitious Name Statement in a newspaper "of general circulation" in the area, the theory being that the public has a right to know with whom they are doing business. The county clerk can provide you with a list of acceptable newspapers. Publication costs can be relatively low if your county has one of those newspapers that specialize in running legal notices (and little else). If not, small-time newspapers almost always charge less than large-circulation dailies.

You will be required to renew your fictitious name periodically, usually once every five years. In many states, the county notifies you when your renewal is due. If you forget to renew, someone else can step in and file for your business name, and you will not be able to use it anymore.

You can usually avoid this form-filling, money-spending procedure by including your name in the "official" business name. My friend Rory Brice who makes redwood water tanks and hot tubs decided to call his business "Clear Heart Tank and Tub" until he found out about the fictitious name requirements. Not being too fond of legal requirements, Rory renamed his business "Brice's Clear Heart Tank and Tub", which took it out of the fictitious name category. This procedure, however, offers no protection against someone else who may decide to call his business "Clear Heart Tank and Tub".

For the specific fictitious name requirements for your locality, contact the county clerk's office, usually located in the county administration building at the county seat.

Corporations, unless operating under a name other than the official name of the corporation, do not need to file a Fictitious Name Statement.

Local Business Licenses

Just about every business in the country must get a local business license, which is merely a permit to do business locally. "Local" may refer to either the municipal or the county level and sometimes to both. Local business licenses can cost anywhere from ten dollars to as much as several hundred dollars and must be renewed annually or bi-annually. Businesses operating under a fictitious name will usually not be able to get the local license until they have filed the Fictitious Name Statement. Contact city hall or the county clerk for specifics.

Bob Matthews, owner of Country Comfort Carpentry: "I never filed a fictitious name statement. I like the name, and right on the checks and letterheads it says 'Country Comfort Carpentry' with my name immediately under it. I felt that's good enough. I never got a business license. I'm in a rural area, twenty miles from town. I feel that business licenses are a tax on people who work in town, to make them conform."

Other Local Permits

Your business may be required to conform to local zoning laws, building codes, health requirements, fire and police regulations. Restaurants, night clubs, taverns, groceries, child care homes and businesses in shopping centers in particular are likely to be subject to these additional regulations. I suggest that you contact your local government *before* you open your doors. You may find the regulations so demanding that you cannot afford to meet them. If you do not get the proper permits or meet the building requirements, the police can and will shut you down.

If we don't have it, you're out of luck.
   —Sign on a tiny general store in the middle of nowhere,
Branscomb, California

If it's in stock, we have it.
   —Sign in farm supply store, Ukiah, California

Key Dickason is a partner in Major Dickason's Blend, a coffee store in Concord, California: "My partner is an honest, law-abiding person, and what he wanted to do is have everything A-OK. Then he found out that to put in what the health inspectors required would cost about twelve hundred dollars: a three-compartment sink, all of the walls smooth in the restrooms, a six-inch moulding all around the bottom of the restrooms. The sink could not be in the location we wanted it, it had to be out in the storage room, the storage room had to be repainted. The main reason, well it's my opinion that the regulatory agencies are loaded with 'genus-clerks', and the only thing that they can see is the letter of the law. 'Genus' is Latin for family. It's a biological term. I say it's a sub-species of homo sapien, and you run across this type of person all the time. When they come in and you're serving coffee, they look up in their book and they say, 'Oh, serving beverages. It's a restaurant.' Then they say that you have to comply with this regulation and so forth and they cite book-and-verse.

"Now we've been in business a year and haven't done any of the things that they've recommended, but it was a big hassle. The reason we didn't do it is because we didn't have the money. When the health inspector comes, he looks around, he says, 'Oh, the place is clean, it's nice', this is it. There's no pressure at all to comply with the written directive which they gave us. If they plan to shut us down, then they'd say, 'You have thirty days in which to comply.' Well, then you do it.

"The laws are written—the health laws, the motor vehicle laws—for health reasons, for safety reasons. In the case of the health laws, it's to prevent people from getting sick from eating restaurant food. So they make these regulations and they apply to restaurants, but if you're just serving coffee in paper cups, well it doesn't apply. But you take a genus-clerk and they've got to enforce the law exactly. To the letter. You run into 'em everywhere. And the spirit of the law is to prevent illness. But, you see, they can't make that distinction.''

State Occupational Licenses

States have traditionally licensed doctors, lawyers, CPA's, contractors and a few other professionals. Recently, however, demand for consumer protection has brought about state licensing of dozens of additional occupations. Auto mechanics, stereo and TV repair shops, marriage counselors, plumbers, even dry cleaners, to name a few, are often licensed. Occupational licenses are usually issued for one or two year periods and, as always, for a fee. Some of the occupational licenses require the licensee to pass a test. Some have education and experience requirements. Contact the state agency administering consumer affairs to inquire about possible licensing of your business. State offices are always located at the state capital and usually in the larger cities around the state.

Sales Tax and Seller's Permits

Unless you live in a state that does not have a sales tax, you will be required to collect sales tax from your customers and remit the tax to the state. Every state's sales tax laws are a bit different. Many states exempt food, labor, and shipping charges from sales tax. Some states tax leased property. Depending on the dollar volume of your business, you will have to prepare monthly, quarterly or annual sales tax returns on which you report your sales and pay the taxes collected. Some states let you keep a portion of the sales tax you collect as a payment for the cost of collecting it.

Every state that collects a sales tax issues "seller's permits" (also called "resale numbers" or "resale permits"), and every business that sells goods must have one. Some states will also require a security deposit from you before issuing you a seller's permit, which is the state's way of guaranteeing that you will collect and remit sales tax when you sell your goods to your customers. States will sometimes allow you to put your security deposit into a special interest-bearing bank account. If you don't want to tie up your own money or if the deposit is more than you can afford, you can often purchase a sales tax bond from an insurance company. The state will accept the bond in lieu of the deposit. When you apply for your seller's permit, the state will give you a full set of sales tax rules and procedures. Service businesses that do not sell parts or inventory are usually not required to obtain a seller's permit.

Besides registering you as a seller, a seller's permit gives you the right to buy goods for resale—both finished products and raw materials—without paying sales tax to your sup-

---

Failure is more frequently from want of energy than want of capital.

—Daniel Webster

plier. Only goods which will be resold in the normal course of business can be purchased in this manner. You may not use your seller's permit to make tax-free purchases of office supplies, tools, or equipment, or for goods to be used for personal, non-business purposes.

Businesses selling wholesale goods and raw materials must also obtain a seller's permit, which allows them to sell their resale goods to another business without charging sales tax. The wholesale business will often be required to keep a detailed record, by customer, of the tax-exempt sales. States usually provide wholesalers with a form for this purpose. A special note: don't confuse the word "wholesale" with "discount". Wholesale refers to a sale of goods by one business to another for resale or manufacture. The ads in the newspapers that say "Wholesale To The Public" or "Wholesale—Factory To You" or some other misuse of the word are actually referring to discount retail sales, that is, sales to the ultimate consumer.

Other State Regulations

In addition to occupational licenses and sales tax laws, some states have various other requirements for small businesses. Some of these state laws parallel or expand upon federal laws, particularly Federal Trade Commission regulations (discussed later). Here is a brief summary of *some* state laws. You are going to have to do some telephoning—try your state's Secretary of State office or Attorney General office for starters—to get answers.

Truckers and taxi cab operators must often register with the Public Utilities Commission. Businesses operating factories or other potential air and water polluting equipment must often meet state Air and Water Resources Commission requirements. Employers may be subject to state wage and hour laws and occupational safety and health laws administered by the state Department of Labor or Department of Industrial Relations. States often have laws regulating finance charges imposed on customers.

Federal Identification Numbers

Your business will be required to identify itself on tax forms and licenses by either of two numbers: your Social Security number or a Federal Employer Identification Number. A Social Security number is all the identification a sole proprietorship needs until you hire employees. Then you will have to get the Federal Employer ID Number. To get an ID number, file Form SS-4 with the IRS. No fee is charged.

If you do file for and receive a Federal Employer Identification Number, the IRS will automatically send you quarterly and year-end payroll tax returns that you must fill out and return even if you have no employees. So don't apply for an Employer ID Number until you become an employer.

Partnerships and corporations must have federal and/or state identification numbers whether they hire employees or not. See the separate chapters in the Growing Up section.

Federal Permits and Regulations

Federal "watch dog" agencies and the rules and regulations generated by these agencies are growing at a tremendous rate. The U.S. Government section of the San Francisco telephone book lists over twenty-four major agencies and departments which in some way regulate or oversee business activity. Most of this government intervention is aimed at large corporations, but some small businesses are also subject to federal licensing and regulation.

Federal Licenses

The federal government licenses all businesses engaged in interstate commerce, common-carrier transportation, radio and television station construction, manufacture of drugs, preparation of meat products and investment counseling. You should contact the Federal Trade Commission, Washington, D.C. 20580 for specific licensing requirements.

Exporting and Importing

Businesses that export goods to foreign countries will, in most cases, be required to fill out a Shipper's Export Declaration (SED). If you export certain military or scarce goods, or if you ship to a handful of trade-restricted countries, you will have to obtain a Validated Export License. More information about exporting is available from the Department of Commerce, Washington D.C. 20233.

You do not need any special permit to import goods into the United States, but you should be aware of customs procedures—which are lengthy if the value of your shipment is over $250 including shipping costs—and customs duties, which can run from nominal amounts to as much as 110 percent of the value of the imported goods (as is the case with carved stones imported from some communist countries). The U.S. Customs Service publishes a booklet, "Importing Into the U.S.", available from the U.S. Government Printing Office, Washington, D.C. 20402.

Employers

Some employers are subject to the minimum wage and equal-opportunity employment laws which come under the Department of Labor's Fair Labor Standards Act. These laws are discussed in the Hiring Help chapter.

Finance Charges

Businesses that impose finance charges on credit customers must explain those charges in carefully worded statements according to the Federal Trade Commission's Truth in Lending Act. Finance charges and Truth in Lending requirements are discussed more in the "Credit Selling" chapter.

More Federal Trade Commission Rules

Small businesses that guarantee merchandise, sell by mail, sell or manufacture clothes or fabrics, sell or manufacture packaged or labeled goods, or do certain types of advertising are subject to Federal Trade Commission regulations. Here is a brief rundown:

Product guarantees and warranties must be specifically worded according to the Consumer Products Warranty Law.

Mail order businesses must comply with a Federal Trade Commission rule designed to crack down on undue mail order shipping delays. Mail order sellers must ship ordered merchandise within their stated time (or thirty days if no time is stated) or notify the buyer of any shipping delay, and give the buyer

---

Form SS–4
(Rev. 9–82)
Department of the Treasury
Internal Revenue Service

Application for Employer Identification Number
(For use by employers and others as explained in the instructions.
Please read the instructions before completing this form.)

OMB No. 1545–0003   Expires 9–30–85

1 Name (True name and not trade name. If partnership, see page 4.)
David Kay

2 Social security no., if sole proprietor
234-00-5678

3 Ending month of accounting year
December

4 Trade name, if any, of business (if different from item 1)
Dekay Engineering

5 General partner's name, if partnership; principal officer's name, if corporation; or grantor's name, if trust

6 Address of principal place of business (Number and street)
1944 Edgewood Road

7 Mailing address, if different

8 City, State, and ZIP code
Aberdeen, Maryland 43229

9 County of principal business location
Baltimore

10 Type of organization
[X] Individual   [ ] Trust   [ ] Partnership   [ ] Other (specify)
[ ] Governmental   [ ] Nonprofit organization   [ ] Corporation

11 Date you acquired or started this business (Mo., day, year)
1-14-84

12 Reason for applying
[ ] Started new business   [ ] Purchased going business   [X] Other (specify) hired employee

13 First date you paid or will pay wages for this business (Mo., day, year)
2-1-85

14 Nature of principal business activity (See instructions on page 4.)
service--consulting

15 Do you operate more than one place of business?   [ ] Yes   [X] No

16 Peak number of employees expected in next 12 months (If none, enter "0") ►
Nonagricultural 1   Agricultural 0   Household 0

17 If nature of business is manufacturing, state principal product and raw material used.

18 To whom do you sell most of your products or services?
[X] Business establishments (wholesale)   [ ] General public (retail)   [ ] Other (specify)

19 Have you ever applied for an identification number for this or any other business?   [ ] Yes   [X] No
If "Yes," enter name and trade name. Also enter approx. date, ► city, and State where you applied and previous number if known. ►

Under penalties of perjury, I declare that I have examined this application, and to the best of my knowledge and belief it is true, correct, and complete.
Signature and Title ► *David Kay*   Date ► 1-18-85

Telephone number (include area code)
301-123-0123

Please leave blank ►   Geo.   Ind.   Class   Size   Reas. for appl.   **Part II**

All employers, partnerships, and corporations must have a federal identification number, obtained by filing Form SS-4 with the IRS.

an option to cancel the order "via an adequate cost-free means".

Textiles, fabric, wool, furs and clothing must be labeled according to a variety of Federal Trade Commission rules. Generally, a label must state (1) the composition of the fabric—the fiber content, (2) the country of origin, (3) the names or registered identification numbers of the manufacturer and the business marketing the fabric, and (4) detailed instructions for care and cleaning.

All packages and labels on goods must conform to the Federal Fair Packaging and Labeling Act. Basically, a label must identify the product, name the manufacturer, packer, or distributor, and show the net quantity of the contents. The Act specifies how the label must be printed and where on the package it must appear.

Some advertising is regulated by the Federal Trade Commission.

Current information on all of the above Federal Trade Commission regulations is available free from the FTC, Washington, D.C. 20580. You should be aware that FTC regulations are constantly changing. If you want to keep up to date on FTC rule changes, you can get a free subscription to "FTC News Notes" from the Federal Trade Commission, Office of Public Affairs, Washington, D.C. 20580.

Although all businesses, big and small, are subject to the various Federal Trade Commission rules, enforcement of the laws is directed primarily at large companies that, due to their size, can and do take advantage of many, many people. As one Federal Trade Commission official explained to me,

---

Red Tape Gone Crazy

"Our small businesses are sinking deeper into a morass of federal rules, regulations, and paper. They are victimized by discriminatory federal income tax laws. They are being driven out of business by confiscatory estate taxes.

"Many federal policies now discourage the formation of new small enterprises, hold down the expansion of existing small firms, and tend to force small family-owned enterprises—including farms, stores, and factories—to quit the business race.

"Paperwork is out of control, imposing a $40 billion yearly burden on the economy, more than half of it borne by small business... federal regulations, such as those contained in the 330-page document on occupational safety and health, are proliferating. They sap the time, funds, and productive energies of small enterprise...major economic legislation, such as the Pension Reform Act, may inflict unintended penalties on smaller firms and their employees because of unnecessary federal paperwork.

"Our own investigation (the Commission on Federal Paperwork) convinced us that paperwork can be substantially reduced—if govern-

ment will devote a fraction of the energy toward reducing and simplifying forms that it has to generating them in the past.

"Changing the 941A employment report from a quarterly to an annual form would eliminate a stack of paper forms over 10,700 feet high—more than two miles—from the annual pile of federal paperwork.

"We are all aware of the larger context of our investigation. Tax policies certainly do determine where capital will flow, which enterprises can be born, which can grow, which will prosper, and which will fail or be merged out of existence in our economic system.

"Those of us who are concerned with the preservation and strengthening of small enterprise are alarmed at the weakness and disrepair of the free enterprise system in this country. Our basic aim must be to recreate a climate in which small business can flourish."

—Former Senator Gaylord Nelson, who was a member of the Senate Select Committee on Small Business. This is excerpted from a speech he gave at the National Legislative Conference of the National Society of Public Accountants.

"We're too busy keeping track of large businesses to worry about a mom-and-pop grocery store in Kansas City which may be violating one of our laws. We've found that small businesses, though they may not adhere to the letter of the law—most of them don't even *know* about a lot of these laws—tend to be much more honest with their customers. We rarely get a complaint about a small business."

Insurance

Before you open your doors, you should thoroughly investigate the insurance needs of your business. Insurance replaces a large, uncertain loss with a small but certain cost—the insurance premium. The different kinds of insurance available to you include:

Basic Fire Insurance covers fire and lightning losses to your equipment and inventory and to your premises. Fire premiums vary widely and are based upon the location of your property and the degree of fire protection in your community, the type of construction of the building, the nature of your business and the nature of neighboring businesses. If you move into a building next to a woodworking, upholstery or dry cleaning shop, your fire premiums will be high even if your business is a low fire risk. A sprinkler system in your building will sharply reduce your premium.

Extended Coverage protects against storms, most explosions, smoke damage, riot, and damage caused by aircraft or vehicles.

Liability Insurance pays lawsuits brought against your business because of bodily injury or damage to others' property. A customer in your store slips and falls, breaks a leg and slaps you with a $100,000 lawsuit; it's not uncommon. Premiums for merchants usually are based upon the square footage in the store. The bigger the store, the higher the premium. If you are a manufacturer or a contractor, premiums increase as your payroll increases.

Property Damage Liability provides coverage for damage to property of others. A fire starts in your small office. The damage is minimal but smoke and water destroyed $30,000 worth of Persian rugs in the business next door. Property damage liability covers this situation. It specifically excludes property leased or rented to you or in your care.

Fire Legal Liability covers fire damage to your landlord's building—the portion you occupy only. The rest of the building would be covered by property damage liability.

Vandalism and Malicious Mischief Insurance.

Theft Coverage provides protection from burglary (theft from your closed and locked business) and robbery (theft using force or threat of violence). The cost of theft insurance depends largely on the type of merchandise you stock and on the type of theft protection on your premises—alarms, bars on the windows, door locks, etc.

An investment in some security protection is certainly as important as an investment in theft insurance.

Products Liability refers to insurance coverage for any product manufactured or sold by the insured once the product leaves the business' hands. It covers the business in case the ultimate user of the product sues for bodily injury or property damage. The courts generally hold manufacturers strictly liable for any injury caused by their product, sometimes even when the product has not been used correctly. Even retail stores and restaurants can sometimes be liable for products they sell. If the insurance company does not consider your product to be hazardous, the premium could be low. Premiums increase as sales increase.

Business Interruption. If your business closes due to fire or some other insurable cause, business interruption insurance will pay you approximately what you normally would have earned. The premiums, especially when part of a complete insurance package, are low. There is similar insurance which provides coverage if you are hospitalized and have to shut down your business. You can also purchase "extra expense" insurance, which pays the extra cost of keeping a business operating (such as renting temporary quarters) after a fire or other building damage.

Bonds. Surety bonds guarantee the performance of a job. If you are unable for any reason to complete a job, your surety company must do so. Many contractors have such bonds to protect their customers and require them of subcontractors. Surety bonds are most often used in the construction industry and are always required on public construction projects. Surety bonds are difficult to obtain unless you have $30,000 or more of liquid assets, such as cash, receivables and inventory.

Fidelity bonds are placed on employees, insuring the employer against theft or embezzlement by the bonded employees.

Workers' Compensation Insurance provides disability and death benefits to employees injured or killed on the job. Most states require employers to carry workers' compensation for all employees. In nearly all states, a state board determines the premiums to be charged, but insurance companies can pay dividends (i.e., refunds) after the policy has expired if you have a satisfactory loss record. Premiums increase as your payroll increases and vary dramatically with the occupation. Workers' compensation insurance for a roofer is roughly ten times higher than for a grocery clerk.

You as the owner of your sole proprietorship usually cannot be covered under workers' compensation. As a partner in a partnership or an officer in a privately owned corporation, you may elect to be included in most states.

Automobile Insurance. Liability coverage is mandatory in many states. The same coverage available to you on your personal auto is available on a business vehicle. The premiums, however, are usually higher for business vehicles. If you use your personal vehicle for business, check with your insurance company to make sure you have coverage that includes business use.

"Non-owned" auto liability insurance protects you if one of your employees injures someone or damages someone's property while driving his own car on your company business. This coverage does not protect the employee, who should have his own insurance as well.

You should check with the state, your landlord and your bank (if you plan to get a loan) to determine what kinds of insurance you *must* carry. Many leases specify that the tenant must carry liability insurance naming the landlord as an additional insured. Landlords often require their tenants to carry plate glass insurance and sometimes even fire insurance on the landlord's building. When banks loan you money, they often require you to carry life insurance naming the bank as beneficiary. They will also require you to insure any property purchased with the loan money. Car and equipment leasing firms often require you to obtain liability and/or property insurance on leased equipment.

Over and above any mandatory insurance, liability coverage is unquestionably the most important to a business. One lawsuit by an irate customer can wipe you out—your business and you personally. Even if you win the lawsuit, without insurance it could still cost thousands of dollars in lawyer's fees.

Most insurance companies offer a "business owner's package", combining many of the above coverages in one policy. Some insurance companies offer "all risk" insurance, which includes fire, extended coverage, vandalism, theft and all other damage not specifically excluded in the policy. Insurance companies are competitive, offering different rates, packages and premium payment plans. It is a good idea to shop around. Talk to several insurance agents.

I am partial to independent agents because they are not tied to one company and can piece together the best insurance package to fit your needs and your pocketbook. I suggest you pick an agent who will devote time to your individual problems, who will at no extra cost survey your entire situation and recommend alternative methods of insurance, pointing out the advantages and disadvantages of each.

Initial Cash Outlays

Getting your business started is going to require cash outlays right at Day One. The largest and most obvious expenses, of course, will be for your initial inventory and equipment purchases, for rent and

Type of Expense	Cost Estimate	Actual Cost
1. Inventory		$ _____
2. Equipment		_____
3. First month's rent		_____
4. Lease deposit		_____
5. Insurance premiums:		
liability	$150–500	
fire and extended coverage	150–300	_____
6. Telephone installation	25–100	_____
7. Telephone deposit	0–50	_____
8. Gas and electric deposit	0–50	_____
9. Seller's permit—fee	0–25	_____
10. Seller's permit—deposit	50–300	_____
11. Local license fee	10–100	_____
12. Fictitious name statement—fee	10–50	_____
13. Fictitious name statement—publication	15–50	_____
14. Business cards, stationery, sales books, check printing, etc.	50–200	_____
TOTAL START UP COSTS		$ _____

possibly a rent deposit for your shop or store, and for insurance premiums. All those licenses and permits—$10 here, $25 there—can also run into a lot of money.

Here is a list of typical start-up expenses, a rough estimate of what the costs may be, and a blank column so you can fill in the actual costs.

Choosing A Business Name

Thinking up a name for your new business can be a lot of fun, an opportunity to let your creativity and your imagination take charge. A business name, however, should be selected with care. I suggest three key guidelines:

1. Choose a name that is both pleasant and easy to pronounce. If your customer chokes on your name every time he mentions it to someone else, fewer people will hear about you.

2. Choose a name that will do a little advertising for you, that will tell people what you do. Wallpapers Plus, Strider Real Estate, Madrone Hand Crafted Jewelry, say what they need to say, clearly and simply. "Acme Enterprises" tells people absolutely nothing.

3. Most important, choose a name that will not severely limit you, a name that will stand up to the passage of time. I know two jewelers who named their business "The Silver Workshop". They made

high quality silver and turquoise necklaces and bracelets. Silver, however, is not as popular as it was three years ago, and The Silver Workshop is now making gold and beaded jewelry. These jewelers now find themselves with an albatross around their necks: the business name. On the one hand, the old customers recognize the name. But new customers, looking for gold jewelry, assume that The Silver Workshop makes silver jewelry, and they stay away.

When you finally settle on a name you like, go to the county office that handles fictitious names and ask to see their alphabetical list of all fictitious names registered with the county. If you live in a large urban area, you may find that your first, second *and* third choices are all already taken. You can, if you want, try to contact the person who owns the business name and find out if the business is still in existence. If it isn't, and if the owner of the name consents, an Abandonment of Fictitious Name Statement can be filed, whereby the prior owner gives up all rights to the name. You may simultaneously file a Fictitious Name Statement for the name. The Abandonment of Fictitious Name Statement procedures are identical to the Fictitious Name Statement procedures, including the requirement to publish the statement in the newspaper. The former owner will probably want you to pay the cost of filing the statement of abandonment and may even want you to pay him a fee for his trouble.

Mike Madsen, Easy Rider Leather: "You talk to people who are outside of business, they don't understand it. You talk to somebody who's on a fixed income or working on a salary or an educator or a student, they don't understand what being in business is. They're not risk takers. They're not striving to make a whole number of things work simultaneously. They go to work in the morning or go to school and have a prescribed routine and they get off at five o'clock, whenever their day's over, and they go home and their business is done. But if you're in business for yourself, you don't turn off the switch when you go home. You're constantly thinking about it.

"In the late sixties, early seventies, business was 'bad' and you got hostility from people who weren't in business. Not to make a profit, not to like dealing with money was a value of the mid-sixties, a Thoreauian concept. Thoreau made a statement that men lead lives of quiet desperation, and the accompanying idea was that the profit motive is associated with that desperation. People also see our dwindling resources as a function of consumption. They think that the profit motive is part of that consumptive behavior, which they know in the long run is not going to be good. I concur with that. But your life has needs, and in this monetary system where money is the medium of exchange, you need it. In order to have the cash to do what you want to do, you gotta have more than just your costs. You have to make a profit."

Section Two
BOOKKEEPING

The best memory is not so firm
as faded ink.

Chinese proverb

"If you take one from three hundred
and sixty-five, what remains?" asked
Humpty Dumpty.
"Three hundred and sixty-four, of
course," said Alice.
Humpty Dumpty looked doubtful. "I'd
rather see that done on paper,"
he said.

Alice In Wonderland by
Lewis Carroll

Warming Up to an Unpopular Subject

Bookkeeping seems to be the one aspect of business that so many people dread. Columns upon columns of numbers, streams of adding machine tape, balancing the books (whatever that means), and "I'm a shopkeeper not an accountant." Whenever I try to explain or defend the paperwork end of business to a new business person, I always feel I have two strikes against me before I even open my mouth. But once a person understands why a business requires a set of ledgers and how these records can be kept with a minimum of time and effort, the fear vanishes, the work—somehow—gets done, and you are left with the satisfaction of seeing the total picture and of having done it yourself. And that is a nice feeling.

Bookkeeping is an integral part of business, of *your* business. To attempt a definition, bookkeeping is a system designed to record, summarize and analyze your financial activity—your sales, purchases, credit accounts, cash, payrolls, inventory, equipment. Your "books"—your ledgers and worksheets—are the bound papers on which the bookkeeping activity is recorded or "posted."

Why Keep a Set of Books?

Most new businesspeople think that they must keep books only because the government (meaning the Internal Revenue Service) requires them to. Well, it's true, the IRS does require every business to keep a set of books. But there is a bit more to bookkeeping than taxes and tax law requirements.

The real reason you'd *want* to keep a set of books, as you will learn soon enough, is because you *need* the information to run your business. Can you ever expect to make a good decision based on incomplete information? Your books are your only source of complete information about your business. It is virtually impossible to keep all your business information in your head. You may think you know your business like the back of your hand, but you would be very surprised to see how much you don't know unless you can see the total financial picture, on paper in front of you. This is especially true of a business operated out of your home where personal and business expenses can get intermingled and confused.

Business failures have been blamed, time and again, on a lack of accurate financial records. Bob Willis, former owner of Booknews, a defunct bookstore: "Our biggest mistake was that we didn't keep a regular set of books. Half of our records were on scraps of paper and receipts. We didn't know whether some accounts were paid or not. We thought we were making a profit, but a good set of books would have shown us the truth: we were going broke. And you know, had I realized that, I could have taken steps to change things, to head us in a better direction."

Without a complete set of books, you find yourself trying to evaluate your business by looking at isolated areas, such as cash and inventory—these being the most observable (and also the most misleading). If, for example, you price your product based solely on its cost to you plus some arbitrary markup—a common mistake with beginners—you could be selling at a loss and not even know it. This happened at Booknews: "We knew what the books were costing us, but we didn't have any real idea of what our total overhead was—rent, insurance, supplies, utilities, payroll taxes, the rest. We sold a lot of books because we sold at a discount, and I thought we were doing well. Do you know it took me four months to realize that every single book we sold, we sold at a loss."

A good bookkeeping system will provide you with information essential to the survival of your business. Only with a complete set of books will you be able to evaluate your business and make any needed changes and plans for the future.

Joe Campbell, Resistance Repair: "Everybody who runs a business should sit down and figure out what it costs them to turn the key in that door every morning. Overhead. And do it on a daily basis. I never knew until I sat down and calculated exactly what my expenses were, what it costs me to have that place down there. And it's fifty dollars a day. When you walk in there in the morning you know exactly what you gotta do before you start putting bread on the table. You gotta make fifty bucks for the man. And then you start making money for yourself."

Setting Up Your Books

Where do you begin? How much bookkeeping do you need? If your business is a one man, one woman or husband and wife operation—no partners, no employees—your records can be kept quite simple. A bank account, a set of income and expenditure ledgers and a few worksheets are about all you will need. Do you sell on account? You will want to keep records of each credit customer. If you hire employees, you will need payroll records for each employee. Partnerships must keep records of each partner's contributions and withdrawals. Partnerships must file separate income tax returns and

are sometimes required to prepare year-end balance sheets. Corporations, even small ones, often need entire forests to supply all the necessary paper to make everything run smoothly.

But let's take things one step at a time. *None* of the bookkeeping records need be too complicated for most people to keep themselves and to understand. This section of *Small Time Operator* will show you, step by step, how to keep your own books and how to use the information once you have it. This bookkeeping section will also virtually make *Small Time Operator* pay for itself, because included in the back of the book are all the income and expenditure ledgers you will need for a full year. Commercially designed business ledgers sell in stationery stores for anywhere from $5 to $20, an unnecessarily high price to pay for some blank, lined pages. You will also learn that you can custom-design your own ledgers from low cost accounting worksheets to meet your special requirements.

Business Bank Account

As soon as you start your business, before you open your doors, go to the bank and open a separate business checking account. Keep your business finances and your personal finances separate. Nothing can be more confusing or cause you more trouble than mixing business with pleasure, financially. If you plan ahead and open your account a few weeks before starting business, you can have your checks all printed up with your business name and address, ready to use on opening day.

Many states require you to have your fictitious name statement before you can open a bank account in your business name. Talk to your banker ahead of time and find out all the legal requirements.

Ask your banker what the bank charges will be. Business accounts are handled differently from personal accounts. At my bank, a personal checking account with a $300 minimum deposit has no service charge. A business account, however, must have a $1,000 minimum deposit to have no service charge. Some banks charge substantially more than others; some offer free checks printed with your business name and address; some will provide you a free rubber stamp for endorsing checks.

There are three Important Rules to follow:

Rule One: *Pay all your business bills by check.* Your expenses are more easily recorded and better documented when paid by check. Some payments, of course, will have to be in cash, but keep them to a minimum. A chapter at the end of this section explains how to set up a petty cash fund for your cash payments.

Rule Two: *Deposit all your income*, checks and cash, into the business bank account. You will have a complete record of your earnings.

Rule Three: When you take money out of the business account for non-business or personal use, it is known as "withdrawal" or "personal draw". When you want to spend some of your hard-earned money on yourself—to meet the car payment, buy groceries, see a movie—withdraw the money from the business account by writing a check payable to yourself or payable to "cash". Either cash the check or deposit the money in your personal account. Never use the business account to pay personal, non-business expenses. It is just too confusing (and doubles the time spent on bookkeeping) when business and personal expenses are paid from the same account.

A few bank account rules-of-thumb:

1. Balance your bank account every month. It is too easy to make an adding error. You certainly don't want to bounce a check on your most important supplier because you thought you were down to the last ten dollars when you were really down to the last dime. Never balanced a bank account? There is a chapter in the Appendix explaining how to do it.

2. Keep your bank statements and cancelled checks at least three years. They are the best documentation you have if you ever need to support your records. Three years is the normal statute of limitations set by the Internal Revenue Service for income tax audits.

3. Never write a check payable to "cash" unless it is a personal draw. Checks written to "cash" leave you with no record of how the money was spent.

4. Expenses that are partly personal and partly business, such as automobile expenses or rent and utilities on your home when you use part of your home for business, should be paid from your *personal* bank account. Adding these expenses to your business ledgers, following the instructions in this bookkeeping section and using the worksheets in the ledger section, will be easier and less confusing than paying the expenses from the business account and then deducting the personal portion.

Joe Campbell, Resistance Repair: "My problem was that I would look in our checking account, our one and only checking account, and I'd say, Jesus Christ, there's a thousand dollars in there. Let's go buy the new tires we need for the bus. And then I'd say the kids can stand to have a new pair of shoes, and I go buy them a new pair of shoes. And I see we still have $700 in the bank; we're in good shape. Then all the parts bills come in, and I owe $800 worth of parts bills. And then I have to put creditors off. Having that parts money in a separate account tells you exactly where you are. And to me it's a tremendous feeling of security. It works like a charm. Plus it's emergency cash if you have to go in and get it."

Bookkeeping Simplified: an Introduction To the Single Entry System

The ledgers in *Small Time Operator* are simple "single entry" ledgers. For any transaction, only one entry is made, either to income or to expenditure. Single entry bookkeeping keeps the paperwork and the arithmetic to a minimum while still providing you with the basic information you need to manage your business and prepare tax returns.

There are two disadvantages to this simple bookkeeping system. Single entry bookkeeping will provide a record of your income and expenditures but will not provide a complete record of inventory on hand, equipment, outstanding loans or other assets and liabilities. The other drawback to single entry bookkeeping is the lack of a built-in double check of arithmetical accuracy. These disadvantages, however, are partially offset by the additional asset records that the depreciation worksheets and the inventory ledgers provide, and also by the Total columns in the ledgers that provide a partial math double check.

The alternative to single entry bookkeeping, the well known and elaborate system called "double entry" bookkeeping, compares to our single entry system as a fancy stereo compares to a portable record player. Double entry is a complete bookkeeping system that provides cross checks and automatic balancing of the books, that minimizes errors, and that transforms business bookkeeping from a part-time nuisance into a full-time occupation. In double entry bookkeeping, every transaction requires two separate entries, a "debit" and a "credit". These terms originated in double entry bookkeeping, along with the expression "balancing the books": total debits must equal total credits for the books to be "in balance".

Double entry bookkeeping is a science. It is *the* perfected bookkeeping system, and it requires a full semester in college to master. Simplicity is our goal. I find that most small businesses are better off without the refinements (and the headaches) of a double entry system.

Cash Accounting Vs. Accrual

Regardless of whether your books are single entry or double entry, you must choose between two accepted accounting methods: "cash" or "accrual". Under the cash method of accounting, income is recorded when the cash is received, and expenses are recorded when paid. (In accounting terminology, the word "cash" refers to checks and money orders as well as currency). Thus, unpaid credit sales and purchases do not show on cash ledgers, which can present a misleading picture of your income and expense. Accrual accounting, by comparison, records all income and expenses whether paid or not. Both credit and cash transactions are recorded when made. Accrual accounting requires a little more bookkeeping effort than cash accounting.

Every sales and manufacturing business and any service business that stocks and sells parts is required by federal tax law to use the accrual method for its inventory. Businesses that have no inventory can use either method, although once a method is selected, it cannot be changed without written approval from the Internal Revenue Service.

The income and expenditure ledgers in the ledger section of *Small Time Operator* can be kept by either the cash or the accrual method. The posting instructions, however, are only for accrual accounting. Since all businesses can and most businesses must use the accrual method, and since accrual accounting provides a more accurate set of books, I feel this is a much better method. Posting instructions for cash accounting are included in the Appendix.

Recording Income

Income is recorded in two steps. Step One: at the time you make a sale, record the sale on an individual invoice, cash receipt or cash register tape. Step Two will be to summarize the sales in your income ledger. Let's first examine Step One in depth.

The manner in which you record each sale depends primarily on your volume of sales. A writer or cabinetmaker, for example, may have only a few sales each month. For this kind of low volume activity, a special invoice can easily be prepared for each sale. Way at the other end of the spectrum, a grocer may have several hundred sales each day and would go plumb crazy if he had to write out a receipt for every sale. The grocer needs a cash register tape to record his sales. The typical small business falls somewhere between the two examples. For most small businesses, use of preprinted cash receipts or invoice books is the simplest and most efficient way to record sales.

Below are step-by-step procedures for recording sales for low, medium and high volume businesses.

Low Volume of Sales

If your business is of the type having only a few sales, you can easily prepare a special billing for each sale. The billing should be marked "Invoice" and prepared in duplicate. The invoice should include:

1. Your name or business name, address and telephone.
2. Date of sale.
3. Customer's name and address.
4. Description of sale.
5. Amount, showing any sales tax separately.
6. A space to indicate when paid.

If you offer return privileges or discounts for prompt payment, these should be spelled out on your invoice. If you offer credit terms, federal law requires you to disclose, clearly and in detail, your credit terms and finance charges (see "Credit Sales").

Give the original invoice to your customer and keep the duplicate copy for your records. Depending on your inclination and your finances, your invoices can be prepared on specially printed and custom-designed forms, or you can just type the information on plain paper.

```
            WESLEY'S FARM FRESH EGGS
               9372 Huckleberry Drive
             Petaluma, California 95432


                                        July 15

INVOICE

Corner Grocery
5th and Market
Petaluma


    30 dozen eggs, brown shell
         at 65¢ per dozen            $19.50
```

A simple, typed invoice may be all you need if you have a low volume of sales.

Medium Volume of Sales

Most everyone is familiar with the small cash receipt books (invoice books) many businesses use to record individual sales. The books contain fifty or one hundred pre-numbered forms, in duplicate—one for the customer, one for you. Such books are ideal for small businesses with more than just a few occassional sales. These books are standardized and available in any stationery store. You can usually order the books with your business name custom-printed at the top; or you can purchase a rubber stamp for about four dollars and mark each receipt individually.

Note: Don't confuse this book of cash receipts with other books labelled "Cash Receipts" which are in fact ledgers for recording income totals.

The procedure for using your cash receipts book is simple:

1. If the receipts are not already pre-numbered, number them as you use them.

2. Use a separate receipt for each sale.

3. Make a carbon copy of each receipt.

4. Write down the date and the amount of the sale. If there is any sales tax, it is very important to show the amount of the tax separately.

5. If this is a credit sale, write "CREDIT SALE" on the receipt.

6. A description of the sale is not necessary unless the customer desires it or you need it for your own information, such as for inventory control discussed at the end of this section).

7. Give the original to your customer. *Leave the duplicate copy in your receipt book.* The duplicate copies will later be summarized and posted to your income ledger.

8. If you void any invoice, do not throw it out. Mark it "VOID" and retain it in your receipt book. Although you should not include the voided receipt in your summary total, you should keep a record of it here.

Typical cash receipt forms, sold in books of 50 or 100.

Some Terminology

Throughout the book, the terms "sales slips," "sales receipts," "cash receipts" and "invoices" are used interchangably. They all refer to individual sales records.

Large Volume of Sales:
Introducing the Cash Register

Few small businesses have a large enough volume of sales to justify the use and the expense of a cash register. But if you are opening a grocery, restaurant, auto parts store, dry cleaners or any similar retail business making a hundred or more small sales a day, a cash register will be indispensable.

Cash registers can be as simple (and as useless, I should add) as the old-fashioned ones where the sale amount "pops up" in the little glass window, the bell jingles and the cash drawer flies out at you—but there's no tape, and no totals are recorded. And they can be as space-age-complicated as the new $5,000 mini-computers that do everything from updating inventory records to automatically weighing vegetables (yet they still overcharged me on the broccoli!). Those monsters are going to be the death of us all yet.

A cash register that is going to be useful to you must be a combination money box and adding machine. Each time you ring up a sale, the amount is recorded on a two-part cash register tape. Everyone is familiar with the part of the tape that pops out when the sale is rung and the cash drawer opens. That part of the tape is the customer's receipt. The other part of the tape, a duplicate of the customer receipt, stays inside the register and becomes the merchant's sales record. At the end of the day, the register is "totaled" and "cleared". Pushing one key on the register will total all the sales rung up during the day and print the total on the tape. Pushing the key also clears the total from the machine so it will start afresh the next day with a zero balance. As you can well imagine, such machines are not cheap. Even used ones will cost at least a few hundred dollars. If your business demands use of a cash register, shop for a machine with the following features:

1. A double tape as described above.

2. A separate total for sales tax if you are required to collect sales tax.

3. If some sales are subject to sales tax and others are not, as is the case with many groceries, an additional mechanism that separates these sales totals. Such a register will give you three totals: sales subject to sales tax, tax on those sales, and sales not subject to sales tax.

You should also realize that even the finest of these mechanical marvels can and do break down once in a while. So be especially careful in selecting a register; be wary of cheap looking or very old machines. Does the register come with a guarantee or a repair contract? Before you buy it, work it fast and hard for a few minutes. Does it operate smoothly? Or does it feel like it's about to jam up any minute?

Recording Income, Step Two: The Income Ledger

The income ledger is a summary record of your sales invoices, cash receipts or cash register tapes. It is one of the most important business records you have. It tells you, monthly and at year-end, how much income you've earned and how much sales tax you've collected. It helps you manage your business by showing you the days and the months that are slow or busy so that you can better plan your expenditures, advertising, sales, even vacations. It is a guide to preparing cash flow information (cash flow and financial management are discussed at the end of this section). The income ledger also saves you time preparing your sales tax reports and your income taxes.

The ledger section in the back of this book includes a year's worth of income ledgers. There is a

INCOME LEDGER Month of _June_

1	2	3	4	5	6	7
DATE	SALES PERIOD	TAXABLE SALES	SALES TAX	NON-TAXABLE SALES FREIGHT	WHOLESALE	TOTAL SALES
1		173 24	10 39			183 63
2		217 36	13 04	7 00		237 40
3						
4						
5	3rd – 5th	577 82	34 67	18 00		630 49
6		118 71	7 12			125 83
7	closed					
8		266 94	16 02	14 19	275 00	572 15
9						

separate ledger page for each month plus a year-end summary page. The ledger pages were designed so they may be adapted to your individual needs and your state sales tax requirement. Each page has seven columns:

1. *Date.* You may post daily or periodically. How often you post the income ledger depends on you and the volume of sales you have. Discussed below.

2. *Sales Period.* Discussed below. This column can also be used for any special notations you may want to make.

3. *Taxable sales,* excluding sales tax. If you live in a state that does not collect sales tax, or if you sell services or goods exempt from sales tax, use this column for total sales and ignore the rest of the columns.

4. *Sales tax collected.*

5 and 6. *Non-taxable sales.* Some states require your non-taxable sales to be broken down into categories, such as labor, freight, wholesale, out-of-state retail, etc. You also have the option of using these columns to separate different types of sales for your own information.

7. *Total sales amount,* including sales tax. This column serves as a double check on your totals: the sum of the amounts in Columns Three, Four, Five and Six should equal the amount in Column Seven.

You will be summarizing your individual sales (from Step One of Recording Income) and posting the summary totals to the income ledger.

Daily Posting

If you have a moderate or heavy volume of sales, you probably should post the income ledger daily. Add up your sales slips for the day and post your totals to the proper columns in the ledger. Compute separate totals for taxable sales (post to Column Three), sales tax (Column Four), non-taxable sales (Columns Five and Six), and total (Column Seven). No need to make any entries under Sales Period (Column Two). After you have posted the ledger, add the daily totals in Columns Three, Four, Five and Six together. They should equal the total in Column Seven, which is the grand total for the day. If you get a different amount, you will have to locate your adding error. The procedure is a lot simpler in the doing than in the explaining. You really should have no trouble getting the hang of it.

Posting Every Few Days or Once a Week

If you have only a few sales each day, you may wish to post the ledger once every few days or once a week. Whatever period you choose, total all your sales for the period, separating taxable sales, sales tax, and non-taxable sales. Enter the totals on the line corresponding with the last day of your sales period. For example, if the sales you are combining are for January 1 through January 5, post your totals on the January 5 line. Under Sales Period (Column Two), note the period: "January 1 through January 5".

Don't feel that you must stick to one method of posting once you have started. If daily posting becomes too tedious, try posting every three days or five days. And if you normally post your income ledger every few days, and a very busy time comes along, switch over to daily posting for the busy period. The posting only becomes a nightmare if the paperwork is allowed to accumulate. All of a sudden there's a three week backlog, all the receipts are mixed up, some billings are missing and, oh, how I hate bookkeeping. It doesn't have to happen that way if you keep your ledger up to date.

How to Post Sales Returns

Sales returns, both cash and credit, should be handled as if they were negative sales:

1. Prepare a separate sales slip for each return, and mark it clearly and in large letters, "RETURN" or "REFUND".

2. Write down all the information which was on the original sales slip, including the amount of sales tax.

3. Include the return slip with your *current* batch of sales receipts.

4. When you add up the current receipts to post to the income ledger, subtract the amounts on the return slips from the total.

End of Month Procedure

No matter how frequently or infrequently you do your posting, run a monthly total at month-end, even though it may not be a full five or seven days since your last regular posting. Never let a posting period cross months. As with your daily or period totals, your monthly totals in Columns 3, 4, 5 and 6 should be cross-checked against the total in Column 7, and any error should be located and corrected.

Year-end Procedure

Record the twelve monthly totals on the year-end summary page. Cross-check your yearly totals in Columns, 3, 4, 5 and 6 to Column 7 and correct any errors. That's all there is to it.

Filing Your Sales Receipts

Keep your sales receipts (and all other business records) at least three years. These are the source documents which support your tax returns, and you may need them if you are ever audited. If your invoices are not already bound, batch and bind them monthly before filing them away.

Return Checks

If a customer's check bounces on you, find out first why the check was returned. Your bank will include an explanation with the returned check. "Insufficient funds" means that there is not enough money in the customer's account to pay the check. Often, this is not an intentionally written bad check. Get in touch with your customer and tell him you will redeposit the check after a certain number of days. If it comes back once more, however, the bank will not accept it a third time. "Account closed" means just that. Your customer either switched banks and had the wrong checks with him by mistake or switched banks and had the wrong checks with him intentionally. If the check came back from the bank marked "Stop Payment", the customer deliberately stopped payment. In either case, try to contact your customer and get payment. "Return to maker" is a general term; usually it means the same as "insufficient funds".

One possible way to collect on a bounced check is to "put it in for collection," a procedure which is very effective when you are dealing with well-meaning customers who are always down to their last penny. You give the bounced check back to your bank and request that it be held for collection. Your bank then sends the check back to your customer's bank which will hold the check for up to a month. If any funds are deposited to the customer's account during this holding period, any checks held for collection will be paid first. Some banks may charge you a dollar or two for this service.

If all attempts at collection prove futile, file the bounced check in a folder marked "Bad Debts". Bad debts will be a year-end expenditure entry, explained in the expenditure ledger instructions. Make no entry in your income ledger.

Other Incoming Funds

The income ledger has one limitation. It is not a complete record of incoming funds. Any loans received and any of your own money put into the business are not recorded on the income ledger. Loans and "contributions" (your own funds) are not income to your business, and you pay no taxes on this money. If you wish to record business loans and personal contributions, do so as a memo entry on the income ledger *below* the total for the month. Do not include these amounts as part of your sales totals.

Credit Sales

A Simple Credit Ledger

If you do not have a large number of credit sales, you can easily set up a credit ledger to keep track of unpaid accounts. The credit ledger must be kept in addition to your income ledger. Credit sales will have to be posted to both. The ledger section in the back of the book includes a sample credit ledger page that you can use as a prototype. The ledger has five columns:

Column One: Date of sale.
Column Two: Customer's name.
Column Three: Invoice number.
Column Four: Total amount of sale (*including sales tax*).
Column Five: Date paid.

Each credit sale should be recorded on a separate line on the credit ledger. Post Columns One through Four from the credit sales slip either when you make the sale or when you post to your income ledger. (Be sure to write the words "CREDIT SALE" on the sales receipt when you make the sale.) Post Column Five when you get paid. At any time, you can glance down your credit ledger and, by looking at Column Five, tell who still owes you money. Now, collecting that money—that's another story.

An Alternative Credit Record

An alternative to the credit ledger is to make extra copies of credit sales receipts and use them in lieu of a ledger. Order your sales receipts in three-part, rather than two-part forms, and use the third copy as your record of credit sales. File all credit sale third copies in a folder marked "Unpaid". When you receive payment, pull the copy from the "Unpaid" folder and then either file it in a "Paid" folder or throw it away. This method eliminates the need for a credit ledger, but it involves more pieces of paper (which can be easily lost) and more expensive forms.

If you only have a two-part sales receipt form (one for the customer, one for you) you should *not* put your one remaining copy in a credit file. It should stay batched with the rest of the sales receipts. If you start shuffling receipts around, some here, some there, and lose numerical control, you are just asking for trouble. The result of such haphazard bookkeeping is usually an incomplete set of records and unsupportable ledgers.

Businesses that regularly make a large number of credit sales may want a more elaborate credit system. Stores with regular credit customers often keep a separate card on each customer with a complete record of sales and payments. Such cards can be informal or can be part of a complicated system

CREDIT LEDGER

1 SALE DATE	2 CUSTOMER	3 INV. NO.	4 TOTAL SALE AMOUNT		5 DATE PAID	6 MEMO
1-18	Brenneman	113	53	12	2-10	
1-23	J. Ross	128	17	92		notice sent 3-1
1-24	Rygh	134	8	82	2-28	
2-12	Miley	186	10	71		

of billings and monthly statements. For you not-so-small time operators who need to keep close track of credit sales, there are several commercially designed systems for recording credit sales. I suggest a visit to a large business-oriented stationery store.

> Remember: Credit sales must be posted to your Income Ledger as well as to any credit ledger. The Income Ledger is your only complete record of income from all sales.

Uncollectible Accounts

At year-end, you should review all unpaid credit sales and determine which are uncollectible. If you keep a credit ledger, write "Uncollectible" and the year in Column Five next to those accounts that are uncollectible. Add up the uncollectible accounts for the year, and record the amount in your Bad Debts folder (see the previous discussion of Return Checks). If you keep the third-part sales receipt copies instead of a credit ledger, pull out the uncollectible receipts from the unpaid file and mark each "Uncollectible". Add up the total sales amount from all the uncollectible receipts. Staple the uncollectible receipts together, write the total on the front (or attach the adding machine tape total), and file in your Bad Debts folder. Bad debts are an expense of your business and are computed at year-end. The additional procedures are explained in the expenditure ledger section.

A note regarding uncollectibility: only include in your list of uncollectible accounts those that you are certain are uncollectible. If you are unsure, let it ride until next year. You can write off a bad debt in any future year that it becomes definitely uncollectible.

You and Your Credit Customers

I have postponed until this point in the book a discussion of the pros and cons of credit selling. One of the bigger headaches involved in extending credit to your customers is the extra bookkeeping. So if the credit ledgers, the extra posting, and the year-end bad debt write-offs haven't convinced you to hang out the "No Credit, No How" sign, let's look at some of the pluses of credit selling, and some more of the minuses.

There is no doubt that offering credit to your customers will increase sales. "Buy Now Pay Later" has virtually replaced "In God We Trust" as America's slogan. Many, many people have come to expect, even demand, that they be allowed to buy on credit. Shoppers may not go out of their way to find a store that offers quality merchandise at low prices, but they will always be on the lookout for a store that will sell to them on credit. And they are often willing to pay higher prices for the privilege: we all know people who will buy gasoline only at a station that takes their credit card, even though the gas is 5 cents per gallon cheaper at the station across the street.

There are, basically, two ways to extend credit: directly, as old-time grocery stores used to do; or via a commercial credit card such as Master Card or VISA.

OUR CREDIT POLICY: 100% DOWN No Monthly Payments!

Direct Credit

Direct credit involves more work and bookkeeping on your part and a much larger expenditure of energy. You must decide who you will and will not extend credit to and how flexible or inflexible your credit policy will be. It is a good idea to have a formal, written credit policy that applies to all customers, although you will find, time and again, that each customer is different and may require special handling. Any customer seeking credit should be made aware of your policy, which should clearly state (1) maximum credit allowed, (2) payment timetable, and (3) finance charges if any.

If you do impose finance charges, you must abide by the rules of the Federal Truth in Lending Act, the Fair Credit Billing Act and the Equal Credit Opportunity Act. The purpose of the Truth in Lending Act, according to the Federal Trade Commission, "is to assure that every customer who has need for consumer credit is given meaningful information with respect to the cost of that credit." The Fair Credit Billing Act requires you to make prompt correction of a billing mistake. Equal Credit Opportunity prohibits discrimination against an applicant for credit on the basis of age, sex, marital status, race, color, religion, national origin, etc.

These acts specify what information must be presented to the customer—right down to the exact wording and size of the print—and when the information must be made available. The acts also regulate advertising of credit terms and handling of cancellations.

The Truth in Lending Act, the most far-reaching of the three laws, states that before the first transaction is made on any open-end credit account (an account with no specified last payment date), the creditor (you, the merchant) must disclose in writing (1) the conditions under which a finance charge may be imposed, (2) the method of determining the balance upon which a finance charge may be imposed, (3) the method of determining the amount of the finance charge, (4) the minimum periodic payment required, and (5) your customer's legal rights regarding possible errors or questions he may have about the bill. Good lord...

In addition to the above laws, you may also have to abide by the Consumer Credit Protection Act, Fair Credit Reporting Act and Fair Debt Collection Practices Act. You can get information about all of these wonderful laws from the Federal Trade Commission, Washington, D.C. 20580.

The hardest part of direct credit is trying to collect past-due accounts from slow or non-paying customers. I can think of no single aspect of business that is more upsetting than trying to deal with people who can't or won't pay their bills. You begin to resent the customers and they begin to resent you. Bad and sometimes bitter feelings build up. You must decide for yourself where you draw the line, where you decide that the money is no longer worth the aggravation.

Credit Cards

Accepting credit cards such as Master Card or VISA will eliminate most of the headaches of direct credit selling. You will not need credit ledgers, and you will never have to hound people to pay up. The banks handle all the paperwork. The fee charged for this service—usually three percent of the sale amount—is, for most businesses, worth the savings in effort and aggravation. There is also usually a one-time sign up fee and an annual rental fee for the imprinter—the machine that imprints the sales slips with the information on the customer's credit card. The bank provides all the forms and the "We Accept..." signs, usually free.

Credit card sales can be handled through your regular checking account if it's in a bank that handles the credit card, or you can set up a special "merchants account" just to process credit cards.

The procedures for processing Master Card and VISA sales are very similar. When you make a credit card sale, you deposit the credit tag in your bank account just as if you were depositing cash. The bank does the rest. They take and process the tags; they credit your account for the amount deposited, less the service charge; once a month, they send you a statement of activity.

You usually will not be responsible for unpaid Master Card or VISA accounts or for stolen or invalid cards if you follow the three procedures required by the banks: (1) check the expiration date on the card, and refuse to accept expired cards without special bank approval; (2) have the customer sign the sales draft and compare the signature to the one on the credit card; and (3) telephone for approval on sales over a certain dollar amount specified by the bank. There are other instructions which will be explained to you when you apply for the cards.

Merchants cannot legally impose a surcharge (an additional fee) on customers who use credit cards. You may, however, offer a discount to buyers who pay by cash or check as long as the offer is made to all your customers.

Lara Stonebraker, Cunningham's Coffee, Oakland: "We thought about having accounts for people who were in the neighborhood and then decided that was just a can of worms. We just didn't want to mess with it. It would take a lot of bookwork, keeping track of these accounts and what they owe and all. But we do have both Master Card and VISA. We have to have both because people just don't carry the cash around any more. We have a $10 minimum. With the 3 percent they take out, it doesn't pay us to do it for smaller amounts. I think people are much more willing to spend money if they can charge it because they kind of feel they won't be billed for a long time."

Nick Mein, owner of Wallpapers Plus in San Francisco: ''I don't think the credit cards are worth it. We must have had $600 of credit sales at the very most. We had to open a separate merchant's account, and it wasn't at my bank. And they take three percent, which is a lot for a mini-merchant like me. Three percent does mount up. I think it's kind of a rip-off. Everybody has a checking account, right? I'd rather take checks than Master Card. In my business it's easy for me to take checks because the kind of people who are going to buy our stuff are usually fairly responsible. We've never had a bounced check.''

The Expenditure Ledger

The expenditure ledger is your record of all business expenses, business loan repayments and personal draws (money you pay to yourself). The most important function of the expenditure ledger is to separate and classify different types of expenditures. The columns in the ledger represent categories of expenditure—such as materials, supplies, rent, etc.—and each item must be posted to its appropriate column. For this reason, you will not be able to summarize a number of transactions on one line as you can with sales in the income ledger.

There are literally hundreds of different categories of expenditure on which small businesses spend their money. The tax section of this book lists 113 of the more typical items. But you certainly don't want to post a ledger with 113 columns, or even with 50 or 25 columns. Visions of green eyeshades, tall stool and columns and columns of numbers. Not necessary. The secret is to use only the categories you need and want. Some categories of expenditures must have their own column because they are required to be shown separately on your income tax return. Other categories should also be listed separately because they are used repeatedly or in large dollar amounts. You will want to know where your big dollars went and so will the tax people. Occasional or small expenses can often be combined under a single title. And, of course, there is good old "miscellaneous" for the ten bucks you "loaned" your brother-in-law that you know you'll never see again. (That's not really a legitimate business expense, but you get the idea.)

The expenditure ledgers in the back of this book have been specially designed for small businesses. They separate expenditures into eleven categories, specific enough to give you a good idea of how your money was spent and provide adequate information for preparing your income taxes, yet general enough to make them useful to a large variety of small businesses with little or no alteration.

As with the income ledger, your own experience will soon guide you to the best schedule for posting the expenditure ledger. To start you off, here is a recommended system of posting that I think will work best for most small businesses:

Payments in currency: Record the expenditure in your ledger when you make the payment. Don't put it off even a few hours—it is too easy to forget.

Payments by check: When you write a check, record the information in your checkbook—check number, date, amount, paid to, and a brief description of what the payment is for. You must then recopy the information from your checkbook into the expenditure ledger. How often you sit down and take the time to do the copy job depends again on you, your time schedule and the volume of checks you write. If you write a large number of checks, post daily. It is a good idea to post your expenditure ledger the same time you post your income ledger. The same warnings about posting apply here: whatever schedule you choose, stick to it. Don't get behind in the paperwork.

Checkbook and Ledger Combined?

Probably some of you are already asking why have both a checkbook and an expenditure ledger. The expenditure ledger provides you with important information that your checkbook does not show, such as expenditures paid by currency and money order and unpaid expenses at year-end. The ledger format also makes it easy to summarize and review your important categories of expenditure. Your checkbook cannot readily show you how much you spent on materials or parts last month, or on office supplies; it doesn't even show the total combined expenditures.

Your checkbook, on the other hand, provides a very important record that the expenditure ledger is not designed to show—your running bank balance. The checkbook also has space for ticking off the cancelled checks, for recording void checks and adding errors, and for posting deposits.

You can buy commercial bookkeeping systems that combine the expenditure ledger and checkbook. A lot of small businesses use and like them. I personally find them unwieldy and too complicated, particularly for people with no bookkeeping experience. The method I describe here takes more time and more pencil pushing, but it is easy for a beginner to understand. Once you have mastered bookkeeping and feel comfortable with your ledgers, which will take three to six months, then you are in a better position to experiment with different methods.

Posting the Expenditure Ledger

There are 12 pages of expenditure ledgers in the ledger section at the back of the book. Each page of the ledger provides space for 39 entries. The first column is for the date. The second column is for the check number. If you pay by currency, write "cash" in this column; if you pay by money order, write "M.O." The third column shows to whom the money was paid. This column can also be used to record any special notation you may need. The fourth column shows the total amount of the payment. This column will provide a double check of your monthly and year-end totals. All payments should be posted to this "Total" column and to one or more of the following detail expenditure columns:

Column One—Merchandise and Materials (Inventory). If you make or sell a product, this column will be the one showing the most activity. Record in Column One all the goods you purchase for resale or for manufacturing, including any delivery charges. Also include all the related materials that go into or are consumed in the process of preparing your product for sale such as a dressmaker's thread and a jeweler's solder. Include packaging materials if they are an integral part of your product. If your packaging costs are only occasional or incidental, record them in Column Two. Do not include in Column One office supplies, tools, equipment or any material purchased for reasons other than resale.

Column Two—Supplies, Postage, Etc. These are expenses incidental to your work. Office supplies, paper, pencils, coffee, small tools that will not last more than a year. Do not include the supplies that become part of your product or are consumed in making your product; such expenses belong in Column One. Draws for Petty Cash should also be posted to Column Two. Petty cash is explained later in this chapter.

Column Three—Labor: Non-Employees. There are two types of payment for labor: payments to employees, where you withhold income taxes, social security, etc.; and payments to non-employees such as outside contractors, where nothing is withheld. The Growing Up section of Small Time Operator includes a chapter, "Hiring Help", that explains in detail the difference between these two types of labor.

EXPENDITURE LEDGER

DATE	CHECK NO.	PAYEE	TOTAL	1 MDSE. & MAT'LS.	2 SUPPLIES, POSTAGE, ETC.	3 LABOR NON-EMPL.	4 EMPLOYEE PAYROLL	5 ADVERTISING	6 RENT	7 UTILITIES	8 TAXES & LICENSES	9	10 MISC.	11 NON-DEDUCT.
1-2	101	Postmaster	12 18		12 18									
1-2	102	R. Jones	150 00						150 00					
1-6	103	Silver Supply	137 50	137 50										
1-7	104	Daily Journal	32 00					32 00						
1-7	105	Acme Supply	83 30	83 30										
1-8	CASH	UPS (delivery)	2 20		2 20									
1-9	106	City of S.F. (bus. license)	35 00								35 00			
1-10	107	Wilson Equip. Co. (drill)	83 69											83 69

To record payments to non-employees, simply write down the full amount of the payment here in Column Three. Employee payroll is recorded in Column Four. Remember, any payments to yourself should not be shown in Column Three or Column Four. Your own "labor" is not an expense of your business. Record payments to yourself in Column Eleven—*Non-Deductible*.

Column Four—Employee Payroll. You must record employee payroll both here in Column Four and in a separate payroll ledger (discussed in the "Hiring Help" chapter). The separate payroll ledger must show the full detail of the payment: gross, amounts withheld and net pay. Column Four, however, should show only the *net* amount of the payroll check (the employee's take-home pay).

Payroll taxes that you withhold from your employees are also recorded in Column Four, but only at the time you pay them to the government. Withheld taxes include federal income, Social Security, state income and possibly state disability. You should not confuse these withheld payroll taxes with payroll taxes that you, the employer, are required to pay, such as employer's portion of Social Security, and federal and state unemployment taxes. Employer-paid payroll taxes are posted to Column Eight—*Taxes and Licenses*. This is a confusing area, especially since employees' and employer's taxes are reported to the government on the same form and usually paid with the same check.

Column Five—Advertising. Includes advertising, promotion, business gifts and entertainment.

Column Six—Rent. When you rent a business premises separate from your home, post the full amount of the rent to Column Six. If, however, you are using a portion of your home for your shop or office, you must follow a different procedure.

First you must determine if you are allowed any deduction at all for an office or shop in your home. The Internal Revenue Service has strict rules limiting home office deductions. These rules are explained in the "Office In The Home" chapter in the tax section.

If you are eligible for a home shop or office and if you own or are buying your home, you still cannot deduct any rent expense. You may only "depreciate" or write off a portion of the cost of your home as a business expense. Depreciation should be calculated once a year, at year-end. It is explained in detail in the tax section of the book.

If you rent your home (and if you qualify for the deduction) you must determine what percentage of

your home is used for business. The percentage must be based on the amount of space devoted to business. For example, if you rent a five-room house and one room is used totally for business, one-fifth or twenty percent of your home can be considered used for business, and twenty percent of your rent expense can be charged to your business.

You should pay your home rent from your personal, and not your business, checking account. But when you pay the rent, post the amount applicable to your business in Column Six. These instructions are long, but when you actually sit down and it, the rent computations will be a lot easier than they sound.

You may not take any rent expense on a separate business premises if you own the building. You may only depreciate a portion of the cost of the building.

Column Seven—Utilities. Utilities include gas, electric, water, garbage and telephone. When your business is operated out of your home, the business portion of your utilities is the same percentage as the business portion of your home (see the discussion under Column Six—*Rent*). But remember, if you are not eligible for an office in the home deduction, you also cannot deduct home utilities.

The percent applicable to telephone is for the basic monthly rate only. Long-distance or message-unit calls should be itemized, business vs. personal. The business amounts should be recorded in Column Seven. As with rent, pay your home utility bills from your personal checking account and then post the business portions here.

Column Eight—Taxes and Licenses. Record any tax payment or license fee here except withheld payroll taxes (see instructions under Column Four). Be sure to note in the "Paid To" column what the payment is for; you will need this information for your income tax return.

Regarding sales tax: the only sales tax that should be posted to Column Eight is the amount you remit to the state, collected from your sales. Any sales tax you pay when purchasing supplies, equipment or anything else should be included as part of the price of the goods purchased. For example, your business cards cost $12.00 plus 72 cents sales tax. You should enter $12.72 in Column Two. Nothing should be entered in Column Eight.

Column Nine is blank. I cannot possibly foresee all your needs, so here is one extra untitled column to use or not to use as you see fit.

Column Ten—Miscellaneous. The ol' catch-all. For unusual expenditures or expenditures that do not recur enough to justify their own column. Include in

Column Ten payments for insurance, bookkeeping and other professional services, dues and organization fees, out-of-town travel, education expenses, minor repairs, loan interest (repayment of the loan principal should be posted to Column Eleven—*Non-Deductible*). A more detailed list of items to post to Column Ten can be found in the tax section. Any expense that you are posting to Column Ten which starts to recur regularly should be moved to its own column. Either use Column Nine or another column you are not using. Feel free to change the heading of any column in the ledger to suit your needs.

Column Eleven—Non-Deductible. Use this column for:

1. Personal draws—money you pay yourself.

2. Furniture, tools, equipment, machinery, buildings and other fixed assets used in your business. These must be depreciated over a period of years. They cannot be written off to expense when purchased. Fixed asset purchases should also be recorded on the depreciation worksheet/equipment ledger in the ledger section. Depreciation and the depreciation worksheet are explained in detail in the tax section.

3. Repayment of business loans—principal only. A loan is not income when received and is not an expense when paid. Any interest paid on a business loan *is* a valid expense and should be posted to Column Ten.

4. Legal fines or penalties, including traffic tickets. These may be "valid" expenses of your business, but they are not deductible for income taxes.

5. Accounts Payable. This relates to year-end adjustments to bring your ledgers up to full accrual. The full details are explained at the end of this chapter.

Recording Automobile Expenses

There are two ways to record automobile expenses. You may keep track of actual expenses, or you can take a standard mileage allowance. The "Automobile Expense" chapter in the tax section explains both methods. If you decide to take the standard mileage allowance, you do not have to make any entries in your expenditure ledger until year-end. If you plan to keep track of actual expenses, you should record all vehicle expenses as they are incurred. Use Column Nine in your expenditure ledger to record these expenses. Note that the cost of the vehicle and any major repairs cannot be

deducted as an expense. They must be depreciated, as explained in the depreciation chapter of the tax section, and posted to Column Eleven—*Non-Deductible*.

Monthly Totals

As with the income ledger, total all the columns of your expenditure ledger each month. Cross-check the monthly totals to the Total column, and correct any errors. Do not, however, start a new expenditure ledger page for each new month. If a month ends and only half a page is used, double-underline your total, skip two lines and start the next month on the same page. There are 12 expenditure ledger pages included in the ledger section, which should be enough for a year. But if you find yourself running out of pages, either photocopy extra pages or purchase some standard twelve-column ledger paper, and write in the column headings. (See the listing of different kinds of ledgers in the Appendix.)

Year-End Procedures

You must make several year-end ledger entries. None are difficult. The Year-End Expenditure Summary in the ledger section has been designed to help you post the year-end entries.

Step One: Post the monthly totals in their proper columns to the summary sheet.

Step Two: Next comes the adjustment to bring your books up to full accrual. You will recall that under accrual accounting, all expenses are recorded whether paid or not. Throughout the year, for ease in posting, only the paid expenses have been recorded. So now you must post any unpaid bills to your ledger. List the bills individually, one to a line, and post to the appropriate columns. As you record each unpaid bill, clearly mark it "ACCOUNTS PAYABLE". Any other unpaid expense for the year just ended, such as payroll taxes, should also be recorded on this year-end summary, one to a line, even if you have not received a bill.

Step Three: Add up the Total column and Columns One through Eleven. Cross-check your totals: the sum of the totals in Columns One through Eleven should equal the total in the Total column.

Step Four: Total the return checks and the uncollectible accounts in your Bad Debts folder (discussed earlier in this section) and post in the Total column.

Step Five: If you use the standard mileage allowance for automobile expenses (discussed in the tax section), calculate the automobile expense on the summary sheet and post to the Total column.

Step Six: Record the depreciation expense from the depreciation worksheets (discussed in the tax section) in the Total column.

Your work is done.

Accounts Payable

The unpaid bills and unbilled expenses that you posted to the Year-End Expenditure Summary require special handling when paid next year. These expenses are deductible the year they were incurred, which is the year just ended. They may not be deducted again next year, even though they will be paid next year. When the bills are paid—you will recognize them because you marked them "ACCOUNTS PAYABLE" when you posted them to the summary—they must be posted to Column Eleven—*Non-Deductible.*

Custom Ledgers

After a year's experience with these ledgers, learning which categories of expense you need and don't need, you can easily design your own ledgers using accounting ledger paper. Ledger paper—also called "accountants' work sheets"—usually comes in fifty-sheet pads, with numbered lines (about 40 to a page), blank spaces for column headings and punched holes for loose-leaf binding. The ledger paper is available with anywhere from two to twenty-five columns. Every stationery store carries a selection of these pads.

Petty Cash

A petty cash fund provides a systematic method for paying and recording out-of-pocket cash payments and payments too small to be made by check. ("Cash" in petty cash refers to currency, *not* to checks; which is just the opposite of my earlier definition. Nobody's perfect.)

I suggest, for starters, that you do not have a petty cash fund. It's more bookkeeping, more paperwork, more procedures to remember. Pay the nickel-and-dime expenditures out of what cash is on hand, and record them directly and *immediately* in your expenditure ledger. Any respectable accountant would roll over in his subsidiary ledgers, so to speak, if he heard me say this. Because the absence of a petty cash fund can result in poor cash control, increasing the possibility of incomplete records and "misappropriation" (that means theft) of funds. But if yours is a one person business or if you alone have access to the money, the importance of cash control is outweighed, I feel, by the need for a simple set of books.

If a petty cash fund is what you want or need, I have devised a relatively simple system for handling petty cash. It is a compromise between no system at all and a bookkeeper's dream, and it requires you to follow three rules. One, keep no more than twenty dollars in the fund. Two, make

Petty Cash Ledger		
3/12	Stamps	$1.30
3/16	C.O.D. Charge	1.87
3/17	Office Supplies	.53
3/20	donation to Boy Scouts	1.00
3/31	coffee for the machine	3.57

payments out of the fund only for miscellaneous supplies and postage—expenses that normally would be posted to Column Two in the expenditure ledger. Three, use the fund as little as possible and only when there is no practical way to write a check instead.

If you promise to follow those ground rules here is the procedure:

1. Write a check payable to "Petty Cash" for $20. Cash the check at your bank and put the money, a piece of accounting worksheet paper and a pencil in a separate cash box or cigar box—whatever is handy and relatively safe.

2. Record the $20 check as an expenditure in your ledger, posting it to Column Eleven—*Non-Deductible.*

3. Every time you make a payment from the petty cash fund, record the date, payee and amount on your accounting worksheet, which has just become your petty cash ledger. Get receipts for the payments if possible and put them in the box with the cash.

4. When the fund starts to get low, total the payments recorded on the worksheet, and add up the remaining cash in the box. The worksheet total and the remaining cash should equal $20. If you are out of balance, you either made an adding error, recorded a payment wrong, failed to record a payment, or else you've been robbed. If you can't find an error, adjust the worksheet total so that your petty cash fund is back in balance. Staple all the petty cash receipts to the worksheet and file it away.

5. Write a check payable to "Petty Cash" equal in amount to the total (or the corrected total if there was an error) from the worksheet. Cash the check and put the money in your petty cash box with a new worksheet. Sharpen the pencil.

6. Record the check in your expenditure ledger in Column Two—*Supplies, Postage, Etc.*

Thereafter, whenever your petty cash fund gets low, and also at year-end, repeat steps Four through Six.

Calculators and Adding Machines

A pocket calculator is an excellent business tool. It can be carried around with you and it will give you instant answers. If you are often computing package deals or bulk prices, figuring discounts, sales tax, etc., a good pocket calculator will be indispensable to you.

But when it comes to posting ledgers, adding columns of figures, balancing bank accounts or any typical business activity involving the addition or subtraction of more than just a few numbers, the pocket calculator leaves much to be desired. Most of the calculators are very small, and their keyboards are tiny. It is easy—*too* easy—to make an adding mistake. Many of the calculators have keyboard buttons smaller than the tip of your finger and no spaces between the buttons. Punch a 6, and your finger strays onto the 5. Try this: get out your calculator and add a column of twenty-five numbers. Note your answer, and then add the numbers a second time. Got two different answers, didn't you? Happens to me all the time. Now, which amount is correct? Here lies another problem inherent in the little calculators. There is no way to check your figures, no tape to look at. An adding machine tape is indispensable for checking your totals, locating errors and keeping a record of your calculations.

The difference between operating a ten-key adding machine and operating a pocket calculator can be compared to the difference between working on a Volkswagen engine and working on the engine of a Ford truck: elbow room; or in our case, finger room. The keys of an adding machine are better spaced to accommodate your hand, allowing maximum speed and minimum error. And, most important, the adding machine provides a tape so you can see what you've done.

Be sure to buy a ten-key machine. Do *not* get stuck with one of those machines that have eighty or a hundred keys on the face. They are relics from the past and will take forever to add a column of numbers. Here are some guidelines to follow when shopping for a ten-key:

1. Test out the machine. Add some numbers and see how the machine feels. The keys should not "stick"—that is, the response should be smooth and rapid. A major difference between quality and cheap adding machines is how well they respond to the touch.

2. Adding machines vary in the number of digits they can handle. Select one with at least an eight-digit capacity.

3. A "repeat" button is an important feature, especially if the machine cannot multiply. The repeat button enables you to input one number and repeat it as many times as you want. For example, if you want to multiply 887 times 5, enter the 887 once and hit the repeat button five times. (A trick for quick multiplying: how much is 887 times 9? Enter 8,870—that's 887 times 10—and then subtract 887 to get the answer).

4. It is very important that your machine be able to handle negative amounts. If you subtract 100 from 90, the machine total should either be a 10 in red or a 10 with a large minus mark next to it, or both. Printing the negative balance in red is preferable because it stands out better. Some older adding machines and some of the very cheap new ones may either give a total of 10 with no indication that it is a minus or else give no total at all. Avoid such a machine.

Basic ten-key adding machines can be purchased new at reasonable prices though a good used machine is better than a cheap new one. The newer electronic adding machines are also calculators capable of anything the pocket calculators can do.

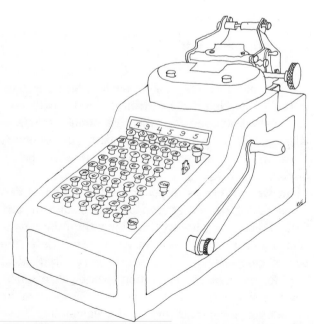

This was the earliest type of adding machine and is still a fixture in many little old grocery stores. It will take you all day long to add a column of numbers. Do not buy one.

A good 10 key machine, well-spaced and uncluttered

Some of the older (pre-electronic age) adding machines can also multiply and divide; but have you ever witnessed an old adding machine do division? It will click and whirr for 20 minutes and then half the time, the answer comes out "E 000" which means Overload, Try Again.

Computers

A small business computer is basically an electronic combination bookkeeper-secretary. A good computer with good programs can help you keep ledgers, organize inventory, prepare invoices, maintain customer files, write letters. Computers cannot organize your business for you, generate sales, increase your profits or scare away the IRS. A computer will provide you with information (all of which is available without a computer). You still have to understand the information, and you still must make your own decisions.

A computer is not just another piece of office equipment like a typewriter or a copier. Mastering a business computer and getting it to provide accurate information the way you want it will require more than just time. It will require a real commitment on your part. The people I know who have used computers successfully in their small businesses all have one thing in common: they like computers. Every one of them looked forward to the challenge of mastering this complex (and, at times, frustrating) machine.

Computers continue to get smaller and less expensive and capable of more and more functions. The needs of any small business, however, can easily be met by today's computers. So in that respect, a computer you buy now—as long as it can meet all your needs—will not become obsolete. But as newer computers are designed and marketed, the older models will probably be discontinued. Parts may be difficult to obtain. Will you have to junk your computer for lack of a $30 plastic gizmo?

Computers do occasionally malfunction, and the results can be anything from a nuisance to a disaster. A "glitch" is a computer term for a temporary malfunction, usually caused by overheating, static electricity or voltage fluctuations in the power lines. Such malfunctions will not shut down the computer but they can destroy programs and wipe out data. You can prevent disaster by making duplicate copies of your programs and records.

You should also be aware of the delicate nature of disks and the need to handle and store them carefully. Dust and dirt or fingerprints on disks can make them unreadable, and so can old age.

The computer itself may break down and require servicing (and how much will that cost you?). If your day-to-day operations are dependent upon your computer, a shut down computer means a shut down business. I personally know a wholesale business that actually had to close its doors for two weeks because its computer malfunctioned and wouldn't properly prepare sales invoices and shipping documents.

I recommend that a new business not acquire a computer at the start. You will have your hands full (and your bank account empty) just getting the business off the ground. After you've gotten to know your business, after it is running smoothly, once you know exactly what information you want and need, and especially once you know what you can and cannot afford, then you are ready to consider a computer. At that point, talk to other business owners who do use computers. Find out what the owners do with their computers, how useful they are, how expensive they are, how difficult they are to master.

Here is a list of considerations when you shop for a computer:

1. Can the computer handle all your needs for now and for the foreseeable future? Every computer is a little different and every one has different capabilities. Some computers are expandable—components can be purchased at a later date giving you

additional functions and added capacity—and some computers cannot be expanded at all. For those that can be expanded, will the computer and its add-on components still be in production a few years later when you are ready to expand?

2. Is the equipment reliable? Well-built computers don't often break down, but every computer will eventually need maintenance or repair. How readily available and how expensive is computer repair? Some manufacturers and retailers offer maintenance contracts though many users find it less expensive to purchase repair work as needed.

3. Most computer manufacturers sell their own prepackaged programs. Many of the best commercially prepared programs, however, are designed and marketed by people who do not manufacture hardware. Can your computer handle these commonly used programs or will it require its own custom-written programs?

4. Every business operates a little differently, so every bookkeeping system is a little different. When you purchase software—a ledger program or an inventory control program—will it give you all you want or will it force you to make compromises you won't like? Can you alter the program to fit your needs? Some programs can be altered and some cannot.

5. Computers and software come with instruction manuals (called "documentation"). You will be referring to the manuals over and over again. It is essential that they make sense to you. Some manuals are well written but some are virtually impossible to understand. If the instructions are talking about "matrix input/output interface" when all you want to find out is how to get your monthly net profit, keep shopping around.

Many people already own small personal computers. Maybe you bought the kids a cheap computer for Christmas last year (along with a dozen video games you hope you never have to see again). Well, that computer probably can perform some business functions, particularly simple bookkeeping. The popular spread-sheet programs (such as VisiCalc) can run on many very small computers. What's more, even though the computer was a non-business purchase, if you use it in your business you are entitled to a business tax write-off (for more information, see the chapters on depreciation and investment credit).

If you use your computer partly for business and partly for non-business use, you must keep a log (dates and hours) of the usage.

Financial Management: Using Your Ledgers

Your books are more than just a record of your business activity and an aid to preparing income tax forms. They are valuable tools to help you manage your business successfully.

Profit-and-Loss Analysis

Without a schedule of profit and loss, it is difficult for the owner of even the smallest business to determine whether or not the business is making a profit. Your cash balances and the day-to-day cash income and outgo, as important as they are, are not a good indication of profit or loss. Cash flow can, in fact, give you a totally misleading picture of how your business is doing.

Simple profit and loss statements, prepared monthly from your ledgers, can tell you a great deal about your business. A profit and loss statement is, basically, a schedule showing your income and your expenses and the difference between the two. Here is a procedure for preparing a very simple profit and loss statement:

Income. The income on the statement is the monthly income total from your ledger (Columns Three, Five and Six in the income ledger). You should exclude sales tax, loan income and any money you put into the business from your own personal funds.

Expenses. Expenses should be separated into two groups: inventory (Column One—*Merchandise and Materials* in the expenditure ledger) and all other expenses (Columns Two through Ten). Column Eleven should not be included.

If you have inventory, you must estimate the cost of the inventory on hand at the end of the month. If it is only an insignificant amount, you can ignore it. The inventory on hand at the beginning of the month, *plus* the current month's purchases from Column One, *less* your estimate of inventory on hand at the end of the month gives you your actual current inventory expense. This expense is called "cost-of-goods-sold" and is covered in much greater depth in the tax section.

"All other expenses" includes everything in Columns Two through Ten except sales tax paid (recorded in Column Eight—*Taxes and Licenses*). Be sure not to include any expenditures from Column Eleven—*Non-Deductible*.

Your income *less* the cost-of-goods-sold (inventory expense) gives you what is known as "gross profit".

```
                    Profit & Loss Statement

                   Bear Soft Pretzel Company

                   January thru September


              Month of September          Year-to-Date


Income from ledger            $2,095              $13,724

Beginning inventory    $  900            $   310

Purchases               1,230             6,710

                       $2,130            $7,020

Estimated inventory
   September 30        (1,000)           (1,000)

      Cost-of-goods-sold        1,130              6,020

         GROSS PROFIT        $   965           $ 7,704

Other expenses:

   Rent                $50               $450

   Supplies             13                74

   Other                 0                27

   Total Other Expenses          63                551

         NET PROFIT          $   902           $ 7,153
```

Gross profit *less* all the other expenses gives you your net profit or loss. By showing both a gross and a net profit or loss, you can tell more easily how your expenses relate to income. If you are losing money, you can readily determine if it is the cost of the inventory (cost-of-goods-sold) or the other expenses that are responsible for the loss. A service business that has no inventory does not have to compute cost-of-goods-sold or gross profit. For such a business, income less "all other expenses" equals net profit or loss.

A statement prepared in the above manner will give you profit and loss information for the month just ended. Some business owners like to see a second column in their profit and loss statements that shows the year-to-date cumulative activity. The year-to-date column is prepared in almost the same way as the monthly column. Year-to-date income is the sum of all the monthly income totals in income ledger Columns Three, Five and Six from January to date, including the month just ended. Cost-of-goods-sold is slightly different. It is the inventory on hand *at January 1, plus* the sum of all the monthly totals in expenditure ledger Column One, *less* the same ending inventory that you estimated for the monthly column. "All other expenses" is the sum of all the monthly totals in Columns Two through Ten (again excluding sales tax payments in Column Eight.)

Your profit and loss statement should look something like the Bear Soft Pretzel Co. illustration. This type of profit and loss statement is only approximate. It does not include unpaid expenses or expenses computed at year-end such as depreciation, and it should not be used for preparing income tax forms.

Cash Flow

One of the most damaging things that can happen to a business is a cash shortage. If you don't have the cash to pay your bills or replenish depleted inventory, your business will suffer. I know of

```
                    Estimated Cash Flow Projection

                           Month of June


                              Cash In      Cash Out      Balance

Cash on hand June 1........                              $800

June 1 rent payment.......                 $250

June 1 utilities..........                  20          $530


Receipts first week.......    $500

Inventory purchase 1st week                $500

Supplies first week.......                  30          $500


Receipts second week......    $500

Payroll second week.......                 $200         $800


Receipts third week.......    $500

Supplies third week.......                 $50          $1,250


Receipts fourth week......    $500

Payroll fourth week.......                 $200

Inventory purch. 4th week..                 500

Personal draw.............                  400         $650


Cash on hand June 30......                              $650
```

profitable businesses actually forced to shut down for a lack of immediate cash.

To help avoid a sudden cash squeeze, many businesses prepare monthly "cash flow projections". Cash flow projections are estimates of cash that will be coming in and cash that must be spent during the upcoming month. These projections show approximately how much cash will be on hand during the month and alert you to possible cash shortages.

During the first few months your business is in operation, cash projections will be difficult for you to make. You cannot yet estimate how much income will be coming in nor will you be familiar enough with your regular expense requirements. But the first few months are a critical time for any business. You should make some attempt to estimate and be prepared for cash needs. Here is a good way to project your first month's cash flow:

First determine how much cash you will need to get your business off to a good start. The chart of start-up costs in the Getting Started section should help you calculate these initial cash outlays.

If yours is a sales or manufacturing business or a service business that stocks parts, estimate how much additional inventory you will need during the first month of business. Unless you initially purchased a large inventory, figure on doubling the original amount.

Next, add the expenses that must be paid during the first month, such as supplies and payroll, and those that must be paid by the first of the next month, such as rent and utilities. Then add another $200 for unanticipated expenses.

The sum of the above items should give you an estimate of your first month's expenses. Now, how much income do you anticipate during the first month of operation? Obviously, this can only be a guess, but be conservative. And once you've arrived at a good guess, knock it down by twenty-five percent—almost all new business owners are over-optimistic.

Comparing the "guess-timated" income to the projected expenses will give you some idea of your cash needs. It is a very rough idea, admittedly; but it is better than no idea at all. Once you have a few months' actual experience behind you, cash flow projections will become easier and more accurate. A good ongoing procedure is to estimate your income and expenditures week by week, showing the balance of cash on hand at the end of each week.

The main purpose of a cash flow statement is to warn you *in advance* when cash might get dangerously low. If you know of a big cash outlay coming up next month—such as a loan payment or a tax payment—or a predictable seasonal drop in sales, the cash flow statement will show you whether your regular income will provide enough cash to meet expenses.

If the statement predicts a cash shortage, you can plan in advance to avoid the problem. Postpone a payment that is not immediately necessary, or plan a sale to generate more income, or seek a short-term loan. Short-term bank loans are relatively easy to get. Banks are usually willing to loan short-term funds (usually thirty days or sixty days) to profitable businesses. What's more, the fact that you have actually prepared a cash flow statement indicates to a banker that you are knowledgeable about your business and, therefore, a better risk than someone who has no financial knowledge at all.

Inventory Control

Any business that sells or manufactures goods and any service business that stocks parts must have some sort of inventory control, some way of knowing what has been ordered, what is on hand, and when it's time to reorder. For a very small business or one selling only a small variety of items, the inventory purchase records in your expenditure ledger (Column One) and your day-to-day observations of the stock on hand will probably provide you all the information you need to maintain

ITEM #3 Silver Buckle

COST $2.00   SUPPLIER Reese

Ordered		Received			
Quantity	Date	Quantity	Date	Sold	Balance
~~50~~	~~1/31~~				~~0~~
15	1/31	35	2/13		35
				~~卌卌III~~	~~22~~
				IIII	18
		15	3/1		33
				~~卌 卌~~	23
				II	21
50	3/12				

adequate inventory control. A periodic count, or "inventory," is the easiest and quickest way to determine what is still on hand and what must be reordered.

Larger businesses and those selling a large selection of merchandise, however, will need more formal procedures for controlling inventory. Such businesses should maintain a written record of all stock ordered, received and sold. "Perpetual inventory" records, as they are called, can be kept on index cards—one card for each type of item in stock—or in inventory ledgers, with a ledger page for each different item. Both the cards and the ledgers have the same format. An up-to-date and accurate inventory record can tell you at a glance your balance on hand, what is still on order, and how long it takes to receive an order.

How to Keep an Inventory Record

When you place your order, record the quantity and the date of the order in the Ordered column. When you receive the order, line out the entry in the Ordered column and enter the information in the Received column. Posting the date received will give you an idea how long it takes your suppliers to send you an ordered item. If you receive only part of your order, record the undelivered back-ordered quantity and the original order date in the Ordered column.

On the sample inventory record, 50 silver buckles were ordered on January 31. A partial shipment of 35 arrived February 13. The 35 received were recorded in the Received column, the order for 50 was lined out, and the balance of 15 still on order was recorded in the Ordered column. The fifteen finally arrived on March 1, at which time the fifteen still showing in the Ordered column was lined out. Got it? The number of items sold should be recorded either when the sale is made or at the end of the day, summarized from the day's sales slips.

At least once a year, and preferably every six months, the perpetual records should be proven by taking a physical count. If there is a discrepancy, the records should be adjusted to agree with the count. If the difference is substantial, you know something is wrong. Either you have not been updating the records correctly, or your inventory is being stolen.

Inventory control, like cash flow, is a management tool only. It is meant to help you run your business. The methods I have described for inventory control are only suggestions. Feel free to alter or ignore them. Any system or non-system that works for you is probably a good one.

Joe Campbell, Resistance Repair: "Here's one example of not running a service business like a regular business. For years I've had parts around, and I'd use one of them and I'd say, 'I think these things cost about fifty cents, so I'll charge 65 cents for them.' But it wasn't at all consistent. I had absolutely no idea how much I was spending for parts. If you get back only what you paid for it, you've lost money. Because it's taken time to order it, write the check for it, put it into stock, keep track of it and pay taxes on it. Now, I've got a little plastic box for every part that I stock. Inside that plastic box is the part and a card telling me where I got it, what the number is, what I paid for it. We use a uniform markup: 100 percent. We're selling things that cost us 30 cents. If we sell them for 40 percent more, for 42 cents, that hasn't even paid for hassling the damn things. Every week when we tally up the income, we break it down into parts and labor. And we get separate totals. We have a separate checking account and we take 60 percent of the parts income total and deposit it into the parts account. This way, we'll be able to replace the part and have 10 percent left over. It gives a little bit of wiggle room. It'll pay our resale taxes. That's about how it works out. Plus we know exactly how much money we've got to buy parts with. You look at it and say the balance is $400 and we need $300 worth of parts. Can we afford it? Yes, we can afford it. It's very simple, it's very efficient, and it works."

Section Three
GROWING UP

Most people would succeed in small things
if they were not troubled with great
ambitions.

—Longfellow

Growing Up

Well, maybe John D. Rockefeller did start with a two-pump filling station and some spectacular ambitions. After all, *bigger and better* has been a trademark of this big country of ours for as long as most of us can remember. For years we have associated big business, big industry, big government with prosperity, happiness and the good life.

But today it seems that America's "powerful places in industry" are just too powerful and are choking—not helping—our economy. In the last few years we have witnessed huge corporations laying off thousands of employees without warning; other corporations doubling and tripling their prices—and their profits—with us apparently powerless to stop them; big city governments unable to pay their bills, on the verge of financial collapse. Bigger is no longer synonymous with better, and big business no longer seems to be able or willing to provide us a good way of life.

Small Time Operator is not going to be much help to those Rockefellers among you with dreams of building your business into "powerful places in industry". I feel that small business can offer you personal satisfaction and a good livelihood. But "small" does not have to mean that you are forever the one person business, unable to grow. Nothing in this world is intrinsically good or bad. Business growth can be a positive and pleasant experience for everyone concerned. Business growth, however, can also be mistimed and miscalculated, turning against you and doing you in.

A few years ago, I was associated briefly with a small music magazine. It was doing well—good circulation, good advertising—and it was making a healthy profit. The owners of the magazine, feeling the power of success, simultaneously launched two other ventures: one was experimental films, the other a fashion magazine. Both new ventures were major undertakings, and both catered to a small audience. And both started losing money immediately and consistently until the entire company, music magazine and all, was at the brink of collapse. Major surgery saved the business. The unsuccessful sidelines were discontinued; friends loaned money to pay the creditors; the number of employees was cut back; and many of the extra luxuries added during the early success were eliminated. Only the original magazine remained, and still being very popular, it saved the company, which eventually emerged again, healthy, happy and much wiser.

He is well paid that is well satisfied.

—Shakespeare from *Merchant of Venice*

Success is heady, and the owners of the successful magazine believed—as many overly ambitious small time operators do—that success necessarily breeds success. They soon learn that things don't always work out that way.

Very often a business expands because a situation presents itself that the owner "just can't pass up": the adjacent store-front becomes vacant, and the landlord offers to knock out the separating partition and rent both stores to you; a competitor is failing and offers to sell his business to you, cheap. Or it may be that your customers have been encouraging expansion, suggesting that you offer some related product or service. And as frequent a reason for expansion as any, you're out to catch a bigger fish; success in your present business is tempting you on to bigger and better success (bigger and better?).

You should put in some real thinking time before making a decision about expanding:

1. Just as your present business was slow going at first, maybe even losing money, the expanded business will take time to get on its own feet. You will probably be making less money for a while, possibly even losing money for a year or two. Are you prepared for a repeat of the early, lean days?

2. Any expansion is going to require more capital. It means investing your savings or borrowing.

3. If you plan to acquire a second business location, be prepared for a *major* increase in the amount and type of work you will have to do. Someone will have to be hired to run one of the stores for you, and suddenly you will find yourself not only buyer, seller, bookkeeper, market analyst and the rest, but manager also. Some real skills are required to manage a multi-store operation, not the least of which is being able to deal with employees—hiring, training, delegating authority and responsibility, and sometimes firing.

4. The paperwork—bookkeeping, payrolls and government forms—will just about double. How well do you handle it now? You may need to hire a book-keeper.

5. Your own leisure time away from business will be reduced and, in the early days, possibly eliminated.

A re-warning about financial commitments: in the eyes of the law, you and your unincorporated business are one and the same. Any liabilities of your business, financial or otherwise, are also personal ones.

Hugo said, "Caution is the eldest child of wisdom." Think this decision through. Don't let any outside factors lure you into a move that you aren't ready for. Whether you choose to stay small or take a chance on expansion, be totally satisfied that you have made the right decision.

Small Time Operator is primarily written as a guide for the very small and the new business. "Growing Up" encompasses a world of new challenges and difficulties, the subject of an entire book itself. It is my purpose in this Growing Up section to discuss three areas that small business people commonly inquire about: hiring help, starting partnerships, and incorporating. This section of the book will familiarize you with these three areas, describe the benefits and drawbacks of each, and list step-by-step procedures for those of you ready for "growing up".

We have assumed that, because the country is big and the economy is big, everything should be big. It has been the conventional wisdom that bigness is goodness. Some bigness is dictated by the nature of things; in manufacturing it can bring wider distribution of goods and potentially lower prices. But a good deal of bigness is bad for the economy and bad for the free enterprise system. The large miscellaneous conglomerates that absorb independent businesses and engage in predatory competitive practices do not serve the best interests of the economy or the country.

—Former Senator Gaylord Nelson from a speech before the
National Society of Public Accountants

Hiring Help—How to Save Time and Money By Not Becoming an Employer

Hiring employees will just about double the amount of your paperwork. As an employer, you must keep separate payroll records for each employee, withhold federal income and Social Security taxes, withhold state income and possibly state disability taxes, prepare quarterly and year-end payroll tax returns, pay employer's portion of Social Security taxes and unemployment taxes, purchase workers' compensation insurance and prepare year-end earnings statements for each employee. It's been estimated that the employer's taxes,

worker's comp insurance and paperwork will cost you an additional thirty percent of your payroll. In other words, if you pay a wage of $4.00 per hour, it's really costing you about $5.20 per hour.

Businesses hiring employees are also more closely controlled and regulated than one-person businesses. Federal and state governments demand prompt payroll tax returns and require strict adherence to employment laws. If you are late filing your income tax return, it might easily be six months or more before you even hear from the government, and then it will just be a letter of inquiry or a bill. If, however, you are late filing your quarterly payroll tax return, in just a few weeks you could find your business under lock and key and your bank account impounded.

Who are employees? From the Internal Revenue Service: "Anyone who performs services that can be controlled by an employer (what will be done and how it will be done) is an employee. This is so even when the employer gives the employee freedom of action, if the employer has the legal right to control the method and result of the services. Employers usually provide the tools and place to work and have the right to fire an employee." In addition, the following people are also considered employees by the IRS regardless of the circumstances: commission truck drivers who deliver laundry, food, or beverages other than milk; full-time life insurance sales people; home workers such as maids and cooks; travelling sales people working full-time for one employer and selling to other businesses (not to consumers).

Some businesses such as restaurants and larger retail stores must have employees; there is no getting around it. You can't possibly do all the work yourself, and the people you hire—dishwashers, waitresses, clerks—definitely fall within the legal definition of "employee".

Some small businesses can sometimes get outside help without hiring employees. These businesses often hire "outside contractors", people in business for themselves, people who sell their services to you. When you hire an outside contractor, you pay the contractor his or her fee in full. You do not withhold taxes, pay employment taxes or file payroll tax returns.

Who is an outside contractor? The IRS says, "Generally, people in business for themselves are not employees. For example, doctors, lawyers, contractors and others who follow an independent trade are usually not employees." In addition, travelling salespeople selling consumer goods (not selling to businesses) and real estate salespeople are considered outside contractors if you have a written agreement with them stating that they are outside contractors and responsible for their own taxes.

Here are two hypothetical examples to illustrate employees vs. non-employees:

Example I: The Clever Leather Company (that's you) needs help making belts. You want someone to cut the leather into two inch wide strips so you can devote your talent to the design work. You hire your buddy for $5.00 an hour, sit him down in your shop, and tell him to cut out 250 two inch wide belts, each three feet long.

The Clever Leather Company has just become a bona-fide employer. When you pay your friend, you must withhold income and Social Security taxes, send the withheld taxes to the government, pay employer Social Security and unemployment taxes, maintain payroll ledgers, prepare earnings statements at year-end. Ugh.

Example II: The More-Clever-Than-Ever Leather Company (that's me) needs help making belts. I want someone to cut the leather into two inch wide strips so I can devote my talent to the design work. I call up the Leather Cutting Company (that's *my* buddy) and order up 250 of his standard two inch wide, three foot long belts. The Leather Cutting Company produces the belts on its own work schedule and delivers the completed order to me.

The More-Clever-Than-Ever Leather company just conducted business with an outside contractor. More-Clever-Than-Ever Leather wrote a check for the full amount billed and recorded it in the expenditure ledger.

Seriously, it is important that you carefully determine the legal status of your hired help. A person who falls within the definition of an employee *is* an employee no matter what you call him. Says the IRS: "If an employer-employee relationship exists, it does not matter what it is called. The employee may be called a partner, agent or independent contractor. It also does not matter how payments are measured or paid, what they are called, or whether the employee works full or part-time."

There is one potentially serious problem if you hire people and treat them as outside contractors when the law says they should be employees. If one of these people gets injured on the job and is not covered by workers' compensation insurance, you could find yourself with medical bills and a large lawsuit.

The IRS puts out a free publication, *Circular E—Employer's Tax Guide*, which includes all of their legal definitions and guidelines. When in doubt about the status of your "employee," you may request a ruling from the IRS on form #SS-8.

If you hire outside contractors, there is one extra bit of paperwork that you must do at year-end. For each person to whom you paid $600 or more during the year, you must file a federal form #1099-MISC. The form shows the contractor's name, address, social security number and amount paid. One copy goes to the IRS and another copy to the contractor. In addition, if your outside contractors are independent sales agents, you must report to the IRS each contractor who purchased $5,000 or more in goods from you. Use form 1099-MISC.

RENTAL AGREEMENT

MONKEYWRENCH MOTORS (hereinafter "Owners"), doing business in Berkeley, California, and _____ (hereinafter "Lessee") in consideration of the premises, agree as follows:

FIRST: Lessee agrees to rent from owner a mechanic's stall and the immediate surrounding area necessary to perform the normal functions of an automobile mechanic for the daily rental of _____ per cent of the lessee's daily gross receipts.

SECOND: Lessee shall provide owner with evidence of sufficient liability insurance coverage.

THIRD: Lessee shall hold harmless owner for any and all losses owing to fire, theft, water hazard, earthquake, or any disaster.

FOURTH: Owner shall provide all supplies and materials necessary for the normal operation of an automobile garage, excepting tools and personal equipment, which shall be supplied by lessee.

FIFTH: Lessee is an independent contractor leasing or renting space in the Monkeywrench Motors' garage for the purpose of conducting the business of an automobile mechanic, and lessee shall be responsible for filing all necessary tax returns.

SIXTH: This rental agreement may be terminated by either party by giving one day's oral notice of the intention to terminate this rental agreement to the other party.

DATED: _____

MONKEYWRENCH MOTORS

_____
                              Owners

_____
                              Lessee

This rental agreement was drafted by a lawyer for the specific purpose of clarifying the relationship between the owner of a garage and the people working in that garage. The lawyer claims that this agreement defining the "lessees" as independent contractors and not as employees will hold up in tax court. The Internal Revenue Service says that the agreement may or may not hold up depending on the actual situation.

PAYER'S name, street address, city, state, and ZIP code	1 Rents	OMB No.1545-0115	Miscellaneous Income
MONKEYWRENCH MOTORS 9345 Cavemont Avenue Berkeley CA 94705	2 Royalties	**1986** Statement for Recipients of	

PAYER'S Federal identification number 123-45-6789	RECIPIENT'S identification number 987-65-4321	3 Prizes and awards	4 Federal income tax withheld	Copy C For Payer
RECIPIENT'S name (first, middle, last) Michael Shine		5 Fishing boat proceeds	6 Medical and health care payments	For Paperwork Reduction Act Notice and instructions for completing this form, see Instructions for Forms 1099, 1098, 5498, 1096 and W-2G.
Street address 1234 Baltimore Street		7 Nonemployee compensation $5,650.00	8 Substitute payments in lieu of dividends or interest	
City, state, and ZIP code Oakland CA 94979		9 Payer made direct sales of $5,000 or more of consumer products to a buyer (recipient) for resale . . . . . ▶ ☐		
Account number (optional)				

Form **1099-MISC**   Department of the Treasury - Internal Revenue Service

Form 1099-MISC must be filed for every outside contractor (non-employee) who received $600 or more during the year and for outside salespeople who purchased $5,000 or more in goods from you.

Form **1096** Department of the Treasury Internal Revenue Service	**Annual Summary and Transmittal of U.S. Information Returns**	OMB No. 1545-0108 **1986**

Type or machine print FILER'S name
  MONKEYWRENCH MOTORS
Street address
  9345 Cavemont Ave.
City, state, and ZIP code
  Berkeley CA 94705

Enter in Box 1 or 2 below the identification number you used as the filer on the attached information returns. Do not fill in both Boxes 1 and 2.

1 Employer identification number none	3 Total number of documents 1
2 Social security number 123-45-6789	4 Federal income tax withheld 0

Check only one box below to indicate the type of forms attached.

W-2G 32	1098 81	1099-A 80	1099-B 79	1099-DIV 91	1099-G 86	1099-INT 92	1099-MISC 95	1099-OID 96	1099-PATR 97	1099-R 98	5498 28
☐	☐	☐	☐	☐	☐	☐	☒	☐	☐	☐	☐

Under penalties of perjury, I declare that I have examined this return and accompanying documents and, to the best of my knowledge and belief, they are true, correct, and complete. In the case of documents without recipients' identification numbers, I have complied with the requirements of the law in attempting to secure such numbers from the recipients.

Signature ▶ *Samuel Thresham*   Title ▶ owner   Date ▶ 1-30-87

A #1096 Summary and Transmittal Form must accompany the 1099 forms sent to the IRS.

Steps to Becoming an Employer

To meet the legal requirements of becoming an employer, you will have to deal with the federal government and the state government, and you will probably have to obtain workers' compensation insurance. These are one-time-only procedures, but they require quite a bit of paperwork. If possible, start these procedures a month before you plan to hire your first employee.

Federal Requirements

1. Contact the Internal Revenue Service and tell them you are about to become an employer. Request Form SS-4, "Application for Employer Identification Number." Ask for a free copy of publication #15, *Circular E—Employer's Tax Guide.* Circular E will give you detailed instructions for complying with federal requirements. Circular E also includes federal withholding tables.

2. Ask the IRS for several copies of Form W-4, "Employees Withholding Allowance Certificate." Each new employee must fill out a W-4 indicating marital status and the number of exemptions claimed. You keep the W-4's in your files.

3. All employers with one or more employees must comply with Occupational Safety & Health Administration (OSHA) regulations. If you have more than ten employees, OSHA will also require you to keep routine job safety records, although some retail businesses with low injury rates are exempt from this requirement. Write OSHA, U.S. Department of Labor, Washington D.C. 20210 for complete information.

4. Most employers are subject to the Fair Labor Standards Act. This act sets a minimum wage of $3.35 per hour for covered employees and sets overtime pay at not less than 1.5 times the regular rate of pay. Generally, the following businesses are covered by the act: businesses that handle, ship or receive goods which have moved or will move in interstate commerce; businesses that regularly use the mail or the telephone for interstate communication; laundries, construction firms, hospitals, nursing homes, schools and preschools; other businesses with annual gross income of $362,500 or more. Specifically exempt from the act are most executives, administrators, professionals and outside sales people and some amusement park employees, switchboard operators, seamen and farm workers. For more details, write the Department of Labor, Washington D.C. 20210.

State Requirements

1. Contact your state department of employment and ask for their forms and instructions.

2. Every state that has an income tax on wages requires employers to withhold state income tax. The states usually publish their own employer's tax guides including state withholding tables. Request a copy of these tables.

3. Some states have other required withholding from employee wages. You should inquire about any such state laws.

4. Most states also have employer-paid state unemployment insurance. Those that do will require you to submit an application and receive an insurance rating. The rates vary from state to state and within states from occupation to occupation. The unemployment insurance rate for your business will initially be based on the prevailing rate in your particular occupation. For future years, your own business experience—that is, how many of your former employees receive unemployment insurance—will determine your rate. A "favorable" record will mean lower rates.

5. Many states require employers to have Worker's Compensation Insurance. Some states provide the insurance themselves, and some require that you obtain Workers' Comp from an insurance company. A detailed explanation of Worker's Compensation Insurance is included in the "Insurance" chapter in the first section of the book.

Form **W-4** (Rev. January 1984)	**Employee's Withholding Allowance Certificate** Department of the Treasury—Internal Revenue Service		OMB No. 1545-0010

1 Type or print your full name
Roslyn Michael

2 Your social security number
234-00-5678

Home address (number and street or rural route)
1964 Scotts Level Road

City or town, State, and ZIP code
Aberdeen, Md 43329

3 Marital Status
[X] Single [ ] Married
[ ] Married, but withhold at higher Single rate
Note: If married, but legally separated, or spouse is a nonresident alien, check the Single box.

4 Total number of allowances you are claiming (from line F of the worksheet on page 2) 1

5 Additional amount, if any, you want deducted from each pay . . . . $ 0

6 I claim exemption from withholding because (see instructions and check boxes below that apply):
 a [ ] Last year I did not owe any Federal income tax and had a right to a full refund of **ALL** income tax withheld, **AND**
 b [ ] This year I do not expect to owe any Federal income tax and expect to have a right to a full refund of **ALL** income tax withheld. If both a and b apply, enter the year effective and "EXEMPT" here ▶   Year
 c If you entered "EXEMPT" on line 6b, are you a full-time student? . . . . [ ]Yes [ ]No

Under penalties of perjury, I certify that I am entitled to the number of withholding allowances claimed on this certificate, or if claiming exemption from withholding, that I am entitled to claim the exempt status.
Employee's signature ▶ *Roslyn Michael*   Date ▶ January 14, 1985

7 Employer's name and address (Employer: Complete 7, 8, and 9 only if sending to IRS)
DEKAY ENGINEERING, 1944 Edgewood, Aberdeen MD 43329

8 Office code

9 Employer identification number
123000123

Each of your employees must fill out a W-4 form.

6. Some states have laws similar to the Federal Fair Labor Standards Act. Again, contact your state department of employment.

Federal Procedures and Taxes for Employers

Outlined here are the basic federal procedures most employers must follow. These laws have changed very little in recent years, but that does not preclude the possibility of changes in the future. It is your responsibility as an employer to read Circular E carefully and comply with all the instructions. Unlike income taxes, there is no "grey" or questionable area where payroll taxes are involved. There is only one way to do it—their way.

1. The Internal Revenue Service requires that you withhold income tax from each employee's paycheck. The amount you withhold is calculated from the tables in Circular E. You must also withhold Social Security tax (officially known as F.I.C.A. which stands for Federal Insurance Contributions Act). Social Security tax is 7.15 percent of the employee's gross up to an annual earnings maximum of $42,000 (1986 rate; look out, this goes up every year.)

Special note to restaurant and nightclub owners: employees must report their tips to you, and you must in turn withhold taxes from them. Businesses with more than ten employees must also report gross income and other information related to tips. Call your local IRS office for more information.

2. You are liable for an employer's portion of Social Security taxes in addition to the tax withheld from your employees. The employer's tax is 7.15 percent of the employee's gross, up to the $42,000 earnings maximum per employee. Do not confuse this employer's Social Security tax with the Self-Employment tax discussed in the tax section of the book. They are different taxes. Employers are liable for both.

3. Federal Payroll Tax Returns (Form #941) are due quarterly on April 30 for January, February and March; July 31 for April, May and June; October 31 for July, August and September; and January 31 for October, November and December. Taxes reported on Form #941 are the withheld income and Social Security taxes and the employer's portion of Social Security taxes. As long as the total taxes due in any one quarter are less than $500, the entire amount can be remitted with the return. If,

however, at the end of any month in the quarter, total taxes due (combined employee and employer portions) are $500 or more, you must deposit the full amount by the fifteenth day of the next month. Deposits are reported on yet another form, #501, "Federal Tax Deposit, Withheld Income and FICA Taxes," and paid to an authorized commercial bank or to a Federal Reserve bank. You can obtain the names of authorized commercial banks at any local bank.

The deposit information is confusing enough to warrant an illustration. (Maybe it's confusing enough to go back and read the chapter, "How Not To Become An Employer.") In January, let's say you withheld from your employees $140 in income tax and $80 in Social Security. Your tax liability at the end of January is the $220 withheld plus $80—your employer's portion of Social Security—for a total of $300. Since this amount is under $500 there is no need to file anything at that time. Okay so far? Now in February, let's say the same taxes recur: $220 withholding and $80 employer's portion, or $300. Your total tax liability is now $600 for the two months. Since you are now over the $500 limit, you must deposit the full $600 with an authorized bank by March 15. Taxes for March, the last month of the quarter, are due when you file the quarterly return on April 30—assuming that March's taxes are less than $500. If your payroll jumped in March, and March's taxes alone are $500 or more, a deposit of the full amount must be made by April 15.

Another and more complicated set of deposit rules apply if your undeposited payroll taxes exceed $3,000. Businesses with payrolls in this bracket should contact the Internal Revenue Service for instructions.

4. As an employer, you are also subject to Federal Unemployment tax (F.U.T.A.) if during the year you, (a) paid wages of $1,500 or more in any calendar quarter, or (b) had one or more employees for some portion of at least one day during each of twenty different calendar weeks (better re-read that slowly). Unemployment tax is imposed on you, the employer. It is not deducted from your employee's wages. An annual return must be filed on Form #940, "Employer's Annual Federal Unemployment Tax Return," on or before January 31 of next year. The rate is 6.2 percent of the first $7,000 of wages paid to each employee during the year. You may receive credit of up to 5.4 percent for state unemployment taxes you pay. So your net federal liability could be as low as 0.8 percent.

5. Ask Internal Revenue to send you several copies of form W-2, "Wage and Tax Statement." The W-2 is a five-part form which you must prepare for each employee, annually at year-end. You must mail or give out the W-2 Forms by January 31. Three copies of the W-2 are given to the employee, one copy you retain, and one copy is sent to the Social Security Administration (the SSA). The SSA copies should be batched and sent with form W-3, "Transmittal of Income and Tax Statements," no later than February 28. W-3's are available from the IRS.

Payroll Ledgers

Every employer must keep a separate payroll ledger in addition to the regular expenditure ledger. The payroll ledger must show all the details of every paycheck for every employee. Payroll ledgers can be purchased pre-lined and all headed up for you, or you can easily design your own. Included in the Ledger section of this book is a sample payroll ledger page that you can use as a prototype.

Use a separate ledger page for each employee. Head the page with the employee's name, address

1 Control number	22222	For Paperwork Reduction Act Notice, see back of Copy D. OMB No. 1545-0008	For Official Use Only	
2 Employer's name, address, and ZIP code DEKAY ENGINEERING 1944 Edgewood Road Aberdeen MD 43329		3 Employer's identification number 123--00-0123	4 Employer's State number CX 1215	
		5 Stat. employee ☐ Deceased ☐ Legal rep. ☐ 942 emp. ☐ Subtotal ☐ Void ☐		
		6 Allocated tips	7 Advance EIC payment	
8 Employee's social security number 234-00-5678	9 Federal income tax withheld $ 327.50	10 Wages, tips, other compensation $ 4,300	11 Social security tax withheld $288.10	
12 Employee's name (first, middle, last)		13 Social security wages $ 4,300	14 Social security tips	
Roslyn Michael 1964 Scotts Level Road Aberdeen MD 43329		16 *		
		17 State income tax $ 67.70	18 State wages, tips, etc. $4,300	19 Name of State MD
		20 Local income tax	21 Local wages, tips, etc.	22 Name of locality
15 Employee's address and ZIP code				

Form **W-2 Wage and Tax Statement** 1985   Copy A For Social Security Administration   * See Instructions for Forms W-2 and W-2P   Department of the Treasury Internal Revenue Service

A W-2 Form must be sent to each employee, listing earnings and deductions for the year.

Please do not staple	1 Control number	33333	OMB No. 1545-0008		
	☐ Kind of Payer and Tax Statements Transmitted ▶	2 941/941E ☒ Military ☐ 943 ☐ CT-1 ☐ 942 ☐ Medicare Fed. emp. ☐	3 W-2 ☒ W-2P ☐	4	5 Number of statements attached 1
	6 Allocated tips	7 Advance EIC payments	8		
	9 Federal income tax withheld $ 327.50	10 Wages, tips, and other compensation $ 4,300.00	11 Social security (FICA) tax withheld $ 288.10		
	12 Employer's State number cx 1215	13 Social security (FICA) wages $ 4,300.00	14 Social security (FICA) tips 0		
	15 Employer's identification number 123 — 00 0123		16 Establishment number		
	17 Employer's name DEKAY ENGINEERING		18 Gross annuity, pension, etc. (Form W-2P) 0		
	1944 Edgewood Road Aberdeen MD 43329		20 Taxable amount (Form W-2P) 0		
	19 Employer's address and ZIP code (If available, place label over boxes 15, 17, and 19.)		21 Income tax withheld by third-party payer 0		

Under penalties of perjury, I declare that I have examined this return and accompanying documents, and to the best of my knowledge and belief, they are true, correct, and complete. In the case of documents without recipients' identifying numbers, I have complied with the requirements of the law in attempting to secure such numbers from the recipients.

Signature ▶ *David Kay*   Title ▶ owner   Date ▶ 2-1-85

Form **W-3** **Transmittal of Income and Tax Statements** 1985   Department of the Treasury Internal Revenue Service

A W-3 must accompany the W-2 forms sent to the Social Security Administration.

PAYROLL LEDGER

Name _____   Social Security _____

Address _____   Pay Rate _____

_____

1	2	3	4	5	6	7	8	9	10	11	12	13
PAYCHECK DATE	CHECK NO.	PAY PERIOD	HOURS REG	O/T	GROSS	F.I.T.	F.I.C.A.	STATE INCOME	OTHER WITHHOLDING			NET PAY

and Social Security number. Year-end W-2 Earnings Statements will be easier to prepare if all this required information is in one place. Also write down the employee's hourly or monthly rate of pay at the top of the page. If the rate changes during the year, show the new rate as well as the old and the date of change.

The payroll ledger should have a column for each of the following:
1. Date of paycheck.
2. Check number.
3. Payroll period.
4. Number of regular hours worked.
5. Number of overtime hours worked.
6. Gross pay.
7. Federal income tax withheld.
8. Social Security (F.I.C.A.) tax withheld.
9. State income tax withheld.
10. through ?. Enough columns to cover any other withholding.
(last column). Net "take-home" pay.

Remember that the *net* pay amount must also be posted to your expenditure ledger in Column Four.

———

Mike Madsen, Easy Rider Leather: "When you're first getting started you don't always hire the best people. You don't know what you are looking for. You might hire somebody who is sympathetic to you or flatters you or somebody who is good looking. But they might not fit the job that you have. You've got to think in terms of what the job is, and hire the people for the job, and not hire friends. I'd say it's better always to make friends of those people that work for you, but never to hire friends."

———

Nick Mein, Wallpapers Plus, San Francisco: "A person's gotta be happy if he or she is going to work for you. The women working for me were terribly unhappy. This one woman who worked for me, who I really liked, was a great saleswoman. She'd been going to a Freudian shrink for about six years, and she switched to a Jungian psychologist. He said, 'Work's bad for you'. So she called up one day and said, 'I won't be in.' A lot of jobs depended on her charm; she brought a lot of people in the store. And she just sort of gave up on it. That's irritating. No 'stick-to-it-ivity' my father calls it; no perseverance.

"It's very difficult to be nice to your employees because they're going to take advantage of you. They're going to start coming in late. All the people who worked for me are perfect examples. I'd say, 'Get in at 9:30, do whatever ordering needs to be done, and open the doors at ten. I want you to be ready to sell at ten.' And they do that for a while, but then they say, 'I want to get in a little later because there's no ordering to do, there's no backlog.' I say okay. And then eventually, they'll be coming in at eleven. Because they felt nobody was coming into the shop until 11:00 or 11:30. And if you're not on it everyday, you get screwed. You have to be on it all the time. And then, they leave early...

If you have somebody working for you you've got to make it absolutely plain that they're being paid for the specified hours. I find that really hard to do, keep people to that, because I'm a little bit like that myself. On a really slow day, I'd say, 'Go ahead, go home early.' Then it always happens: next day some woman would call and say, 'I came by your shop at 5:20 and you weren't there.' That's bad service."

Partnerships

Partnerships offer opportunities often not available to the one-person business: more capital, more skills and ideas, the extra energy generated when two or more people are working together. Partnerships are the traditional meeting ground of the "idea" person and the "money" person. Having a partner can relieve the sole proprietor pressures of having to do everything yourself. And, at last, you can take a little vacation without having to shut down the business.

Partnerships have their drawbacks as well. The independence and sole decision making that only the sole proprietor has must now be shared. There is more paperwork. Inter-personal relations with your partner or partners may require both time and tact. Most important, the legal consequences of having one or more partners can be serious.

Legal Aspects of General Partnerships

A partnership, like a sole proprietorship, is legally inseparable from the owners, the partners. Individual partners can be held responsible for financial debts and legal obligations of the partnership. The most important legal aspect of a general partnership is that all partners can be held personally, individually liable for the acts of any one partner acting on partnership business. If your partner, representing the business, goes to the bank and borrows $5,000, you can be personally responsible to repay the debt, even if you didn't sign the papers yourself, even if you didn't know about the loan. In a more serious situation, if your partner gets into legal trouble while on partnership business, you may also be in legal trouble.

Like sole proprietors, partners cannot be employees of their partnerships. Partners can draw a "wage" (called a "guaranteed payment"), or they can merely share in the profits of the partnership or some combination of the two. Profits and guaranteed payments are taxable to the individual partners.

A partnership must have its own federal identification number, obtained by filing Form SS-4, "Employer's Federal Identification Number." If the partnership will have no employees, note on the form that it is "FOR IDENTIFICATION ONLY." This will alert the IRS not to send you payroll forms.

Partnerships must file a partnership income tax return, although the partnership itself pays no taxes. Partnerships will need business licenses, seller's permits, and if operating under fictitious names, fictitious name statements. Partnerships pay sales, employment, inventory and local taxes.

Death or withdrawal of one partner or the addition of a new partner legally terminates a partnership. The business need not be liquidated, however. A new partnership agreement can be made. The original partnership agreement can include provisions for continuation of a partnership (discussed below).

Partnership Agreements

A partnership agreement is an "understanding" between partners as to how the business will be conducted. Many partnership agreements are nothing more than a handshake and a "Let's do it;" and often such agreements turn out to be more of a *mis*understanding than anything else. A written partnership agreement is not required by law, but it is something no partnership should be without. It reduces the possibilities of misunderstanding and future problems.

A written partnership agreement should be signed by all the partners and should specify:

1. What the business is and what are its goals. Be succinct: you should be able to pin this down in one paragraph. A simple, *written* statement of business goals is the first and most important step in any partnership agreement. Long range goals should be included as well. For example, one partner may want a business that will provide a good livelihood for many years; while the other partner may be dreaming of building up the business and when it becomes successful and established, selling it for a big profit. These two partners obviously have a serious conflict of interest. If partners do not agree on the basics, the partnership is doomed from the start.

2. How much each partner will contribute—in cash, in property and in labor. There are no federal laws requiring partners to make equal or simultaneous contributions.

3. How each partner will share in the profits and losses. The easiest and most common arrangement is an equal division of profits between partners. You may wish, however, to provide for an unequal division of profits to compensate for differences in time or money contributed or for differences in ability and experience. A partner can also draw a wage to reflect actual time spent running the business. The wage is known as a "guaranteed payment to partner." It is not a regular employee wage for tax purposes. There is no withholding, employee social security or unemployment insurance. It is part of the partner's total partnership income. Paying a wage is common when one partner works day-to-day at the business and the other doesn't or when partners do not put in equal time. After the wage is paid, any remaining profit (or loss) for the year is then divided between the partners according to your agreement. Specify in the agreement who gets a wage and the amount.

4. Procedures for withdrawal of funds and payments of profits—how much and when. Such an understanding will prevent situations in which one partner can arbitrarily withdraw substantial amounts of money from the partnership. There is no federal law requiring partners to make equal or simultaneous withdrawals.

5. Provisions for continuing the business if one

partner dies or wants out. A prearranged agreement to buy out a departing partner can prevent the shutdown of the business. Your biggest problem is determining how much money the departing partner (or his estate) should receive and over what period of time. For example, the business may be worth a lot of money because it is established and successful or because it owns a lot of inventory and equipment, but there may be little cash on hand to pay the departing partner.

Your agreement should state how a partner's share of the business is to be valued. Is it based on the value of the business assets; that it, what you actually have invested in the business? Or is it based on what the going business is worth on the open market, what an eager new owner might pay for it? And who will be the lucky person to determine this "worth"? Also, there are tax consequences to a partner buy-out and they vary depending on how the agreement is worded. The tax interests of the remaining and outgoing partners are often diametrically opposed. This tax aspect can be substantial if the business is worth a lot of money; it will require professional help.

6. You may also want a clause specifying the financial and legal powers of each partner. Such a clause will not relieve any partner of partnership obligations entered into by other partners. It only reduces the possibility of future problems.

Most of the professional advice I have heard suggests that you hire a lawyer to draw up any partnership agreement. Certainly a *knowledgeable* lawyer—not all lawyers are familiar with partnership problems—will draft up an "iron-clad" agreement that leaves nothing to doubt. But you will pay a high fee for this service. I feel it is not really necessary to see a lawyer if the partnership agreement is a simple one (such as 50-50, equal sharing, equal contributions) and if you know your partner well enough to be confident you aren't being used.

You and Your Partners

My friend Rory said, "Having a partner is just like having a wife, only more so." Well, Rory is a long-time loner, but his words are basically true. Partnerships are more than business. They are often complex inter-personal relationships. And like marriages, partnerships can bring out the best and the worst in people. By acquiring a partner you are adding a whole new dimension to your business venture, one you should be fully prepared to deal with.

Anyone who has lost a friend after an argument can quickly realize the possible problems and complications of having a business partner. It is not uncommon for partners to have a disagreement, a difference of opinion, or worse. You may feel that your partner is not working as hard as he should (and he may be feeling the same about you!). When trouble arises between partners, the most logical step is to try to work it out: sit down with your partner, get the problems "out front", and hopefully get them solved. Much more easily said than done. Like divorces, partnership dissolutions are more common than ever and often just as problematical. The alternatives—dividing up the assets and going out of business, or one partner buying out the other—can be difficult even with a good written agreement, can require lawyers, and almost always cause the business to suffer.

Marriage counselors can sometimes save a marriage. But it's a little out of my field, and there is little advice I can give you retrospectively. Knowing that such things happen should warn you to take every precaution prior to going into a partnership to reduce the possibility of problems later on. The best advice I can offer is to pick your partner or partners *very* carefully. This advice may seem basic, just common sense; but a poor choice of partners is the root cause of many partnership failures. How well do you know your prospective partner? Are you old friends? Have you worked together before? What business experience does your partner have? What is his or her "track record"?

General vs. Limited Partnerships

The type of partnership just described is known as a "general" partnership and is by far the most common form of partnership. A "limited" partnership is a refinement of the general partnership concept. Limited partnerships allow investors to become partners without assuming unlimited liability. Limited partners usually risk only their investment in the business. There still must be at least one general partner in a limited partnership with full legal and financial responsibility.

Limited partnerships are subject to much greater government scrutiny than general partnerships. Most states require limited partnerships to be registered with the county or the state. The Internal Revenue Service has special income tax rules for limited partnerships.

Limited partnerships are also discussed under "Investors" in the "Getting Started" section. The unique legal and tax requirements of limited partnerships are not covered in *Small Time Operator*. You should consult a tax accountant or a lawyer to help you set up the partnership and to explain the tax consequences.

Partnership Bookkeeping

The basic bookkeeping for a partnership is the same as for a sole proprietorship. You will be able to use the ledgers and worksheets in the ledger section with no alteration. In addition to the income and expenditure ledgers, partnerships must keep a separate "partners' capital ledger" which provides a complete record, by partner, of all contributions and withdrawals and of each partner's share of profit or loss.

The partners' capital ledger has two columns for each partner. One column shows *activity* in the partner's account—contributions, withdrawals and the partner's share of profit or loss. The second column is the *balance* of the partner's capital remaining with the partnership. Contributions and

WESLEY'S Farm Fresh Eggs
PARTNERS' CAPITAL LEDGER

ENTRY		HUCK (PARTNER A) Activity	Balance	PIPPI (PARTNER B) Activity	Balance	TOTAL BALANCE
①	Contrib. 1-1-85	$500	$500	$500	$500	$1,000
②	Contrib. 3-31-85	300	800	200	700	1500
③	1985 Income	600	1400	300	1000	2400
④	w/Draw 2-5-86	(400)	1000			2000
⑤	w/Draw 5-1-86			(350)	650	1650

withdrawals should be recorded when they occur. Contributions are shown as positive amounts and increase the partner's balance. Withdrawals are shown as negative, bracketed amounts and decrease the partner's balance. Each partner's share of the partnership profit or loss is posted to the partners' capital ledger once a year at year-end. A profit is posted to the Activity column as a positive amount; a loss is shown as a negative, bracketed amount. Profits and losses increase and decrease a partner's balance accordingly. The Total Balance column is the sum of all the individual partners' Balance columns.

The sample partners' capital ledger shows activity for 1985 and part of 1986 for Wesley's Farm Fresh Eggs, a new partnership owned by two partners.

Entry 1: The partnership began on January 1, 1985. Each partner contributed $500 to the business. Each partner's balance is $500, and the total balance is $1,000.

Entry 2: On March 31, Huck (Partner A) contributed another $300, and Pippi (Partner B) contributed another $200.

Entry 3: The partnership made a $900 profit in 1985. At December 31, 1985, the partners' shares of the profit were posted to their individual accounts.

Entry 4: On February 5, 1986, Huck withdrew $400 from the business. This is the first money either partner has taken out of the business.

Entry 5: On May 1, 1986, Pippi withdrew $350 from the business.

With each entry, the partners' individual balances and the total balance were adjusted.

A partnership income tax return must sometimes include a balance sheet (explained in the Appendix) and schedule of partners' capital. The Appendix also includes a chapter on husband and wife partnerships. For more tax information about partnerships, ask the IRS for a free copy of Pub. 541, "Tax Information on Partnerships."

PARTNERSHIP POST MORTEM

Lara Stonebraker, former partner in Aromatica, Walnut Creek, California: "It's been my experience that partnerships rarely work, especially if there is an odd number of partners. Because it's always going to be two against one in all decision making, and there's always going to be an odd man out. Unless you have such well matched personalities that everybody is always good friends, it just creates incredible hassles. That was the most anxiety-ridden period of my life. There were three of us and I happened to be the odd one, because I was living in Berkeley and the other two were right there on the premises.

"And then one of the partners turned out to be a Jesus freak and was really just impossible to deal with. She'd bring her Bible to the store and talk to the customers about it, and there was just no way of stopping it. Finally she decided that she had to go to this retreat in the mountains to prepare for the holocaust, so she sold her partnership. I blotted out a lot of that whole experience."

Key Dickason, former partner in Xanadu, Concord, California: "I was in a partnership once before, and my partner and I disagreed, not on the running of the business, but on the way we handle employees. We bought out a data processing service bureau which had two employees, a key puncher and an operator/supervisor. One of the conditions of the sale was that we continue the old employees on and honor their vacations. But when the operator/supervisor got married and gave us notice she was quitting, my partner said, 'No one quits on me,' and he refused to pay her vacation. So I wrote a check for her vacation money.

"The keypuncher working for us got a four-year, fully-paid scholarship from the university; in May, she told us she would be leaving in August. And my partner fired her on the spot. That was fifteen years ago and I've never had another keypuncher who even approached her. He just arbitrarily fired her. Because I disagreed on that, it eventually led to the dissolution of the partnership.

"I also discovered that he was putting his personal debts into the business. I finally went to a CPA. He looked at the books and said, 'I'd advise you to see an attorney.' So I went to see my attorney, and he told me that if I got out of the business, closed the business up, I would be liable for all the debts, and the business would be defunct. So I just signed all the assets and everything over to my partner. The only way I could try and get my money out of it, which was gone, was to sue for dissolution of the partnership. Then once you go into litigation, according to my attorney, everything's tied up.

"The partnership agreement doesn't mean a thing unless both parties want to honor it. Jack and I disagreed on a philosophical—a better word is ethical—aspect of employee-employer relationships. To Jack, an employee was somebody you used and discarded. To me an employee was somebody you used but you also had an obligation and a commitment to. If you have this basic disagreement, no partnership agreement will handle it. Do you put in there, 'You agree to treat employees fairly?' Well, that doesn't mean anything. 'Cause to Jack, Jack was treating them fairly.

"The biggest mistake in the world is to start a partnership if there is disagreement in the beginning when you're laying the groundwork for the formation of the business. If you enter into basic disagreement on ethics, business management, or whatever the objective of the business is, if you disagree on that then you shouldn't go into business together. Putting your doubts about the situation into a partnership agreement doesn't accomplish anything unless you're prepared to fight, which isn't what it's all about."

Jan Lowe, former partner in Midnight Sewing Machine, Mendocino, California: "I went into business with my sister who is a dear person, and who taught me everything I know. I didn't sew a stitch in my life before we bought this dress shop, and she handed me a pattern and scissors and said, 'I'm going to lunch now. If you have any problems, let me know.' So I started off real cold there, which is no way to do it. I'd run into problems when people would want something very intricate done or they'd want something altered, and I wouldn't know how to handle it. I wasn't really prepared to do what I did for living.

"One of our basic problems was non-communication. My partner would borrow money from someone and I didn't know about it, which I thought was a cheap shot. You've got to be in constant communication. If somebody's going to lunch, they've got to tell you. We didn't have anything in writing between us. How things were going to be run was not made clear and that I think was another downfall. That should be made clear right from the start—exactly what do you want to see happen, how is it going to happen, who's going to make what work, who is best at handling what; and stick to it. I think you should be willing to bend when that system does not work. Face it immediately and try something else. To hang onto a system that doesn't work can get you into a lot of trouble, too.''

And a Partnership That Works

''Kipple is a made-up word that means, um, kipple, the dumb stuff that you gather around you that you can't live without.'' Pat Ellington is a partner in Kipple, a small antique store in Berkeley, California: ''We function pretty well as a four-way partnership. Miriam and I are old friends—friends for fifteen years or more. Her downstairs neighbor is the third partner, and a friend of hers is the fourth. Everybody's really working part time. But this way we can operate a full time business.

''When we first came into this, I was the only one with any kind of skill, any kind of business skill. Miriam never really worked at a job. Pam worked at a recycling center. She never held an office job or a business job of any type. Ann has been a housewife all her life.

''We've had personality troubles, but not serious ones, because we squashed them right away. The inter-personal stuff can be worked out if everybody agrees it's going to happen, that there's no blame attached to differences of opinion or feelings. We all agreed when we set out that everybody was going to make mistakes—some of them are going to cost us money—but no blame should be attached to anybody, and we would not throw it up to each other. When Ann joined us, Miriam made a lot of noises, 'She did this wrong, she bought that thing, she never should have bought it...' Pam and I would say, 'Miriam, you made your mistakes too, back off.' And she slowly but surely got over that. She felt, being the one partner with the most money in at that point, like the business was hers. None of this was conscious. People don't consciously set out to be that way about things, it's sort of inbred. The system's run that way, and no matter what your philosophy is, we all have moments of 'mine' mentality: 'That's mine. She's threatening it.'

''Miriam is a crackerjack sales woman. She can sell anybody anything. But she couldn't keep a set of books to save her soul. She can't balance a checkbook. But she can sell. That's a real asset. She doesn't have to keep books if she can do that. Pam's got a good eye when it comes to buying. She's good at that. And Ann, who's much better organized than the other two when it comes to shows and things like that, she's the one who says, 'Uh huh, we're going to do it,' and she sits down and makes out a list: we're gonna need lights, we're gonna need display material, we need this, we need that. Pam says, 'Well, we need so much inventory; where's the rest of it?' These are skills. And I'm the bookkeeper. And between the four of us we can really operate.''

You, Incorporated: A Corporation Primer

The corporation is truly a misunderstood animal. People, even business people, have more misconceptions about corporations than about any other form of business. Some small time operations will benefit by incorporating; most will not. But in order for you to make an intelligent choice between ''You'' and ''You, Incorporated'', you will need a basic understanding of what a corporation is and what can and cannot be accomplished by incorporating.

''In Twenty-Five Words or Less''

A corporation is... just another business. The basic day-to-day operations, the management, the bookkeeping, are virtually no different from the operations of an unincorporated business. A corporation can be as tiny as the tiniest unincorporated business. It can be loose and easy and very personal. Just as there are grey-suits-and-elevators corporations, there are blue-jeans-and-pure-funk corporations.

A corporation is just another business... but the rules of the game are different. The two main differences between corporations and other businesses are the tax laws and the laws governing liability.

Corporate Myth Number One: You're going to lower you taxes by incorporating. Not so. The fact is, most small businesses will not save tax money by incorporating. Corporate profits are taxed *twice*: once as corporate income and again when distributed to the shareholders (owners) as dividends. In contrast, the profits from your unincorporated sole proprietorship or partnership are taxable only to you, the owner; the business itself pays no tax. So even though corporate tax rates are in some cases lower than individual tax rates, the effective corporate tax rate because of the double taxation is always higher. Small corporations do have a few ways to reduce the combined corporation and shareholder taxes (discussed later in this chapter), but none will result in taxes lower than those paid by an unincorporated business.

Rules regarding liability are also different for corporations. These liability rules, which offer protection to the owners of corporations from lawsuits and creditors, are the most convincing reason—and, I feel, the only reason—for you to consider incorporating your small business.

A corporation is recognized by law as a "legal entity", which means that the business is legally separate from its owners, just as a person over twenty-one years of age is legally separate from his parents. If you are in debt and unable to pay, your creditors cannot get their money from your parents. Likewise, if your corporation does not pay its debts, the creditors cannot get their money from your personal, non-business assets. In most cases you will not be personally liable for lawsuits brought against your corporation. Sole proprietorships and partnerships, on the other hand, are legally inseparable from their owners; the owners are personally liable for all business debts and obligations.

High-risk businesses, even very small ones, often incorporate solely to protect the owners from personal loss. Businesses borrowing a lot of "risk" capital and businesses that will owe a lot of money to their suppliers often fall in this category. Businesses with a more than average likelihood of being sued—such as security businesses and manufacturers of potentially dangerous products—also incorporate for the liability protection offered. Partnerships often incorporate to protect individual partners against possible lawsuit and losses resulting from the action of other partners.

Limited corporate liability, however, is not "blanket" or all encompassing. Officers of a corporation (in a small corporation, the officers are the owners) can be personally liable for claims against their corporations in some situations. A corporation will not shield you from personal liability that you normally should be responsible for, such as not having car insurance or acting with gross negligence. Professionals such as doctors cannot hide behind corporations to protect themselves from malpractice suits. And as to financial commitments, any bank lending money to a small corporation will require the stockholders or officers to co-sign as personal guarantors of the loan.

If you plan to incorporate solely or primarily with the intention of limiting your legal liability, I suggest you find out first, before you invest the time and money in incorporation, exactly how limited the liability really is for your particular venture. Hire a knowledgeable lawyer to give you a written opinion as to the extent of personal vs. limited liability you could incur.

There are three other significant differences between corporations and other forms of business. None are as important as the limited liability rules, but all three are worth considering.

Number One: Incorporating a business eliminates most of the legal and tax complications of a change in ownership. Sale of stock or death of a shareholder will not end the business. The same corporation can continue in business with new shareholders. By comparison, a sole proprietorship ceases to exist when the owner closes the business or dies. A partnership ceases to exist when one partner quits or dies. Of course, a sole proprietorship or a partnership can be sold or otherwise acquired by new owners. But the result, legally, is a new business requiring new records, new valuation of assets and liabilities, new business licenses, etc.

Difference Number Two: A corporation is the only form of business that can hire its owners as employees. Corporations can pay their owner-employees a wage and even offer company-paid fringe benefits such as health insurance. Owners of sole proprietorships and partnerships, you'll remember, can never be employees of their businesses. The income tax consequences of hiring owner-employees are numerous and difficult to explain. Briefly—I don't want to bog you down in corporate tax law before you have even decided to incorporate—hiring owner-employees is one method of reducing corporate income taxes. Every employee's wages, including owner-employee's, are deductible expenses of the business. Expenses reduce profits, which means lower income taxes for the corporation. The wages, of course, are taxable to the owner-employee as personal income. But unlike regular corporate profits, which are taxable to the corporation and again to the owners, wages paid to owner-employees are not subject to the double taxation. Any fringe benefits paid to owner-employees are also tax deductible expenses of the corporation. There is even a greater tax savings with company-paid fringe benefits because the fringe benefits are not taxable to the employees at all. The area of owner-employees is complex. The laws, their applications and tax consequences fill volumes. Rather than turn this primer into an accounting textbook, I suggest two things: One, don't consider the owner-employee aspects as a major reason for or against incorporating, because for most small businesses they aren't; and Two, if you do feel, after reading this chapter, that you probably will benefit from incorporation, then talk to your lawyer or accountant and consider *all* the aspects and details of incorporating.

The remaining significant difference between incorporated and unincorporated business is the corporation's legal ability to retain undistributed profits within the company, and not pay the profits out to the owners. Though the corporation must pay income tax on these "retained earnings," as they are called, the owners do not have to pay the "double" or second tax because the profits have not been paid out to them. Retained earnings can be reinvested in the business, distributed to the shareholders at a later date or retained indefinitely by the company. An unincorporated business can also retain the profits in the business, but the owners must pay income tax on the profits whether distributed to them or not. The laws regarding retained earnings are even more complex than those regarding owner-employees. Among other rules, there are strict limitations on the amounts which can be retained. I again feel that this aspect of corporate law, like the provision for owner-employees, is not a major consideration for or against incorporating your small business. If and when you do decide to incorporate, retained earnings is one more potentially complicated area to deal with.

S Corporations

There is a form of corporation different from the type just described. It is sort of a hybrid between a traditional corporation and a partnership, with some of the advantages of both.

The S corporation (formerly called Subchapter S or Sub S) has the same basic structure as a regular corporation and offers the same limited liability protection to the stockholders. The S corporation, however, pays no corporate income tax. Like a partnership, all the profits of the S corporation pass through to the owners who are taxed at their regular individual rates.

Unlike a partnership, owner-employees of S corporations are treated similarly to owner-employees of regular corporations. You are on the payroll with regular payroll deductions, and you receive a W-2 at year-end. S corporation profits (in excess of your salary) are not subject to self-employment tax. As an employee, you are also entitled to some tax-deductible fringe benefits.

There are two main tax advantages to an S corporation. The first and most obvious is the elimination of the double taxation. The other advantage is due to some complex tax laws which allow current business losses to be carried back to prior years to offset prior years' taxes, bringing immediate tax refunds. Any business, corporation or otherwise, can avail itself of operating loss carryback laws (which are explained in more detail in the tax section). But if a corporation is brand new and sustains a loss, there are no prior years to carry the loss back to. In the case of an S corporation, the loss passes through to the stockholders, and they in turn can carry the loss back to their personal prior years' returns even though the business did not exist then. Losses of a regular corporation (or any other business) that cannot be carried back can be carried forward to offset future years' earnings, but the business must wait a full year or more to get the refund.

Only "closely held" corporations—those having 35 or fewer stockholders—can elect to become S corporations. There are special and very stringent requirements as to who may be a stockholder, how profits are to be distributed, how and when the election to become an S corporation must be made.

For state income tax purposes, some states do not recognize the S status and tax these businesses as regular corporations.

For more information on the federal requirements, ask the IRS for a free copy of publication #589, "Tax Information on S Corporations."

Steps to Incorporating a Business

The states, not the federal government, license corporations. The requirements vary greatly from state to state, as do the fees, which can run from $10 in some states to as high as $2,500 in others. And unless you are willing and able to study all the incorporation laws, which can get complicated, and file all the necessary forms yourself, add another $200 to $400 for a lawyer's assistance.

Generally, the first and most important step in the required incorporation procedures is the preparation of a "certificate" or "articles" of incorporation. This document usually must show the following information:

1. The proposed name of the corporation. The state can reject your proposed name if it is too similar to another corporation's name or if it is deceptive so as to mislead the public—like if you called your corporation "Germinal Motors" or "U.S. Government Licensing Co." or something.

2. The purposes for which the corporation is formed. In some states, the wording of this section can be critical and, if improperly worded, can severely limit the type of business you can conduct.

3. Names and addresses of incorporators.

4. Location of the principal office of the corporation. Most small corporations obtain their charter from the state in which the greater part of their business is conducted. Benefits may be gained, however, from incorporating in another state. Such factors as organization fees, state taxes, restrictions on corporate powers and types of business, and capital requirements may make states other than your own more attractive for incorporation. If you decide to obtain your charter from another state, you will be required to have an office in that state. Rather than actually establishing an office there, you may appoint an agent to act for you. The agent will be required only to represent your corporation,

maintain a duplicate list of stockholders and receive or reply to suits brought against the corporation (what a game, eh?).

5. The names of subscribers (future shareholders) and the number of share to which each subscribes. This is known as a "limited offering" of stock. Corporate stock is issued either as a "limited offering" or as a "public offering". Most small corporations make limited offering of stock, with each shareholder individually named in the articles of incorporation. After the initial issuance of stock, you will need special permission from the state to sell new shares or to sell old shares to new stockholders. A corporation that is "going public"—making a public offering—can sell stock to anyone. States charge much higher fees to charter public corporations. Public corporations must register with the Federal Securities and Exchange Commission (the SEC) and hire CPA's to prepare annual audited financial statements.

6. The type and maximum amount of capital stock to be issued. Stock is typically classed as "common" or "preferred." Holders of preferred stock generally have prior or "preferred" claim on corporate assets over common stockholders. Preferred stockholders are often just investors with no interest in the corporation other than making money on their money. Stock can also have a "par value"—an arbitrary value per share—or "no-par value."

7. Capital required at time of incorporation. This is another important decision and requires a knowledge of corporate "equity", which is comprised of "stated capital" and "paid-in surplus." "Stated capital" is, basically, an amount of money that belongs to the corporation and cannot be paid out to stockholders until the corporation is liquidated. All corporations must have some stated capital. Some states specify the dollar minimum. Some states require the corporation to bank the stated capital in cash. Since stated capital is money with only limited use, most corporations try to keep stated capital as small as possible. "Paid-in surplus" is money in excess of stated capital and generally is not restricted.

In addition to filing the articles or certificate of incorporation, many states require one or more of the following procedures:

1. Reserving a name with the state. This step, if required, precedes the filing of the articles of incorporation.

2. Filing a statement naming the elected officers. This usually must be filed after the first board of directors meeting.

3. Requesting formal permission to issue stock. This may require a description of how the stock will be distributed and how the proceeds from the sale will be used.

If a lot of this sounds like a duplication of information already included in the articles of incorporation, you're right—it is. But the states still require separate forms (and additional fees).

In most states, one person can incorporate a business. Some states require two or three people. But be it a one person corporation or a huge conglomerate, if you are going to incorporate you must play the corporate game entirely. You must hold meetings and keep written minutes of the meetings. Your corporation must have stockholders who elect directors (you must have directors), who are a policy making and overseeing group. The directors appoint officers (that's right, you must have officers), who run the business. Officers, in turn hire employees, who do the work. In a small corporation, one person often wears all four hats: stockholder, director, officer and employee.

It may all sound ludicrous to you, but that's the corporate game, and that's the way it must be played.

Joe's Janitorial, Inc.

Charles Dorton is an amazing man. He is a full-time school teacher, enrolled in a doctoral program at the University of San Francisco, and raising a teenage daughter. And ''on the side'', Mr. Dorton operates Dorton Security, Inc., which grossed about $35,000 in its first year of operation:

''Starting a corporation was no big deal. I think most people misinterpret the law, or they feel that they've got to have an attorney do everything. I looked into the possibility of going to a lawyer. He wanted $400. I decided to see what I could do myself instead. I thought, well, I've got to find out something about state requirements. So I called one state agency and they said I had to call another agency, the Secretary of State's office. I called San Francisco, and they said if I want some information I have to write to Sacramento. They gave me the address, and I wrote. They sent back a little brochure indicating what the state required in terms of their articles of incorporation. It's very simple. I think there are about five articles that the state will accept. If you write in anything else, they'll have you take it out.

''I got my articles written up and took them up to Sacramento. The thing that bothered me, it costs $65 to file, but if you go to Sacramento and have them process your papers while you're waiting, it's $70—a $5 handling fee, which to me was sort of a rip-off. I started looking at all the other things in terms of a rip-off. You must pay $200 prepaid franchise tax. Every corporation has to pay that, even if you are floundering financially. Every year you have to pay that $200. Because my typewriter ribbon wasn't dark enough, I had to have my articles typed over. In the state building there's someone renting one of the offices—a public stenographer they call her—and I had to pay $9 for two and a half pages. And that burned me too—nine dollars, which was totally ridiculous. And I'm probably a more proficient typist than this lady. Just a matter of having a darker ribbon. So I paid that, and I got out of there.

''After the articles were filed, the Secretary of State's Office sent out another little form. They wanted additional information about the officers, which is a duplicate of what was sent in on the articles anyway. That's an additional $3.50. So right down the line, they're constantly getting your money.''

**Section Four
TAXES**

"If the adjustments required by section 481(a) and Regulation 1.481-1 are attributable to a change in method of accounting initiated by the taxpayer, the amount of such adjustments, to the extent such amount does not exceed the net amount which would have been required if the change had been made in the first taxable year beginning after December 31, 1953, and ending after August 16, 1954, shall be taken into account by the taxpayer in computing taxable income in the manner provided in section 481 (b) (4) (B) and paragraph (b) of this section."

—Internal Revenue Code

Well as through this world I've rambled
I've seen lots of funny men
Some will rob you with a six-gun
And some with a fountain pen.

—Woody Guthrie*

Deep In the Heart of Taxes

Throughout *Small Time Operator* I've made enough comments-maybe more than enough-about the intrusion of government into all our affairs. And an introduction to Taxes is an ideal setting to get into it again. But I think enough's been said. The revolution doesn't seem to be coming, and the "system" is not quite ready to collapse yet. So it seems that taxes are here to stay awhile. Rather than criticize or defend them, I'd just like to give you some information to help you deal with them.

This tax section of *Small Time Operator* will discuss the federal income, self-employment and excise taxes; state income taxes; gross receipts taxes; and inventory taxes. Sales taxes and the various licenses and permits required of small businesses have already been covered in the "Technicalities and Legalities" chapter. Employment taxes were discussed in the Growing Up section.

Because of the nature of the beast—the non-stop modifications and the complexity of the tax laws—this tax section is handled differently from the rest of the book. The tax section is like a third grade reader, simple and basic. Rather than presenting a step-by-step "all you need to know" guide to taxes (which would require at least five times the space), the tax section will provide you with a general education about taxes, including specifics of some of the basic and more important federal laws. The results, I feel, will provide enough information for most small business people to prepare their own tax returns.

Even if you decide to take your tax problems to an accountant, I think you should familiarize yourself with the information in this tax section. There is more to taxes than just filling out the tax forms every April 15. Many of the tax laws outlined in this section relate directly to every day management of your business. The federal income tax laws affect your bookkeeping and, through a knowledge of which expenditures are and are not tax deductible, your business profit. What's more, you will be of greater help to your tax accountant—which means your tax accountant can be of greater help to you—if you have at least some familiarity with the federal income tax laws. In fact, the information here may help you think of some tax savings that your accountant may have overlooked.

The Tax Laws As They Apply to You

Many of the federal tax laws are designed solely to keep you from cheating the government out of what they think is rightfully theirs—your money. But a lot of these laws were enacted to save you money, to give you some sort of tax break. The Internal Revenue Service does make an effort—albeit a lame one—to educate people about beneficial tax laws; but basically it's up to you to dig in and find out how to save yourself tax dollars. The problem is that income tax laws tend to overwhelm most people, because of their complexity and because of their sheer volume—so many different possibilities, so many "if's, and's and but's."

A lot of special effort has been put into this section of the book to help you understand the tax laws without getting trapped in the octopus tentacles of exceptions. This is accomplished by a four-step procedure:

Step 1: The basic tax rules—those that apply to most small businesses—are explained as simply as possible in plain English; no accounting double-talk and no "if's, and's and but's."

Step 2: Following the basic rules, any special situations, exceptions or tricky catches in the law are separately headed up—labeled "The Fine Print"—and explained. This is designed so you can skim over them rapidly and spot an area that may apply to you.

Step 3: Unusual and complex rules, most of which apply only to a minority of people, are mentioned in order to alert you to their existence but are not explained in detail.

Step 4: Free sources of complete tax information are listed so that you can pursue the subjects you need and want to know more thoroughly.

A Warning

This tax section does *not* provide complete information on all federal tax laws nor was it ever intended to. It is meant to be a general guideline to help you wade through the maze of rules and regulations that our government in its wisdom has seen fit to enact into law. Read the tax section with this warning in mind, and I think you will find it helpful and informative. And remember, the tax laws are in a constant state of change. It is your responsibility—and it could be to your benefit financially—to keep abreast of current tax law.

I list in the Appendix, but I think it appropriate to mention here, an excellent tax guide that is both complete and fairly easy to read. *Tax Guide For Small Business* (Publication #334) is prepared by the Internal Revenue Service and is available free from any IRS office. The *Guide*, which is revised each year, contains about 200 pages and covers income, excise and employment taxes for sole proprietors, partnerships and corporations. If you use the IRS's *Tax Guide* in conjunction with this tax section of *Small Time Operator* you shouldn't go wrong.

Accounting Period:
Calendar Year vs. Fiscal Year

Every business must decide whether to keep books and file tax returns on a "calendar year" or a "fiscal year." A calendar year begins on January 1 and ends on December 31. Calendar year tax returns are due on April 15 for the prior January through December. A fiscal year is a twelve month period ending on the last day of any month other than December. Fiscal year tax returns are due on the fifteenth day of the fourth month following the end of the fiscal year.

Most small businesses choose the calendar year simply because it's easier. All of the federal and state tax procedures are geared to the calendar year: issuance of W-2's, 1099's and dividend and interest statements, and publication of the new tax forms and instructions. A change to fiscal year accounting requires special permission from the IRS and also requires filing a "short period" return for the transition period.

Fiscal year accounting does offer benefits to many businesses. Large retail businesses such as department stores traditionally use a January 31 fiscal year because they don't want to be troubled with closing their books and taking inventory at the end of December, their busiest time of year. CPA firms sometimes offer lower rates to clients ending their business year other than during the January to April "busy season." Some businesses have definite yearly cycles and find that coordinating their business year with the business cycle better reflects actual income and expenses. Corporations also often choose a fiscal year, coinciding with the date the business first began operation, in order to avoid a short-period (part-year) tax return and extra taxes the first year.

Some shrewd business people prefer fiscal year accounting because it can sometimes bring tax savings—sort of a hidden tax loophole. Tax laws change every year, and new laws usually mean higher taxes (regardless of what they call the laws—I've never seen a "Tax Reform Act" or a "Tax Reduction Act" that lowered anyone's taxes). When Congress sets an effective date for a new tax law, very often the wording states that the law "applies to tax years beginnning after December 31, such-and-such year". For a calendar year taxpayer, that means the new law goes in effect January 1. But for a fiscal year business whose tax year begins, say, July 1, the new tax law does not take effect until July 1. That fiscal year business gets to operate six more months under the old law, at the old and usually lower tax rate. Personally, I'm not convinced that the tax savings is worth the extra effort and complication of switching to a fiscal year. Besides, the IRS will not allow a business to switch to a fiscal year if the reason is to beat taxes; there must be some other valid business reason.

There is another form of fiscal year called the "52/53 Week Year". Some businesses (usually large ones) want their tax year to be so-many weeks instead of twelve months—to start, say, on a Monday and end on a Sunday—usually because their business cycles or their corporation procedures are rigidly tied to a weekly schedule. These businesses can adopt a fiscal year beginning on any day of the week they choose, with 52 or 53 weeks in the fiscal year. The number of weeks varies year to year, depending on how close to the end of the month their Monday (or Tuesday or whatever day they choose) falls. Enough of this? If you are really interested, talk to an accountant.

The tax laws discussed in this tax section apply to both calendar year and fiscal year taxpayers.

Tax Calendar for Businesses

The tax calendar lists due dates for federal and state tax reports. Each date shown is the last day on which to perform the required action without penalty. The calendar reflects federal and state laws in effect in 1984 and 1985.

In order to help you spot the dates applicable to your business and skip over those not applicable, the first word in each description will tell who the information applies to, such as "Employers", "Corporations", etc. "Individuals" refers to sole proprietors, partners (not partnerships), and corporate stockholders (not the corporations).

If the due date for filing a return, making a tax payment, etc. falls on a Saturday, Sunday or legal holiday, the date is moved to the next regular work day.

Tax deposits which are due weekly and monthly throughout the year are listed at the end of the calendar.

Fiscal year taxpayers: these dates apply to calendar year only. Consult the Internal Revenue Service for fiscal year dates.

JANUARY 1 — MARCH 16

Corporations that meet certain requirements may elect, during this period, to be treated as S corporations during current and future years. Use form 2553.

JANUARY 15

Individuals must either pay the balance due on prior year's estimated income tax, or file an income tax return (Form 1040) on or before January 31 and pay the full amount of the tax due. See January 31.

Farmers and fishermen may elect to file declaration of estimated income tax (Form 1040-ES) for prior year and pay estimated tax in full, and file income tax return (Form 1040) by April 15. If declaration of estimated tax is not filed, see February 28.

JANUARY 31

Individuals should file an income tax return for prior year and pay the tax due, if the balance due on their prior year's estimated tax was not paid by January 15. Use Form 1040. Farmers and fishermen, see February 28.

Employers' last day for giving every employee Form W-2 showing income and social security information. Also see February 28.

Employers deposit federal unemployment tax (FUTA) at an authorized bank if the tax is more than $100. If the amount is $100 or less, you are not required to deposit it, but you must add it to the taxes for the next quarter. Then, in the next quarter, if the total undeposited tax is more than $100, deposit it by the last day of the month following the quarter. Use Form 508.

Employers file Form 941 for income tax withheld and social security taxes for the 4th quarter of the prior year and pay any taxes due. If timely deposits were made, see February 10.

Businesses liable for excise taxes must file quarterly excise tax return. Use Form 720.

Employers subject to federal unemployment tax file annual return for the prior year. Use Form 940. If timely deposits were made in full payment of the tax, see February 10.

All businesses: most state sales tax returns for the 4th quarter of last year are due.

Corporations that paid $10 or more in dividends or interest must prepare Form 1099 & give one copy to each recipient. See also Feb. 28.

All businesses that paid $600 or more to an individual in commissions, fees or other compensation including payments to subcontractors must prepare Form 1099 & give one copy to each recipient. See also Feb. 28.

All businesses that sold $5,000 or more of goods to independent sales agents must prepare Form 1099 and give one copy to each agent. See also Feb. 28.

FEBRUARY 10

Extended date for certain returns:

Employers who made timely deposits in full payment of all income taxes withheld and social security taxes due for the 4th quarter of the prior year file 4th quarter return. Use Form 941.

Employers subject to federal unemployment tax who made timely deposits in full payment of the tax file annual return for the prior year. Use Form 940.

FEBRUARY 28

All businesses that prepared Form 1099 (See Jan. 31) must file the 1099's along with transmittal Form 1096 with the IRS.

Employers must file Form W-3, Transmittal of Income and Tax Statements, with the Social Security Administration if you have issued Form W-2 (See Jan. 31). Copy A of each W-2 must accompany Form W-3.

Employers whose employees receive tips must report those tips on Form 8027.

Farmers and fishermen who did not elect to file declaration of estimated tax on January 15 should file final income tax return (Form 1040) for prior year.

MARCH 15

Corporations must file federal income tax return, Form 1120, or application for extension, Form 7004, and pay to a depositary the balance of tax still due.

Corporations that have elected to be treated as S corporations must file federal income tax Form 1120S.

Corporations must file state income tax returns for the following states: Ala., Alaska, Calif., D.C., Ill., Maine, Mass., Md., Minn., Miss., Nebr., N.H., N. Mex., N.Y., N.C., Okla., R.I., S.C., Vt., W. Va., Wis.

MARCH 31

Corporations must file state income tax returns for the following states: Conn., Del., Fla., Ohio, Tenn.

APRIL 15

Individuals must file a federal income tax return for the prior calendar year. The tax due must be paid in full with this return. Schedule C must be filed (Schedule F for farmers), and in addition, Schedule SE must be completed. If you desire an automatic 4-month extension, file Form 4868 accompanied by payment of your estimated unpaid income tax liability.

Individuals must file a declaration of estimated income tax (including self-employment tax) for the current year and pay at least 25 percent of such tax. Use Form 1040-ES.

Partnerships must file a return for the prior calendar year. Use Form 1065 (no tax due).

Corporations must pay 25 percent of their current year estimated income tax to a depositary.

Individuals must file a state income tax return for all states collecting income tax except Ark., Del., Hawaii, Va., La., and Iowa.

Corporations must file state income tax returns for the following states: Ariz., Colo., Ga., Idaho, Ind., Kans., Ky., Mo., N.J., N.D., Oreg., Pa., Utah, Va.

APRIL 20

Individuals living in Hawaii must file a state income tax return.

Corporations in Hawaii must file state income tax returns.

APRIL 30

Individuals living in Del., Va. or Iowa must file a state income tax return.

Corporations in Mich. and Iowa must file state income tax returns.

All businesses: most states sales tax returns for the first quarter are due.

Employers file Form 941 for income tax withheld and social security taxes for the 1st quarter and pay any taxes due. If timely deposits were made, see May 10.

Employers deposit federal unemployment tax (FUTA) at an authorized bank if the tax is more than $100. If the amount is $100 or less, you are not required to deposit it, but you must add it to the taxes for the next quarter. Then, in the next quarter, if the total undeposited tax is more than $100, deposit it by the last day of the month following the quarter. Use Form 508.

Businesses liable for excise taxes must file quarterly excise tax return. Use Form 720.

MAY 10

Extended date for quarterly returns:

Employers who made timely deposits in full payment of income tax withheld and social security taxes due for the 1st quarter, file 1st quarter return. Use Form 941.

MAY 15

Individuals living in Ark. or La. must file state income tax returns.

Corporations in Ark., La. or Mont. must file state income tax returns.

JUNE 15

Individuals must pay 2nd installment of estimated income tax.

Corporations must pay second installment of 25 percent of estimated income tax liability. Payments are made to a depositary.

JULY 31

Employers file Form 941 for income tax withheld and social security taxes for the 2nd quarter and pay any taxes due. If timely deposits were made, see August 10.

Businesses liable for excise taxes must file quarterly excise tax return. Use Form 720.

Employers deposit federal unemployment tax (FUTA) at an authorized bank if the tax is more than $100. If the amount is $100 or less, you are not required to deposit it, but you must add it to the taxes for the next quarter. Then, in the next quarter, if the total undeposited tax is more than $100, deposit it by the last day of the month following the quarter. Use Form 508.

All businesses: most state sales tax returns for the 2nd quarter are due.

AUGUST 10

Extended date for quarterly returns:

Employers who made timely deposits in full payment of all income tax withheld and social security taxes due for the 2nd quarter, file 2nd quarter return. Use Form 941.

AUGUST 31

Heavy-duty truck owners and operators must pay the federal use tax on highway motor vehicles used on the public highways. Use Form 2290.

SEPTEMBER 15

Individuals must pay 3rd installment of estimated income tax. Use Form 1040-ES.

Corporations must pay to a depositary 3rd installment of 25 percent of estimated income tax.

OCTOBER 31

Employers file Form 941 for income tax withheld and social security taxes for the 3rd quarter and pay any taxes due. If timely deposits were made, see November 10.

All businesses: most state sales tax returns for the 3rd quarter are due.

Businesses liable for excise taxes must file quarterly excise tax return. Use Form 720.

Employers deposit federal unemployment tax (FUTA) at an authorized bank if the tax is more than $100. If the amount is $100 or less, you are not required to deposit it, but you must add it to the taxes for the next quarter. Then, in the next quarter, if the total undeposited tax is more than $100, deposit it by the last day of the month following the quarter. Use Form 508.

NOVEMBER

Employers should request a new Form W-4 from each employee whose withholding exemptions will be different next year.

NOVEMBER 10

Extended date for quarterly returns:

Employers who made timely deposits in full payment of income tax withheld and social security taxes due for the 3rd quarter, file 3rd quarter return. Use Form 941.

DECEMBER 15

Corporations must pay to a depository the 4th installment of 25 percent estimated income tax.

WEEKLY AND MONTHLY ALL YEAR

Corporations that meet certain requirements may elect, any time during the year, to be treated as S corporations in future years. Use Form 2553. To be treated as an S corporation this year, see Jan. 1.

Employers: tax deposits of social security (NOT self-employment) and withheld income taxes required monthly (by the 15th of the following month) whenever amounts due are $500 or more; required 8 times a month whenever amounts due are $3000 or more.

Businesses liable for excise taxes are required to make monthly deposits on the last day of the month when more than $100 in excise taxes is collected. For more information, see IRS publication #510.

Who Must File a Tax Return

You must file a federal income tax return if your *gross* income is $3,430 or more (for a single person) or $5,620 or more (for a married couple filing jointly). "Gross" income means your income before any business deductions. It is your total sales, fees, commissions. Gross income also includes any non-business income you may have.

You must file a federal income tax return if your *net* earnings from self-employment (your business *net* profit) is $400 or more. Business income minus expenses equals *net* profit. If you operate more than one business, combine the profits and losses of the different businesses to arrive at the total net profit.

These dollar minimums change from year to year.

Business Expenses

All legitimate business expenses, with a few important exceptions, are deductible in computing your taxable income as long as they meet the Internal Revenue Service's four basic rules:

One: The expenses must be incurred in connection with your business. Personal, non-business expenses are not deductible.

Two: The expenses must be, in the words of the IRS, "ordinary and necessary." "Ordinary" does not mean that the expenses must be recurring or habitual; only that similar expenses are common or accepted in your particular type of business. A "necessary" expense, according to the IRS, is one "that is appropriate and helpful in developing and maintaining your trade or business."

Three: The expenses must not be for items that will be used over several years, such as equipment, tools and furniture. You must prorate (depreciate) these expenses over a period of years. Depreciation is explained later in this section of the book.

Four: The amount must be "reasonable."

Business expenses incurred before you start your business (called "start-up" expenses) cannot be deducted 100 percent the year you incur them. You have the option to capitalize them, which means no deduction at all until you quit or sell your business, or to amortize (depreciate) them over a five-year period.

Expenditures that are partly personal (non-business) and partly business can be prorated and the business portion expensed or depreciated. Sometimes your home or your automobile fall in this category. Proration of rent was explained in the bookkeeping section. Proration of automobile expenses is explained in this tax section.

Any asset that you originally purchased and used for non-business purposes that you are now using for business or using partly for business can be depreciated as of the date you began using the asset in your business. It does not matter when you purchased the item. The depreciation chapter has complete information.

Below is an alphabetical listing of 113 typical business expenses which can be deducted on your income tax return. Those items marked with an asterisk (*) are explained in more detail on the following pages. The number following each expense corresponds to the column number in you expenditure ledger, so you can tell at a glance in which column to post the expense. "Y/E" after an item means that the expense is recorded on the year-end summary only. Year-end procedures were explained in the bookkeeping section.

A list of typical business expenses can never be complete. *Any* expense that meets the IRS's four rules (incurred in connection with your business; complies with "ordinary and necessary" test; meets depreciation requirements; is "reasonable"), if not specifically disallowed, should be taken whether it is on this list or not. Those expenses specifically disallowed are listed later in this section.

SCHEDULE C (Form 1040) Department of the Treasury Internal Revenue Service	**Profit or (Loss) From Business or Profession** (Sole Proprietorship) Partnerships, Joint Ventures, etc., Must File Form 1065. ▶ Attach to Form 1040 or Form 1041. ▶ See Instructions for Schedule C (Form 1040).	OMB No 1545 0074 **1985** 09

Name of proprietor	Social security number
Samuel Thesham	123 : 45 : 6789

A	Principal business or profession, including product or service (see Instructions)	B	Principal business code from page 2
	auto repair		8854

C Business name and address ▶ Monkeywrench Motors
9346 Cavemont, Berkeley CA 94705

D Employer ID number NONE

E Method(s) used to value closing inventory:
(1) ☒ Cost   (2) ☐ Lower of cost or market   (3) ☐ Other (attach explanation)

F Accounting method: (1) ☐ Cash   (2) ☒ Accrual   (3) ☐ Other (specify) ▶

		Yes	No
G	Was there any change in determining quantities, costs, or valuations between opening and closing inventory?.		X
	If "Yes," attach explanation.		
H	Did you deduct expenses for an office in your home?.		X

Part I Income

1 a	Gross receipts or sales	**1a**	$22,364
b	Less: Returns and allowances	**1b**	0
c	Subtract line 1b from line 1a and enter the balance here	**1c**	$22,364
2	Cost of goods sold and/or operations (from Part III, line 8)	**2**	2,008
3	Subtract line 2 from line 1c and enter the **gross profit** here	**3**	$20,356
4 a	Windfall Profit Tax Credit or Refund received in 1985 (see Instructions) . . .	**4a**	
b	Other income	**4b**	
5	Add lines 3, 4a, and 4b. This is the **gross income** . . . . ▶	**5**	$20,356

Part II Deductions

6	Advertising	150	22	Pension and profit-sharing plans . .	
7	Bad debts from sales or services (Cash method taxpayers, see Instructions)		23	Rent on business property	1,200
			24	Repairs	
8	Bank service charges.		25	Supplies (not included in Part III below)	218
9	Car and truck expenses	480	26	Taxes (Do not include Windfall Profit Tax here. See line 30.) . . .	130
10	Commissions	5,650			
11	Depletion		27	Travel and entertainment	
12	Depreciation and section 179 deduction from Form 4562 (not included in Part III below)	136	28	Utilities and telephone	221
			29 a	Wages	
			b	Jobs credit	
13	Dues and publications		c	Subtract line 29b from 29a . . .	
14	Employee benefit programs		30	Windfall Profit Tax withheld in 1985	
15	Freight (not included in Part III below) .		31	Other expenses (specify):	
16	Insurance	650	a	1986 shop manuals	34
17	Laundry and cleaning	137	b	misc.	36
18	Legal and professional services . . .		c		
19	Mortgage interest paid to financial institutions (see Instructions)		d		
20	Office expense.	78	e		
21	Other interest	637	f		
			g		

32	Add amounts in columns for lines 6 through 31g. These are the **total deductions** . . . . ▶	**32**	$ 9,757
33	**Net profit or (loss).** Subtract line 32 from line 5 and enter the result. If a profit, enter on Form 1040, line 12, and on Schedule SE, Part I, line 2 (or Form 1041, line 5). If a loss, you **MUST** go on to line 34	**33**	$10,599

34 If you have a loss, you **MUST** answer this question: "Do you have amounts for which you are not at risk in this business (see Instructions)?" ☐ Yes ☐ No
If "Yes," you **MUST** attach **Form 6198.** If "No," enter the loss on Form 1040, line 12, and on Schedule SE, Part I, line 2 (or Form 1041, line 5).

Part III Cost of Goods Sold and/or Operations (See Schedule C Instructions for Part III)

1	Inventory at beginning of year (if different from last year's closing inventory, attach explanation)	**1**	$ 100
2	Purchases less cost of items withdrawn for personal use	**2**	1,958
3	Cost of labor (do not include salary paid to yourself)	**3**	
4	Materials and supplies	**4**	
5	Other costs	**5**	
6	Add lines 1 through 5	**6**	$2,058
7	Less: Inventory at end of year	**7**	50
8	Cost of goods sold and/or operations. Subtract line 7 from line 6. Enter here and in Part I, line 2, above. . .	**8**	$2,008

For Paperwork Reduction Act Notice, see Form 1040 Instructions.   Schedule C (Form 1040) 1985

Account books (2)

Accounting fees (10)

Advertising (5)

Auditing fees (10)

*Automobile expenses (9 or Y/E) (see discussion)

*Bad debts (Y/E)

Bank service charges (2)

Bonding fees (10)

Bookkeeping services (10)

Books (useful life one year or less; see Depreciation) (2)

Burglar alarm service (10)

Burglary (see Casualty losses)

Business associations (10)

Business cards (5)

*Business gifts (5)

Business interruption insurance (see Insurance) (10)

Business license (8)

*Casualty losses (see discussion)

Charitable contributions (10)

Cleaning (2)

Clothing, special (not regular street clothes) (2)

Coffee service (2)

Collection expense (10)

Commissions (3)

Consultant fees (3)

Contractor's fees (3)

Conventions (see Travel away from home) (10)

*Cost of goods sold (1)

Credit bureau fees (10)

Credit card fees for merchants (10)

*Depreciation (Y/E)

Dues, business associations (10)

Dues, professional societies (10)

Dues, union (10)

*Education expenses (10)

Electricity (see Utilities) (7)

Employer's taxes (8)

Employment agency fees (10)

*Entertainment (5)

Equipment (see Depreciation)(Y/E)

Extended coverage insurance
See Insurance) (10)
Fees for services (3)
Fees to organizations (10)
Fire insurance (see Insurance)(10)
Fire losses (see Casualty losses)
*Floor tax (inventory tax) (8)
*Freight (1 or 2—see discussion)
Garbage (see Utilities) (7)
Gas (see Utilities) (7)
Gross receipts tax (8)
Heating (see Utilities) (7)
*Insurance (10)
Interest on business debt (10)
*Inventory (see Cost of Goods
Sold) (1)
Inventory (floor) tax (8)
Janitorial service (10)
Ledgers (2)
Legal expenses (10)
Liability insurance (see
Insurance) (10)
License fees (8)
Loss on sale of business assets
(Y/E)
Loss of useful value (see
Depreciation) (Y/E)
Machinery (see Depreciation)
(Y/E)

Magazines (2)
Merchant's associations (10)
Minor repairs (10)
*Moving expenses (10)
Night watch service (10)
Office furnishings (see Depr.)(Y/E)
*Office in home (see discussion)
Office supplies (2)
Passport fees for business trip (10)
Patents (10)
Payroll and withheld payroll
taxes (4)
Periodicals (2)
Permit fees (8)
Postage (2)
Professional fees (10)
Professional journals (2)
Professional organizations (10)
Property taxes (8)
Publications (2)
Reference books (useful life 1 yr
or less; see Depreciation) (2)
Rent (6)
*Repairs (subject to certain
requirements) (10)
Research and experimentation (10)
Robbery (see Casualty losses)
Safe deposit box (2)
Salaries (4)

Sales tax (8)
Service charges (2)
Shipping (see Freight) (1 or 2)
Shoplifting (see Casualty losses)
Small tools (useful life of 1 yr or
less; see Depreciation) (2)
State income tax (not deductible
on the state return) (8)
Stationery (2)
Supplies (2)
Telephone (7)
Theft (see Casualty losses)
Theft insurance (see Insurance) (10)
This book (2)
Tools (useful life one year or
less; see Depreciation) (2)
Trademarks (10)
*Travel away from home (10)
Uniforms (2)
Unincorporated business tax (8)
Union dues (10)
Utilities (7)
Vandalism (see Casualty losses)
Vehicles (see Automobile)
(9 or Y/E; see discussion)
Wages (4)
Water (see Utilities) (7)
Worthless inventory (see Cost
of goods sold)

Automobile Expenses

All expenses of operating a vehicle for business purposes are deductible except regular commuting expenses between your home and usual place of business, which the IRS considers personal and not deductible. There are two ways of figuring automobile expenses. As in so many other situations, one is difficult and one is easy.

Method One: You can keep itemized records of all your automobile expenses. These include gasoline, oil, lubrication, maintenance, repairs, insurance, parking and tolls, garage rents, license and registration fees, even auto club dues. The purchase price of the vehicle cannot be deducted in total but must be depreciated. The cost of major repairs such as an engine overhaul must also be depreciated. See the depreciation chapter in this section of the book.

Automobile expenses must be prorated between personal use (not deductible) and business use (ful-

ly deductible). The most common method of proration is based on miles driven. For example, let's say you drove 10,000 miles last year of which 2,500 miles was in connection with business. Twenty-five percent of all your auto expenses are deductible, and twenty-five percent of the cost of your vehicle can be depreciated.

Keeping itemized records of all your vehicle expenses is tedious work. The Internal Revenue Service realizes this also. In one of their rare helpful moods they have come up with ...

Method Two: An optional Standard Mileage Allowance. Instead of recording each fill up and every oil change, you may take a standard 21 cents per mile for every business mile driven. Using the example in Method One, you would have a deductible expense of $525.00 (2,500 miles at 21 cents per mile). The standard mileage allowance is in lieu of depreciation and all your automobile expenses except parking, tolls, interest and state and local taxes, which are deductible in addition to the mileage allowance. If your vehicle is eligible for an Investment Credit (discussed later), you may take the credit as well as the mileage allowance. The 21 cents per mile is on the first 15,000 business miles each year. Above 15,000 miles a year, you can only deduct 11 cents per mile. Above 60,000 total business miles on one vehicle (all years combined) you also are limited to 11 cents per mile. Check with the IRS before relying on these figures. Every year or two, the IRS changes the rates.

If you drive a new or expensive vehicle, your actual expenses will most likely be higher than the standard mileage allowance. You will have to decide for yourself whether the tax you might save by itemizing is worth the extra work of keeping all those records. The best advice I can give the budding bookkeeper who does want to itemize: get a gasoline credit card and keep the receipts. It is much easier to keep track of one or two monthly payments rather than dozens of individual purchases.

Regardless of the method you choose, you must keep a log of the business and personal use of your vehicle—dates and mileage.

The Fine Print

You may not use the standard mileage allowance if you lease the vehicle, if your business operates more than one vehicle at a time, or if you use the vehicle for hire such as for a taxi. Business vehicles that do not qualify for the standard mileage allowance may still make use of Method One, itemizing actual expenses.

The method you choose the first year you use your vehicle for business determines what methods you can use in future years (for that particular vehicle). If you use Method One (itemizing expenses) the first year, you must stay with that method as long as you use that vehicle. If you use the mileage allowance the first year, you can switch back and forth if you want, itemizing some years and using the mileage allowance other years. If you do switch from the mileage allowance to itemizing, you must use straight line depreciation. You may not use accelerated (ACRS) depreciation.

Depreciation and investment credit are limited if the vehicle costs over a certain dollar amount or if the vehicle is used 50 percent or less for business. This is covered in the "Depreciation" and "Investment Tax Credit" chapters.

Bad Debts

Business bad debts—bounced checks and other uncollectible accounts—are fully deductible. The bookkeeping section, under the headings "Return Checks" and "Uncollectible Accounts", tells how to set up a bad debts folder.

Special Note: businesses using the cash method of accounting cannot take a bad debt expense for unpaid and uncollectible accounts, because the income was not recorded in the first place. Bounced checks, however, are deductible bad debts, because they were posted to the income ledgers.

Business Gifts

Tax deductions for business gifts are limited to $25 per recipient in any one year. Keep records of who the gifts were given to, how much and why.

Casualty Losses/Theft Losses

Business losses from fire, storm or other casualty, or from theft, shoplifting or vandalism are fully deductible to the extent they are not covered by insurance. There is no limitation as in the case of nonbusiness losses.

Inventory that is stolen or destroyed should not be shown as a casualty loss. The inventory loss is part of your cost-of-goods-sold (discussed in this section) and cannot be deducted a second time. Stolen or destroyed depreciable property can be deducted as a casualty loss, but only to the extent of the undepreciated balance. For example, let's say your box of tools was stolen. You paid $200 for it two years ago and have already taken $40 depreciation on it. You may show a theft loss of only $160 ($200 less the $40).

Education Expenses

Here is a good opportunity to get some additional education and charge the cost to your business—if you are careful in selecting your courses of study. The cost of education and any related expenses are deductible only if the education maintains or improves a skill required in your business. Education expenses are *not* allowed if the education is required to meet minimum educational requirements of your present business or if the education will qualify you for a new trade or business.

A welder in business for himself who takes a course in a new welding method can charge the expense to his business. A self-employed dance teacher who also takes dance lessons can charge the cost of the lessons to the dance business. On the other hand, a leather craftsperson who takes a course in massage cannot deduct the expenses. The education must be directly related to the business you have already begun to operate. Taking a course in pottery *before* opening your pottery shop is not deductible. By the way, any self-employed person can take a course in bookkeeping and deduct the cost as a business expense.

Education expenses include tuition, course fees, books, laboratory fees, travel, and meals and lodging while away from home overnight.

Entertainment

Entertainment is one of those expenses the Internal Revenue Service will look over twice. Be sure to keep detailed records of all entertainment expenses and be prepared to justify them.

Generally, any entertainment expense directly related to the business is deductible. The famous "business lunch" (wining and dining a prospective client) is allowable. Get a receipt and note on it who you took to lunch and why. The cost of a party to advertise your business or drum up new business is also deductible. Food served at a business meeting and food provided to employees on the business

premises are legitimate entertainment expenses.

Remember: Have fun, but keep records.

Freight

"Freight" refers to all shipping charges. "Freight-in" is shipping to you; "freight-out" is shipping of goods you sell. Freight-in on merchandise and materials (inventory) purchased for resale must be included as part of the cost of the inventory. Freight-in on depreciable fixed assets (equipment, furniture and fixtures, etc.) should be added to the cost of the asset and depreciated. Freight-out and shipping charges on goods you sell are fully deductible expenses.

Insurance

All current business related insurance premiums are deductible, including fire, extended coverage, liability, theft, business interruption, automobile (but see "Automobile Expenses"), worker's compensation, group insurance premiums for employees, unemployment, surety and fidelity bonds. Personal health insurance premiums and life insurance premiums are not deductible.

If you pay an insurance premium covering more than one year, you may deduct only the current year's portion. Even if you use the cash method of accounting and paid the cash this year, the IRS will not allow a deduction for prepaid insurance extending beyond one year.

Moving Expenses

A New Place of Business

You may deduct all the expenses of moving your shop from one location to another. This is an ordinary business expense. There are no special requirements.

Moving to a New Home

The costs of moving to a new home are also deductible if you meet certain requirements. The move must coincide with a move to a new business location where you plan to stay and work for at least 78 weeks. There is also a distance requirement: the distance between your *new shop* and your *old home* must be at least 35 miles greater than the distance between your *old shop* and your *old home*. (Better read that again.)

Try it this way:

(a) What is the distance from your *former* residence to your *new* business location? _____ miles.

(b) What is the distance from your *former* residence to your *former* business location? _____ miles.

If the distance in (a) is 35 or more miles *farther than* the distance in (b), you will be eligible for a moving expense deduction. If the distance is *less than* 35 miles, you are not eligible.

If your old workshop, for example, was five miles from your old home, in order to deduct the cost of moving to your new home, your new shop must be at least 40 miles from your old home. It does not matter where your new home is located.

Where home and shop are combined, the move must be at least 35 miles. If the move is less than 35 miles, you may still prorate and deduct the business portion of your moving expenses.

If you move to a new home but keep the same place of business, you may not deduct any moving expense no matter how far you move.

Detail of Allowable Moving Expenses

The allowable deductions for a move to a new home include:

1. Transportation for you, your family, furniture and all your possessions. If you drive your car, you may deduct either the actual out-of-pocket expenses (gas, oil, repairs, etc.; but not depreciation or any portion of auto insurance) or a standard 9 cents per mile.

2. Meals and lodging in route.

There are also allowable deductions for temporary living expenses up to thirty days, travel in search of a new residence (*after* you have located your new shop), and incidental expenses connected with the sale, purchase or lease of your residence.

The Fine Print

Moving expense deductions are subject to specific limitations in scope and in amount. The Internal Revenue Service publishes a free pamphlet, #521, "Tax Information on Moving Expenses", which explains the entire law in detail.

Repairs

Minor repairs on any of your business property, tools and equipment are fully deductible as a current expense.

Major repairs, however, that either add to the value or extend the useful life of an asset must be treated as a permanent investment and handled in the same manner as the purchase of a depreciable asset. The cost of the repair must be depreciated. See "Depreciation."

Travel Away From Home

Charge the expense of your vacation to your business? Many small business people plan to take that long dreamed-of tour of the Far East, make a few business "contacts" along the way, and deduct the entire trip as a business expense. The IRS says "NO!" Legitimate business travel expenses are deductible, but the rules are very specific.

If the reason for your trip is *primarily* personal, NONE of the travelling expenses to and from your destination are deductible. Only expenses directly related to your business may be deducted.

The cost of a business trip inside the United States is *entirely* deductible even if some of the trip is for pleasure.

More stringent rules apply to travel outside the U.S. You must allocate travel expenses between the business portion of your trip and the personal portion. If, however, the trip is no more than one week *or* the time spent for pleasure is less than 25 percent, the entire cost of travel is deductible.

There are special rules if you attend overseas conventions, seminars or other business meetings outside North America. A tax deduction is allowed only if the meeting is directly related to your business and if, in the IRS' opinion, there is a valid business reason for holding the meeting overseas.

If you attend a business convention aboard a cruise ship, additional rules apply. No deduction is allowed for attending conventions on international cruise ships, regardless of the legitimacy of the meeting. If your convention is held on a U.S. registered ship making calls at U.S. ports only, you are allowed a deduction, but not to exceed $2,000.

Travel expenses typically include:

1. Cost of transportation for yourself and your luggage to and from your destination.

2. Meals and lodging (must not be "lavish or extravagant")

3. Cost of transportation while away from home (taxi fares, auto rentals, etc.)

4. Business entertainment.

5. Personal services such as laundry and dry cleaning, barbering, etc.

For more information see IRS publication 463, "Travel, Entertainment, and Gift Expenses."

Inventory, and Something Very Important Called Cost-Of-Goods-Sold

"Inventory" refers to merchandise and materials that are held for sale in the normal course of business. It is the sale of inventory that normally provides a business (unless it is a service business) with its main source of revenue. Inventory includes finished products, work in process, raw materials and any materials that will go into the making of a finished product. Inventory does *not* include your tools, equipment, office supplies or anything else purchased for reasons other than resale.

Not all of your inventory purchases can be deducted as current year expenses. Only the cost of those goods actually sold is deductible. This is a very important distinction, and you should understand it completely. The cost of inventory *un*sold at year-end is an asset owned by you and will not be a deductible expense until sold (or until it becomes worthless, which will be covered later in the chapter).

Let's first use a simple example of cost-of-goods-sold. My friends John and Karen Resykle buy antiques, junk and old clothes at garage and rummage

sales and then resell the merchandise at a profit at flea markets. Last year, John and Karen purchased a total of $4,200 worth of merchandise (cost to them). At year-end, they still had $300 worth of merchandise on hand and unsold. John and Karen's deductible cost-of-goods-sold is $3,900 ($4,200 purchased, less $300 unsold). Note that the selling price of the inventory has no bearing on the calculation of cost-of-goods-sold.

The above example assumes that there was no inventory on hand at the beginning of the year. Let's now say there was $400 on hand at January 1. John and Karen's cost-of-goods-sold is now $4,300:

Inventory on hand at January 1	$ 400
Add: Inventory purchased during the year	4,200
Total inventory available for sale	$4,600
Subtract: Inventory on hand at December 31	(300)
Cost-of-goods-sold	$4,300

Taking Inventory

As you can see, at the end of the year you will need to make a list of inventory on hand. This is called "taking inventory" or "taking a physical inventory." (Business folk use the word "inventory" to refer both to the goods and to the procedure of counting the goods.) *Do not value the inventory at sale price.* The inventory should be valued at your cost.

If you are a manufacturer, computing the cost of your inventory will be a difficult task, for two reasons. First, you must calculate your cost not only of your raw materials but of your finished and partially finished goods as well. This will require a lot of educated guesswork it always does. Remember, value your inventory at its dollars-and-cents cost to you. That cost includes materials, supplies and paid labor. It does not, however, include the value of your own labor.

The other complication in computing cost-of-goods-sold, for manufacturers only, is a nasty law the Internal Revenue Service calls "Full Absorption Accounting." The IRS says that the cost of a manufacturer's inventory must include the cost of overhead, such as rent and utilities, which is attributable to the manufacturing operation. Such manufacturing overhead becomes part of the cost of the manufactured product and cannot be deducted as an expense until the product is sold. "Overhead" in this context refers specifically to the following expenses if they are "incident to and necessary for the production process": repairs, maintenance, utilities, rent, indirect labor and production supervisory wages, indirect materials, tools and equipment (useful life less than one year), and quality control costs.

I'll try a "simple" example: let's say that the space in your shop is divided, half for manufacturing and half for sales. Your expenses for the year included $1,200 for rent and utilities, and $5,000 for inventory. At the beginning of the year, there was no inventory. At year-end, there was $500 (cost) on hand. Your cost-of-goods-sold must be computed as follows:

Inventory on hand January 1	$ 0
Inventory purchased during year	5,000
One-half rent and utilities (manufacturing portion)	600
Cost of goods available for sale	$5,600
Subtract: inventory on hand Dec. 31	(500)
($500 is ten percent of the inventory purchased during the year; therefore, you must assume that ten percent of the overhead is also still "on hand".) Subtract: ten percent of the manufacturing portion of rent and utilities	(60)
Cost-of-goods-sold	$5,040

This $560 inventory (goods and overhead) "on hand" at year-end will become the inventory on hand January 1 of next year. It's a crazy way to have to calculate cost-of-goods-sold, I know, but it's the law. If ever the tax people have gone out of their way to unnecessarily complicate income taxes, they've sure done it to us here.

What this country needs is a dime that will buy a good 5 cent cigar.
                                                        —Pogo

Inventory Loss of Value

In computing cost-of-goods-sold, inventory on hand at year-end is usually valued at its cost to you and not at its sales price which, in normal circumstances, is higher than its cost. If for any reason your year-end inventory is *worth less* than what you paid, the inventory should be valued at this lesser amount. "Worth" refers to its retail value—what you can sell it for. Clothes which are no longer in fashion, damaged or destroyed goods, goods unsalable for any reason—all such items should be reduced to their market (sales) value. If year-end inventory is totally worthless, it should be valued at zero. This inventory valuation method is known as "lower of cost or market."

You may have figured out by now that reducing the value of your inventory—"writing it off" as a loss—increases your expenses, thereby decreasing your profits and your taxes. Let's look again at our first example, John and Karen Resykle, the flea market entrepreneurs. Their purchases during the year were $4,200; cost of inventory on hand at year-end was $300. Originally, their cost-of-goods-sold was $3,900 ($4,200 less the $300 on hand). Karen finds, however, that she made some bad purchases, and the inventory on hand at year-end for which she paid $300 cannot be sold for more than $200. Year-end inventory is therefore reduced to $200, that being the lower of cost or market. The cost-of-goods-sold, instead of being $3,900, is now $4,000 ($4,200 purchased, less $200). The additional $100 cost-of-goods-sold increases deductible expense by $100. Since John and Karen's income is unchanged, the additional expense reduces their profits by $100 and, therefore, reduces their taxes also.

When you value inventory below cost, the IRS requires you to prove your figures by offering the devalued inventory for sale within 30 days after the end of the year. *Excess inventory* (also called "overstock"—more goods on hand than you can sell) must be valued at original cost or replacement cost—not market value—whichever is lower. The accountants refer to this rule as the Thor decision, based on a Supreme Court case, IRS vs. Thor Power Tool Co. Thor lost.

Cost-of-goods-sold is your most important and usually your largest item of expense. The federal income tax form #1040-C has two main categories of expense: (1) cost-of-goods-sold, and (2) all other. You will be required to show on your tax return how you calculated your cost-of-goods-sold.

Inventory Valuation—LIFO & FIFO

Businesses may value inventory using the first-in, first-out method (FIFO), which is calculated as though the oldest inventory is sold first and the newest inventory is on the shelves; or the last-in, first-out method (LIFO), which is calculated as though the newly purchased inventory is sold before the older inventory. The actual inventory on hand doesn't have to be the last purchased in order to use the LIFO method; you may actually sell your inventory first-in, first-out and still use LIFO.

The tax consequences of FIFO versus LIFO can be significant. Remember, inventory on hand and unsold is an asset owned by you and cannot be written off as an expense until sold. In times of inflation, the inventory purchased last week might be much more expensive than the same inventory purchased a year ago. If the old inventory sold first, and the new more expensive inventory is unsold—which is what the FIFO, first-in, first-out method assumes—your-cost-of-goods-sold expense is the older, less expensive inventory. If, on the other hand, the newer inventory sold first, and the older, less expensive inventory is unsold—LIFO, last-in, first-out—the more expensive inventory gets written off as a cost-of-goods-sold expense. Under LIFO the result is a lower dollar value of inventory on hand (the older inventory), a higher dollar value of inventory sold (the newer inventory), a higher cost-of-goods-sold expense, and—this is where we're heading—lower taxes.

Despite LIFO tax savings, many businesses prefer the FIFO method because it is easier to figure the cost of year-end inventory. You simply look up the most recent bills from your suppliers. Hunting up old bills to figure LIFO can take more time than it's worth, particularly if you have a large or varied inventory. The IRS has lent a sympathetic ear to this problem. They have a standard formula you can use to convert FIFO figures to LIFO.

The IRS's LIFO rules are a good deal more complex than the FIFO rules. Also, switching from one method to the other requires a special adjustment. Contact the IRS for more information.

Problems worthy of attack, Prove their worth by fighting back.

—Piet Hein

Depreciation

An asset that will be useful to you over a period of years cannot be fully deducted as a business expense the year it is purchased. For tax purposes, the cost of such an asset must be spread out over several years. Each year, a portion of the cost of the asset can be deducted. The method by which this is accomplished is commonly known as "depreciation" and the assets are variously called "fixed" or "capital" or "depreciable" assets.

A mechanic's tools and equipment, a contractor's machinery, a writer's typewriter are examples of assets that must be depreciated. Display cases, furniture and fixtures, and major improvements to your shop are depreciable assets. Major repairs that increase the value or extend the life of an asset must be depreciated. Your automobile or truck can be depreciated providing you do not take the optional standard mileage allowance (see "Automobile Expenses").

All materials and supplies and all inventory, regardless of cost, are not capital assets and may not be depreciated. Stationery, business cards, small and inexpensive tools, anything that will be consumed in a year should be deducted as an expense the year it is purchased.

If your business is located in a building that you own (including your own home), you can depreciate the portion of the building being used for business. If you rent, your rent is a direct expense, and there is no need to compute building depreciation. A special note: the land apart from the improvements cannot be depreciated. Land is considered a permanent asset that cannot be expensed until sold.

Depreciable assets used in your business that were purchased before going into business can also be depreciated regardless of when acquired. Depreciable assets used partly for business and partly for pleasure can be depreciated to the extent used for business.

Actually, for accounting and tax purposes, the term "depreciation" is obsolete. The legal term is "cost recovery", and the system for depreciating assets is called the "cost recovery system" or the "accelerated cost recovery system" (ACRS). But everybody in business, including the accountants, still call it "depreciation".

Depreciation rules change from year to year. The entire depreciation system was completely changed in 1981 (that's when we first got "cost recovery") and has been tinkered with several times since.

Generally, whatever rule was in effect when you purchased an asset (or when you first used it in business if you purchased it before going into business) is the rule you must use for as long as you own the asset. The depreciation rules explained below are only for newly-acquired assets.

How Much Can Be Depreciated?

Generally speaking, you are allowed to depreciate the cost of your depreciable asset. "Cost" is the actual purchase price and includes freight charges and any installation charges. If you bought your equipment very inexpensively, your cost is still what you paid, not what the equipment is "worth". Sales tax can be deducted entirely the year you buy the equipment. When equipment is purchased in installments (on time) the cost is the total purchase price—as if you had paid cash for it—*excluding* the finance or interest charges. The finance charges are a separate business expense, fully deductible the year paid.

Special Note: A depreciable asset owned prior to going into business must be valued at its cost or at its market value at the time the asset is first converted to business use, *whichever is less*. If your old box of hand tools, which cost you $200 in 1979, was only worth $50 (market value) when you first used those tools in your business, you may only depreciate $50.

Many depreciable assets, in addition to being depreciated, are eligible for a special tax deduction called the "investment credit" (explained in a separate chapter). If you choose to take the full investment credit on a depreciable asset, you may not depreciate the full cost of that asset. You must reduce the cost by 50 percent of the investment credit before calculating depreciation. As an alternative, you have the option of taking a lower investment credit (2 percent lower) and taking full depreciation. These alternatives are explained in the chapter on investment credit.

Write Off Period

There are four categories of assets and each has a different write off period (also called a "recovery period").

Three Year Property: automobiles, light trucks (under 13,000#), highway semis (tractor units, not the trailers), small tools, equipment used for research and experimentation, hogs, some race horses.

Five Year Property: equipment, machinery, furniture, fixtures, display cases, signs, heavy general purpose trucks (over 13,000#), trailers, buses, aircraft, cattle, horses, sheep, goats.

Ten Year Property: This category is primarily for public utility property but also includes theme park structures, railroad tank cars, certain residential manufactured (mobile) homes.

Nineteen Year Property: Buildings (owned, not rented, excluding land)

ACRS DEPRECIATION TABLE
Assets Other Than Real Estate

Year	Percentage		
	3 Year	5 Year	10 Year
1.	25%	15%	8%
2.	38	22	14
3.	37	21	12
4.		21	10
5.		21	10
6.			10
7.			9
8.			9
9.			9
10.			9

Methods of Computing Depreciation

You may choose one of two methods for depreciating property: the ACRS method (Accelerated Cost Recovery System) or the Straight Line method. ACRS is more commonly used and has less restrictions than Straight Line.

To use the ACRS method for assets other than real estate, use the ACRS Depreciation Table to calculate annual depreciation. The percentages refer to the percent of the cost you can write off each year. It doesn't matter when during the year you purchased the property; you use the same percentages for property bought in December as you do for property bought in January. The "Year" in the table refers to the calendar year, not to the first twelve months you own the property.

The ACRS depreciation for nineteen-year real estate is calculated differently. The percent deduction for a given building depends on the month the building was purchased. A building purchased in February will have a totally different depreciation schedule than a building purchased in November. Consult the IRS for their nineteen-year ACRS tables. Remember, land is not depreciable.

Straight Line

The Straight Line method distributes the depreciation equally over the write off period. Each year the same amount is depreciated. For three-, five- and ten-year property, you may take only one-half year's depreciation the first year you own the asset but you get an additional half year's depreciation at the end of the write off period. For nineteen-year real estate, the first year's deduction must be prorated for the number of months you own the property.

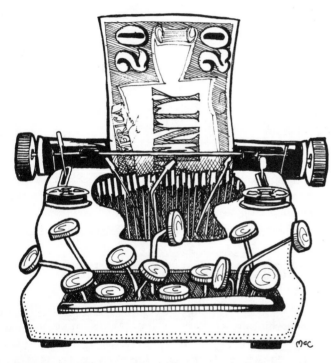

With Straight Line depreciation you also have the option of using longer write off periods. For 3 year assets, you may choose a 3, 5 or 12 year period. For 5 year assets, 5, 12 or 25 years. For 10 year assets, 10, 25 or 35 years. For 19 year assets, 19, 35 or 45 years.

A few special rules apply only to Straight Line depreciation: (1) If you sell the asset before the end of the write off period, no depreciation is allowed for that asset the year of sale. (2) Within a given category—three-year, five-year or ten-year—the same write off period (whatever write off period you choose) must be used for all assets purchased that year. For nineteen-year real estate, the choice

can be made asset by asset. (3) Once you choose Straight Line and a write off period for a particular asset, you may not change to the ACRS method or change the write off period without prior approval from the IRS.

Why would you choose Straight Line depreciation over the ACRS method? In the early days of a business, expenses are often high and income low. Many businesses lose money the first year or two or three. You may owe little or no income tax and therefore have no real use for the additional tax deduction ACRS depreciation brings. It might be better for you to get the bulk of the depreciation expense a few years down the road when you could use it to reduce taxes. The difference between Straight Line and ACRS depreciation is significant, however, only if you choose a longer write off period. Five years Straight Line versus 5 years ACRS—there is little difference. But 12 years Straight Line versus 5 years ACRS will give you substantially more depreciation in future years under the Straight Line method.

Let's take the example of a piece of equipment you purchase for $1,200. It's a 5 year asset. Under ACRS depreciation it must be depreciated over 5 years. Under Straight Line, you can choose a write off period of 5, 12 or 25 years. Let's say you choose a 12 year period. Here is how depreciation deductions compare:

	Accelerated	*Straight Line*
1st year	$180	$ 50
2nd	264	100
3rd	252	100
4th	252	100
5th	252	100
6th	0	100
7th	0	100
8th	0	100
9th	0	100
10th	0	100
11th	0	100
12th	0	100
13th	0	50
Total	$1,200	$1,200

Writing Off Assets the Year of Purchase

You have yet another tax option for fixed assets. Rather than depreciate them at all, you may write off the entire cost of some of them, as an expense, the year you purchase them. There is a $5000 limitation on the total write off allowed in any one year.

There is a major pitfall here. Most depreciable assets are eligible for the investment credit which can result in a substantial tax savings. If you choose this write off instead of depreciation, you lose the investment credit on the assets written off. You want to be sure that the tax savings you get by writing off rather than depreciating assets isn't lost because you gave up the investment credit.

Part Business, Part Personal

Depreciation, both ACRS and Straight Line, may be computed only for the business portion of a depreciable asset. If your tools are used half for work and half for pleasure, you may compute depreciation only on half the cost.

Special rules apply to vehicles and computers used only partly for business. If your vehicle or computer is used more than 50 percent for business, you prorate the depreciation as you would for any other asset used partly for business. If, however, your vehicle or computer is used 50 percent or less for business, you may not use ACRS depreciation, and you may not use the normal number of years. For the car, you must use five-year (or longer) Straight Line depreciation, prorated between business and non-business use. (This rule applies only if you are depreciating your car. If you take the standard mileage allowance—see the chapter "Automobile Expenses" in this tax section—you can ignore this rule.) For the computer used 50 percent or less for business, you must use twelve-year (or longer) Straight Line depreciation, again prorated between business and non-business. You must keep detailed records—dates and hours for the computer, dates and mileage for the car—to verify your business use.

Similar restrictions also apply to property used for entertainment, recreation or amusement.

Limitations on Automobiles

Regardless of the percent used for business or the depreciation method used, automobile depreciation is limited to a maximum of $3,200 the first year and $4,800 a year in future years (these amounts will change annually). Due to this limitation, expensive cars cannot be fully depreciated in the three years normally allowed. The depreciation will have to be spread out over a longer period.

This "luxury car rule," as it is known, applies to four-wheel vehicles rated at 6,000 pounds or less. It does not apply to ambulances, hearses, trucks, vans, cabs or other vehicles used to transport people or property for compensation or hire.

The Depreciation Worksheet

The combination depreciation worksheet and equipment ledger in the Ledger section has been designed to help you compute depreciation. Depreciation must be reported to the IRS on a separate depreciation schedule, Form #4562. But instead of filling out the IRS form in detail, you can attach a copy of this worksheet to Form #4562 and save yourself a lot of tedious copying.

EQUIPMENT LEDGER AND DEPRECIATION WORKSHEETS

1 DATE	2 DESCRIPTION	3 METH.	4 WRITE OFF PERIOD	5 NEW OR USED	6 %	7 COST	8 REDUCTION FOR INV. CREDIT	9 WRITE OFF	10 BAL. TO BE DEPR.	11 DEPR. 19__	12 BAL. TO BE DEPR.	13 DEPR. 19__	14 BAL. TO BE DEPR.	15 DEPR. 19__	16 BAL. TO BE DEPR.	17 DEPR. 19__	18 BAL. TO BE DEPR.
1-10	Drill	Acc.	3	N	100	83 69	Ø	Ø	83 69	20 92	62 77						
3-1	Desk + Chair	Acc.	5	N	100	250 00	Ø	Ø	250 00	37 50	212 50						
7-1	Welding Unit	Acc.	5	N	100	663 00	Ø	Ø	663 00	99 45	563 55						

Use a separate line on the worksheet for each depreciable asset. Fill out all the columns when you purchase an asset, and you will never have to hunt up the information a second time. Even if you hire an accountant to prepare your taxes, you will save the accountant time—and save yourself money—if you fill out Columns 1, 2, 5, 6 and 7 (the basic information) so that it will be readily available.

Enter the information as follows:

Column 1, Date. Date purchased or date first used in business.

Column 2, Description. Be specific enough to distinguish this particular asset from all others. If the asset is your one and only welding torch, the description "welding torch" is sufficient. If, however, you have four welding torches, "welding torch, serial no. 34-15" or some other specific designation is needed.

Column 3, Method. ACRS or Straight Line.

Column 4, Write Off Period. Three, five, ten or nineteen years or, if you use Straight Line depreciation, possibly longer.

Column 5, New or Used.

Column 6, Percent Used for Business. One hundred percent if the asset is used solely for business; a smaller percent if partly personal.

Column 7, Cost. See the discussion of cost in this chapter.

Column 8, Reduction for Investment Credit. If you take the full investment credit (see the "Investment Credit" chapter) enter 50 percent of the investment credit in this column.

Column 9, Write Off. If you take the option of writing off rather than depreciating some of your assets (see the discussion in this chapter), fill out the amount in this column. This column is not for depreciation.

Column 10, Balance to be Depreciated. Column 6 x Column 7 - Column 8 - Column 9 = Column 10. This column is actually the cost adjusted for the percentage used for business, investment credit and first-year write off. The amount you arrive at here is commonly called the "cost basis." This is the amount that is actually depreciated.

The four sets of paired columns, 11 and 12, 13 and 14, 15 and 16, and 17 and 18, provide four years of depreciation scheduling for each asset. The first column in a pair is the depreciation for the year, and the following column is the remaining undepreciated balance. Column 10 less Column 11 equals Column 12, and so on.

Office in the Home

You will not be able to deduct any expenses for a home office unless it is used on a regular basis as your principal place of business or a place of business that is used by your patients, clients or customers in the normal course of business. If your business is also operated out of another location such as a storefront, you cannot deduct the cost of a home office unless your customers normally come to your home.

Joe Campbell, who owns Resistance Repair, does his repair work in a rented repair shop but does all his bookkeeping at home because there is no extra space in the shop and because the bookkeeping requires quiet, uninterrupted thinking time which is impossible at the shop. All legitimate, for sure, but his home office is not deductible. Another friend of mine who is an attorney has her office in downtown San Francisco but also sees her clients on a regular basis in her home. Her home office is deductible.

If you work a day job and run your home business in the evenings or if you have a regular business away from home and a second business in the home, you are allowed the home office deduction for the home business as long as it meets the other requirements.

To be eligible for the home office deduction, a specific part of your home must be used exclusively for business. It can be a separate room or even part of a room as long as it is designated for business and nothing else.

There are two exceptions to the exclusive rule. If your home is your sole fixed location for a retail sales business and if you regularly store your merchandise in your home, the expense of maintaining the storage area is deductible. If you operate a licensed child care business at your home, you also do not have to meet the exclusive test.

The deduction for a home office cannot exceed your gross income from the business—total income before any expenses—reduced by the business percentage of the mortgage interest and property taxes if you own your own home.

As already discussed in the Bookkeeping section under "Rent" and "Utilities" and in this Tax section under "Depreciation", expenses related to office in the home include a percentage of your rent if you rent your home or a percentage of the depreciation if you own your home, and an equal percentage of home utilities, property taxes, mortgage interest and insurance.

If you own your home and are depreciating a part of it as a business office, you will run into tax complications when you sell the house. In computing the profit on the sale, you are required to reduce your cost basis by the amount of the depreciation, which has the effect of increasing your profit and your taxes on the sale. Also, some of the profit may be considered regular income (instead of capital gains) and subject to a higher tax rate.

The IRS requires you to indicate on Schedule C whether or not you are claiming a deduction for a home office. For more information, ask the IRS for a free copy of Publication #587, "Business Use of Your Home."

Non-Deductible Expenses

Certain expenses are specifically disallowed by law and cannot be deducted on your income tax return, no way, no how:

1. Expenses not related to your business, and business expenses not meeting the "ordinary and necessary" or the "reasonable" test.

2. Federal income tax, self-employment tax or any tax penalties. Interest on back taxes is deductible. State income tax is deductible on your federal return but not on your state return.

3. Any fines for violation of the law. Even though you were parked on business, you cannot deduct that parking ticket. If you got towed away, the towing charge is deductible, for what little consolation that may offer.

4. Payments to yourself. The profit from your business is not an expense of running your business; and when you pay yourself, it is not deductible. The only way you may pay yourself a wage and deduct it as an expense is to incorporate (see the chapter on corporations.)

5. Loan repayments. The loan was not income when received and is not expense when paid. Any interest on the loan, however, is a deductible expense.

6. Clothing, unless used exclusively for work and unsuitable for street wear.

7. Meals at work. If, however, you are traveling away from home on business overnight, the cost of meals is deductible. Business lunches to entertain customers or prospective customers are also deductible.

8. Regular commuting expenses between your home and usual place of business.

9. Cost of land, until you sell it. Only the structure on the land may be depreciated.

Investment Tax Credit (ITC)

Any business that purchases tools, equipment, furniture or similar fixed assets with a useful life of three years or more is allowed a tax credit—a direct income tax reduction—the year of the purchase. The credit is called the "investment tax credit" or "investment credit" and it's like getting a government financed discount on your fixed assets.

The investment credit is a credit against federal income taxes equal to a percentage of the cost of certain fixed assets. The credit is allowed the year the assets are first used in business. Assets eligible for the investment credit must be tangible property other than real estate used in your business. Equipment, tools, office furnishings—new or used—are all eligible. Real estate and any improvements, such as built-in cabinets or remodeling, usually do not qualify.

The investment credit is 10 percent of the cost of eligible property with a five or ten-year write off period. For property with a three-year write off period, the investment credit is 6 percent (except for commuter highway vehicles which are eligible for a 10 percent credit). An investment credit is allowed for rehabilitating old buildings: 15 percent for buildings 30-39 years old, 20 percent for buildings at least 40 years old, 25 percent for certified historic structures. No investment credit is allowed on assets written off to expense rather than depreciated (see the chapter on depreciation).

The investment credit is not a totally free gift. If you take the full investment credit on an asset, you must decrease the amount of depreciation on that asset. The cost of the asset (the basis for determining depreciation) must be reduced by 50 percent of the investment credit. Take an example of a piece of equipment which cost $5,000 and which is eligible for a 10 percent investment credit. If you don't take the credit (it is optional) you may depreciate the full $5,000. If you do take the 10 percent credit, you may depreciate only $4,750 ($5,000 cost less 50 percent of the $500 credit). As an alternative, you may reduce the investment credit by 2 percent—in the above example, to 8 percent or $400 instead of $500—and take full depreciation. This 8 percent alternative applies only to the regular investment credit. If you take the energy investment credit or the building rehabilitation credit, you still must reduce the cost basis of the asset even if you reduce the regular investment credit.

Form 3468

Department of the Treasury
Internal Revenue Service

Computation of Investment Credit

▶ Attach to your tax return.
▶ Schedule B (Business Energy Investment Credit) on back.

OMB No. 1545-0155

1985

Name(s) as shown on return

Samuel Thesham

Identifying number
123-45-6789

Part I — Elections (Check the box(es) below that apply to you (See Instruction D).)

A I elect to increase my qualified investment to 100% for certain commuter highway vehicles placed in service before January 1, 1986 (section 46(c)(6)) ☐

B I elect to increase my qualified investment by all qualified progress expenditures made this and all later tax years . . . . ☐
Enter total qualified progress expenditures included in column (4), Part II ▶ . . . .

C I claim full credit on certain ships under section 46(g)(3) (See **Instruction B** for details.) . . . . ☐

Part II — Qualified Investment (See instructions for rules on automobiles and other property with any personal use)

1 Recovery Property			Line	(1) Class of Property	(2) Cost or Other Basis	(3) Applicable Percentage	(4) Qualified Investment (Column 2 x column 3)
Regular Percentage	New Property		(a)	3-year		60	
			(b)	Other	$467	100	$467
	Used Property		(c)	3-year		60	
			(d)	Other		100	
Section 48(q) Election to Reduce Credit (instead of adjusting basis)	New Property		(e)	3-year		40	
			(f)	Other		80	
	Used Property		(g)	3-year		40	
			(h)	Other		80	

2	Nonrecovery property—Enter total qualified investment (See instructions for line 2)	2	
3	New commuter highway vehicle—Enter total qualified investment (See Instruction D(1))	3	
4	Used commuter highway vehicle—Enter total qualified investment (See Instruction D(1))	4	
5	**Total qualified investment in 10% property**—Add lines 1(a) through 1(h), 2, 3, and 4 (See instructions for special limits)	5	$467
6	Qualified rehabilitation expenditures—Enter total qualified investment for:		
a	30-year-old buildings	6a	
b	40-year-old buildings	6b	
c	Certified historic structures (You must attach NPS certification—see instructions)	6c	

Part III — Tentative Regular Investment Credit

7	10% of line 5	7	$ 47
8	15% of line 6a	8	
9	20% of line 6b	9	
10	25% of line 6c	10	
11	Credit from cooperatives—Enter regular investment credit from cooperatives	11	
12	Regular investment credit—Add lines 7 through 11	12	$ 47
13	Business energy investment credit—From line 11 of Schedule B (see back of this form)	13	
14	Current year investment credit—Add lines 12 and 13	14	$ 47

Note: If you have a 1985 jobs credit (Form 5884), credit for alcohol used as fuel (Form 6478), or employee stock ownership plan (ESOP) credit (Form 8007) in addition to your 1985 investment credit, or if you have a carryback or carryforward of any general business credit, stop here and go to **Form 3800**, General Business Credit, to claim your 1985 investment credit. If you have only a 1985 investment credit (which may include business energy investment credit), you may continue with lines 15 through 20 to claim your credit.

Part IV — Tax Liability Limitations

15	a Individuals—From Form 1040, enter amount from line 46 . . . . ⎫		
	b Corporations—From Form 1120, Schedule J, enter tax from line 3 (or Form 1120-A, Part I, line 1). ⎬	15	$2,732
	c Other filers—Enter income tax before credits from return. . . . . ⎭		
16	a Individuals—From Form 1040, enter credit from line 47, plus any orphan drug, nonconventional source fuel, and research credits included on line 49 . . . . ⎫		
	b Corporations—From Form 1120, Schedule J, enter credits from lines 4(a) through 4(e) (Form 1120-A filers, enter zero) . . . . ⎬	16	0
	c Other filers—See instructions for line 16c . . . . ⎭		
17	Income tax liability as adjusted (subtract line 16 from line 15)	17	$2,732
18	a Enter smaller of line 17 or $25,000. (See instructions for line 18)	18a	$2,732
	b If line 17 is more than $25,000—Enter 85% of the excess	18b	
19	Investment credit limitation—Add lines 18a and 18b	19	$2,732
20	Total allowed credit—Enter the smaller of line 14 or line 19. This is your **General Business Credit** for 1985. Enter here and on Form 1040, line 48; Form 1120, Schedule J, line 4(f); Form 1120-A, Part I, line 2 ; or the proper line of other returns	20	$ 47

For Paperwork Reduction Act Notice, see separate instructions.

Form **3468** (1985)

Five- and ten-year property must be kept five years, and three-year property must be kept three years to earn the full investment credit. If you sell the property before the five years (or three years) some of the investment credit must be paid back ("recaptured") the year of sale.

The investment credit cannot exceed your federal income tax liability. If the credit is greater than your income tax, there are provisions for carryback to prior years and carryover to future years. The credit does not apply against the self-employment tax or state income tax. Investment credit is neither business income nor expense.

If property eligible for the investment credit (other than cars and computers) is used partly for business and partly for pleasure, you are allowed a partial investment credit. If, for example, your tools are used 25 percent for business, you are allowed 25 percent of the normal investment credit. Cars and computers, however, must be used more than 50 percent for business to be eligible for any investment credit. If you use your computer 51 percent for business, you can take 51 percent of the normal investment credit. But if you use that computer 50 percent for business, you get no investment credit.

The investment credit for automobiles, normally 6 percent of the cost, is limited to a maximum of $675. If you use a 4 percent investment credit instead of 6 percent, the maximum investment credit is 2/3 what it normally would be, or $450. Like the "luxury car rule" explained in the Depreciation chapter, these maximums will change in future years. These maximums apply only to four-wheel vehicles rated at 6,000 pounds or less. They do not apply to ambulances, hearses, trucks, vans, cabs or other vehicles used to transport people or property for compensation or hire.

The Fine Print

The many "if's" and "but's" in the investment credit rules are complex but are unlikely to apply to most small businesses:

1. The investment credit is limited if your income taxes exceed $25,000 ($12,500 for married couples filing separate returns).

2. Property used in the operation of an apartment or boarding house does not qualify.

3. Livestock must meet special requirements.

4. In a few limited situations, leased property is eligible if the owner elects to pass the credit to you.

5. Property acquired from a relative may not qualify.

6. Property purchased for use outside the U.S. generally will not qualify.

7. Used property eligible for the credit is limited to $125,000.

8. Some livestock and horticulture buildings are eligible for the investment credit.

The Internal Revenue Service has a special tax form, #3468, for computing investment credit. The full details of the investment credit law are explained in a free IRS pamphlet, #572, "Tax Information on Investment Credit."

Self-Employment Tax

Self-employment tax is Social Security tax for self-employed individuals. Independent business people pay the highest Social Security rate of all, and it goes up every year. The 1986 rate is 12.3 percent on profits up to a maximum of $42,000 — a maximum tax of $5,166.00.

Sole proprietors, partners and independent contractors are liable for self-employment tax. Corporate stockholders are not liable. Rental income and royalty income are not subject to self-employment tax.

You will owe no self-employment tax if your profits were $400 or less. But if you net $401, you pay 12.3 percent on the entire $401, not just on the one dollar over the $400 minimum (go back and round off those pennies).

Self-employment tax is apart from and in addition to federal income tax. You may owe no income taxes but still be liable for self-employment tax. Retirement deductions and tax credits such as the investment credit, which reduce income taxes, cannot be used to reduce self-employment tax.

If a husband and wife operate a business together, who pays self-employment tax depends on how the business is set up. If the business is a partnership, formally set up as such and filing partnership tax returns, both spouses pay self-employment tax. If the business is a sole proprietorship, only one spouse pays self-employment tax—the one who is the primary operator of the business. This is covered in more detail in a chapter in the Appendix, "Husband and Wife Partnerships."

Self-employed people who are also holding down jobs where Social Security is withheld from their pay should combine the two incomes to arrive at the self-employment tax maximum. An example will explain best:

My brother Michael is employed as a salesman and earns $39,000 a year. His employer withholds Social Security tax on these earnings. Michael also operates his own small mail order business out of his home. The business made a profit in 1986 of $4,500. The self-employment tax is computed as follows:

Maximum income eligible for tax	$42,000
Deduct earnings from employment, which are already taxed	(39,000)
Maximum applicable to the self-employment tax	$3,000

Since Michael's business earnings, $4,500, are in excess of the maximum, Michael owes self-employment tax only on $3,000, or $369 (12.3 percent of $3,000)

Let's change the example around a little and say Michael earned only $2,000 in his mail order business. He would now owe self-employment tax on

SCHEDULE SE
(Form 1040)

Department of the Treasury
Internal Revenue Service

Computation of Social Security Self-Employment Tax

▶ See Instructions for Schedule SE (Form 1040).
▶ Attach to Form 1040.

OMB No. 1545-0074

1985

18

Name of **self-employed** person (as shown on social security card) Samuel Thesham	Social security number of **self-employed** person ▶	123 : 45 : 6789

Part I — Regular Computation of Net Earnings From Self-Employment

Note: *If you performed services for certain churches or church-controlled organizations and you are not a minister or a member of a religious order, see the instructions.*

1 Net farm profit or (loss) from Schedule F (Form 1040), line 39, and farm partnerships, Schedule K–1 (Form 1065), line 13a	**1**	
2 Net profit or (loss) from Schedule C (Form 1040), line 33, Schedule K–1 (Form 1065), line 13a (other than farming), and Form W–2 wages of $100 or more from an electing church or church-controlled organization. (See instructions for other income to report.)	**2**	$10,599

Note: ☐ *Check here if you are **exempt** from self-employment tax on your earnings as a minister, member of a religious order, or Christian Science practitioner because you filed **Form 4361**.*
See instructions for kinds of income to report. If you have other earnings of $400 or more that are subject to self-employment tax, include those earnings on line 2.

Part II — Optional Computation of Net Earnings From Self-Employment (See "Who Can Use Schedule SE")

Generally, this part may be used **only** if you meet any of the following tests:

A Your gross farm income (Schedule F (Form 1040), line 12) was not more than $2,400; or

B Your gross farm income (Schedule F (Form 1040), line 12) was more than $2,400 and your net farm profits (Schedule F (Form 1040), line 39) were less than $1,600; or

C Your net nonfarm profits (Schedule C (Form 1040), line 33) were less than $1,600 and also less than two-thirds (⅔) of your gross nonfarm income (Schedule C (Form 1040), line 5).
See instructions for other limitations.

3 Maximum income for optional methods	**3**	$1,600 00
4 Farm Optional Method—If you meet test A or B above, enter: the smaller of two-thirds (⅔) of gross farm income from Schedule F (Form 1040), line 12, and farm partnerships, Schedule K–1 (Form 1065), line 13b; or $1,600	**4**	
5 Subtract line 4 from line 3	**5**	
6 Nonfarm Optional Method—If you meet test C above, enter: the smallest of two-thirds (⅔) of gross nonfarm income from Schedule C (Form 1040), line 5, and Schedule K–1 (Form 1065), line 13c (other than farming); or $1,600; or, if you elected the farm optional method, the amount on line 5	**6**	

Part III — Computation of Social Security Self-Employment Tax

7 Enter the amount from Part I, line 1, or, if you elected the farm optional method, Part II, line 4 . . .	**7**	
8 Enter the amount from Part I, line 2, or, if you elected the nonfarm optional method, Part II, line 6 . . .	**8**	$10,599
9 Add lines 7 and 8. If less than $400, do not fill in the rest of the schedule because you are not subject to self-employment tax. (**Exception:** If this line is less than $400 and you are an employee of an electing church or church-controlled organization, complete the schedule unless this line is a loss. See instructions.)	**9**	$10,599
10 The largest amount of combined wages and self-employment earnings subject to social security or railroad retirement tax (Tier 1) for 1985 is	**10**	$39,600 00
11 a Total social security wages and tips from Forms W–2 and railroad retirement compensation (Tier 1). **Note:** *U.S. Government employees whose wages are only subject to the 1.35% hospital insurance benefits tax (Medicare) and employees of certain church or church-controlled organizations should not include those wages on this line (see instructions)* **11a**		
b Unreported tips subject to social security tax from Form 4137, line 9, or to railroad retirement tax (Tier 1) **11b**		
c Add lines 11a and 11b	**11c**	0
12 a Subtract line 11c from line 10	**12a**	$39,600
b Enter your "qualified" U.S. Government wages if you are required to use the worksheet in Part III of the instructions. **12b**		
c Enter your Form W-2 wages from an electing church or church-controlled organization. **12c**		
13 Enter the smaller of line 9 or line 12a	**13**	$10,599
If line 13 is $39,600, fill in $4,672.80 on line 14. Otherwise, multiply line 13 by .118 and enter the result on line 14		.118
14 Self-employment tax. Enter this amount on Form 1040, line 51	**14**	$1,251

For Paperwork Reduction Act Notice, see Form 1040 Instructions.

Schedule SE (Form 1040) 1985

---

the full $2,000, since it is under the $3,000 maximum. His self-employment tax would be $246 (12.3 percent of $2,000)

Let's change the example a last time and say that Michael's earnings as an employed salesman were $45,000. Since these earnings are now in excess of the $42,000 maximum, Michael will owe *no* self-employment tax on the profits of his little mail order business no matter how much his business makes.

Self-employment tax is computed on your regular federal income tax return, using form #1040-SE.

There are alternative ways to compute self-employment tax if your earnings were below the $400 minimum and you still want to pay into Social Security. For more information, request a free copy of IRS Publication #553, "Information on Self-Employment Tax."

Retirement Deductions

The Internal Revenue Service allows you to invest a portion of your business profits in a special retirement plan, called a "Keogh" or "H.R. 10" plan. You pay no federal income taxes on the money you invest or the interest earned until you retire and withdraw the funds.

There are different types of Keogh retirement plans and they all have lengthy, complicated rules. Under the most common of these plans, the "defined contribution"plan, you are allowed to invest up to 20 percent of your profits every year, up to a maximum investment of $30,000. These figures are annual allowable maximums. You may choose to invest less than the maximum or nothing at all, even after you have already started the plan. Once you have invested in a retirement plan, the invested money and the interest may not be withdrawn without penalty until you reach age 59½ except in special cases of death or disability.

What real benefits does this special retirement plan hold for you now? An example will help explain:

Charles Checkout who owns Chuck's Chicken and Ribs did pretty well last year, netting a $20,000 profit from his business. Chuck is married and has one kid, and he takes the standard deduction. Without any retirement deduction, Chuck would owe $2,041 in federal income taxes. Chuck, however, is a man concerned about his future. He joined a retirement plan and contributed the maximum, which was $4,000 (20 percent of $20,000). His taxable income was reduced by the $4,000 and his income taxes were reduced by $701. That's a big savings! Chuck will have to pay income taxes on his investment and the earned interest when he withdraws the money after he retires. But the taxes he pays then will probably be lower, due to several tax breaks available to retired people.

Roses have thorns as well as flowers. And so do retirement deductions:

1. The most obvious disadvantage is that you do not have current use of that money. You have invested it and cannot withdraw it without penalty for possibly twenty to thirty years. And we won't even discuss inflation and what that does to the value of future money.

2. If you have regular employees who have worked for you three years or more, you *must* include them in the retirement plan. You must pay for their retirement contributions out of your own pocket; you cannot deduct it from their wages. Any money invested for employees is a tax-deductible business expense.

3. Investing in a retirement plan will not reduce the amount of your self-employment tax. Self-employment tax is computed on the profits of your business before the retirement deduction. Charles Checkout in our example will still owe self-employment tax on $20,000 profit, not on the reduced amount.

4. Not all states allow the retirement deduction in calculating state income tax. You may still owe state income tax on the full amount of your profit.

You should remember that all of these restrictions are only applicable if you invest in a special retirement plan as described above. You still may continue to invest your profits however you please without having to invest money on behalf of employees, but you must pay the regular income taxes on the profits so invested.

How do you join a special retirement plan? Many banks, savings and loan associations, insurance companies and investment companies offer such plans to the public. The U.S. Treasury also offers a special series of U.S. bonds you may invest in. Each plan may be a little different, and the interest you earn will vary depending on where and in what amounts you invest your money. If you are interested in joining a retirement plan, it is certainly worth shopping around. Make sure that the plan you select is approved by the Internal Revenue Service (have the bank show you a formal, written approval from the IRS), and be sure you are dealing with reputable people. Read all the fine print in the contract, and get an explanation for anything you do not understand.

You can also open an IRA (Individual Retirement Account) in addition to a Keogh plan, for even greater tax savings. Self-employed people are allowed to have both Keoghs and IRA's. Ask the IRS for more information.

The IRS publishes a free booklet, "Self Employed Retirement Plans" (Publication #560).

Owner of a small factory in New Orleans offered a $25 bonus to employees for money saving ideas. First winner paid was the man who suggested the bonus be cut to $10.

—reported in the San Francisco Chronicle

Estimated taxes are filed on Form 1040-ES.

Estimated Tax Payments

If your federal tax for the current year, income and self-employment combined, is estimated to be $500 or more, you may be required to pay your taxes in quarterly installments. The government wants your tax money just like the taxes withheld from employees' paychecks. The four quarterly payments are due April 15, June 15, September 15 and the following January 15. You do not have to pay the fourth estimate if you file your tax return by January 31 and pay the balance due.

How do you estimate your taxes? You can base your estimate on your prior year's taxes, even if you were not in business then. Whatever your total tax came to last year, divide it by four and send the IRS four equal installments. If your total tax last year (including self-employment) was less than $500, you are not required to make any estimated tax payments.

You also have the option to estimate your taxes based on your current year's income. Four times a year, you figure your taxable income for the quarter and send in the correct tax. As you can imagine, this is not an easy task. Under this method you may be hit with an interest penalty if you underestimate by more than 20 percent.

When you compute your actual tax at year-end, any overpayment of estimated taxes will, at your option, either be refunded or applied to the following year's estimates.

If you pay very low estimated taxes or none at all, and if you are having a profitable year, be prepared when April 15 rolls around. You may have to come up with a lot of cash to pay all of this year's taxes _and_ to pay next year's first quarterly estimate; both are due the same day. You may want to make voluntary estimated payments or set some money aside in a separate bank account to cushion the blow.

Estimated taxes are filed on a four-part form, #1040-ES. For more information, see IRS Publication #505, "Tax Withholding And Estimated Taxes."

The Fine Print

The above rules apply to sole proprietors and partners. There is a different set of rules for corporations and a third set of rules for farmers and fishermen. If you base your estimates on the prior year's taxes, you must have been a U.S. citizen or resident for the entire previous year. If you are hit with an underpayment penalty, talk to the IRS or your accountant about it; there are several situations where the IRS will waive the penalty.

Operating Losses

If your business suffers a loss this year, you will owe no income taxes, which I'm sure you know. But did you know that you can use this year's loss to offset profits from other years? You are allowed to carry back what the IRS calls a "Net Operating

Loss'' from a trade or business to apply against prior income and receive a refund of prior years' taxes, even if you were not in business then. The loss can be carried back three years. And if your taxable income for the three prior years is not sufficient to absorb the entire loss, you may carry the balance forward to apply to as many as fifteen future years.

Net Operating Loss is not simply the business loss shown on your tax return. It is a complicated combination of business and non-business income and deductions. Although the Net Operating Loss rules are long and complex, they can save you a substantial amount of money.

Net Operating Loss is computed as follows:

First, business profits and losses for the year are netted together to determine your "net business loss," which is only part of Net Operating Loss. Included in "net business loss" are the profits and losses from all your unincorporated businesses, any partnership profit or loss, S corporation losses (S corporation profits are not included here), any salary or wage you earned working for someone else, and any personal casualty loss shown on your itemized deductions (after the $100 exclusion and percentage limitation).

Second, all other income, called "non-business income," is added together. "Non-business income" includes dividends, interest, capital gains (full amounts), and S corporations income (but not S corporation losses; don't ask me why).

Third, the "non-business income" is reduced by your "non-business deductions." These include your itemized deductions, excluding casualty losses, if you itemized; or the standard deduction (now called the "zero bracket amount") if you did not itemize. Non-business deductions also include contributions to a self-employed retirement plan. "Non-business income" less "non-business deductions" gives us a "net non-business income." Net non-business income cannot be less than zero.

Finally, the "net business loss" from the first step is reduced by the "net non-business income" from the third step to arrive, at last, at the Net Operating Loss.

Got it? No? Maybe an example will help. An old friend of mine whom I will call Roscoe (he really wants to remain anonymous) purchased an entire truckload of Magic Miracle Ten-in-One Kitchen Wonders and proceeded to find out that Mrs. Housewife was not as gullible as he was. To make a long story short, ol' Roscoe lost his shirt, to the amount of $6,000. Had this been Roscoe's only

source of income, his Net Operating Loss would have been $6,000. Roscoe, however, also held a part-time job that paid him $2,500, he earned $300 in bank interest and he made a $3,000 profit on some stock he sold. With me so far? To complete the illustration, Roscoe's itemized deductions were $3,000, which included a casualty loss of $200.

First, Roscoe's "Net Business Loss" is computed as follows:

Loss from his business	($6,000)
Casualty loss	(200)
Salary	2,500
Net Business Loss	($3,700)

Next, the "Net Non-Business Income":

Capital Gains	$3,000
Bank Interest	300
Non-Business Income	$3,300
LESS:	
Itemized Deductions (excluding the Casualty Loss)	(2,800)
Net Non-Business Income	$ 500

The Net Operating Loss is the Net Business Loss reduced by the Net Non-Business Income:

Net Business Loss	($3,700)
Net Non-Business Income	500
NET OPERATING LOSS	$3,200

The Net Operating Loss is first applied to the *taxable income* per your tax return of the third preceding year (that is, three years ago). It does not matter whether you were in business that year or not—the Net Operating Loss applies against all taxable income. To the extent that the taxable income for the third preceding year is less than the NOL carryback, the balance may be applied to the second preceding year; then the most recent prior year. If there is still a remaining NOL balance, it can be applied to next year's taxable income, and then the next, and so on, up to 15 years.

The IRS allows you, at your option, to forego the three year carryback period and apply your Net Operating Loss entirely to the 15 future years.

The Internal Revenue Service has a special Form #1045 for filing a claim and receiving "prompt" (*their* word) refund of taxes. Have you ever known a government agency to be prompt about anything?

The Fine Print

In your computation of Net Operating Loss:

1. You may not deduct Net Operating Loss carryover or carryback from any other year.

2. Capital losses may not exceed capital gains.

3. Capital gains must be included in their entirety; no 60 percent exclusion.

4. You may not claim the deductible portion of the excess of net long-term capital gains over net short-term capital losses.

5. You may not include any personal exemptions or exemptions for dependents in the calculations.

6. Your non-business deductions may not exceed your non-business income. (If they do, show the amount as zero.)

7. Corporations are also allowed NOL deductions. The corporate rules however, are different.

The Internal Revenue Service and You

Small Time Operator is not a manual for beating the IRS at their own game nor is it intended to be another "101 Ways To Reduce Your Taxes." Still, a general knowledge of the Internal Revenue Service and its inner workings may benefit you in your dealings with the agency and may even add to your peace of mind.

Most people, including most small businesses, file their tax returns and never get audited. The IRS audits less than 2 percent of all tax returns. IRS agents have to earn their keep and they are not going to be nickel-and-diming every little business that files a return. In almost all instances, returns selected for audit are those obviously out of line with Internal Revenue's idea of the "norm." The IRS does audit a random sample of tax returns every year, but the number is very small.

All tax returns, big and small, are automatically checked on the computer for errors—addition, multiplication, tax computation. If there is an arithmetical error, you will be notified of the error and any change in your taxes due to it. This is not an audit; and if you make an error, it does not increase your chances of being audited.

All federal income tax returns are recorded on reels of computer tape at the regional IRS Service Centers and sent to the National Computer Center in Martinsburg, West Virginia. There, the returns are inspected and compared to what is known as the "Discriminate Input Function Formula", a computer program of the average American's financial profile. If your return falls within the "DIF" formula, you will be deemed An Honest Taxpayer. Your return will be filed away in the deep recesses of computer storage and will probably never be seen again. If, on the other hand, the computer "kicks out" your return—flags it for a possible audit—it will be sent back to your local IRS district office. An agent in the local office will review the return and decide whether or not to initiate an audit. Not every tax return rejected by the computer is audited; only those the agent feels are potential "money makers" for the IRS are selected.

It is hard to specify those items the IRS will be looking for when examining the return of a small business, but generally, you can expect them to look for the following:

1. A reasonable profit, comparing total expenses to total sales. If your sales are $10,000 and your expenses $9,990, you may arouse suspicion that all is not right.

2. Consistency from one year to the next. Large fluctuations or unusual changes from year to year will almost surely invite an audit.

3. Unusual or unreasonable expenses. Large expenses not usually found in your type of business will be suspect. Large deductions for entertainment, conventions or travel away from home often invite audits.

If you have been audited in the past and wound up owing more tax, your chances of being audited again are increased. On the other hand, if prior

"MOST PEOPLE BRING THEIR ACCOUNTANT!"

Notice of an IRS audit.

audits did not result in more tax, you probably will not get audited again even if the computer does "kick out" your return.

Another possible audit situation comes about due to an undertaking known as the State Income Tax Information Exchange Program. The IRS has an agreement with most states to exchange tax information including information about audits. If your state income tax return was audited, the state may notify the IRS about your audit: the year involved, the reason for the audit and the results. The exchange program works both ways. The IRS may also notify the participating states about the results of IRS audits.

A business loss on your tax return is by no means a sure cause for audit, though your return is more likely to be examined than one showing a healthy profit. It is not uncommon for a new business to sustain a loss the first year, with all the start-up costs combined with early, slow business. A warning, however, to people who manage to show a loss year after year: if you do not show a profit for at least two out of five consecutive years, the IRS can declare your business to be a hobby ("an activity not engaged in for profit") and disallow any losses. This is not a firm rule, however. A business can deduct losses for several years in a row without ever being challenged by the IRS. In the event of an audit, the IRS will allow the ongoing losses if they are convinced that you are operating a real business and trying, though unsuccessfully, to make a profit.

Notice of An Audit

Your first notice of an audit will be a letter from the IRS informing you of the audit and the year or years to be examined. You may be asked to come in person to a meeting with an agent or merely to send in certain written information. They may request to see a specific bill to support a specific item of expense, or they may request your entire set of ledgers. And you may be asked to bring or mail in copies of your tax returns for other years that are still open to audit.

If your books are in order and your bills are available, there is no need to fear an audit, and there is no real reason to hire an accountant or a tax lawyer to escort you to the meeting. And if you know you've been "caught," there is not much you can do but pay up and go home to lick your wounds. There is probably little or nothing even the most expensive accountant can do for you. Should you, however, find yourself in legitimate disagreement with the IRS, or you feel that matters are getting too complicated, it may be time to seek professional help (see the chapter in the Appendix, "Seeking Professional Help"). The IRS code is extremely complex, and IRS agents have been known to make mistakes. Do not accept a ruling you disagree with. The IRS provides all taxpayers an elaborate system of appeals, starting with informal meetings with agents and going right up to the Supreme Court.

Generally, no penalties are assessed where there is an honest mistake on a tax return. You will owe only the back taxes and interest—as long as you pay up when the IRS says pay up.

There *are* a large variety of IRS penalties, some mild and some severe, for various offenses: failure to file (the penalty increases significantly after 60 days); failure to pay (the more you owe, the bigger the penalty); "negligence"; "intentional disregard of rules and regulations without intent to defraud"; "willful attempt to evade or defeat taxes" — i.e. fraud. Where fraud is involved, the IRS can impose both "civil" penalties and "criminal" penalties. Civil penalties can be imposed in the normal course of an audit. Criminal penalties (very large fines and/or jail) may only be imposed after full due-process of law, a trial, etc.

If you cannot afford to pay the taxes when your tax return is due, file the return on time anyway. The penalties will probably be less. Quite often, the IRS will waive penalties where failure to file a return or failure to pay the tax is due to "reasonable cause."

Except for special situations, the general statute of limitations—the length of time the IRS has to audit a return and assess back taxes—is three years from the time the return is filed. If you omit from your return more than twenty-five percent of your gross income, the statute of limitations is increased to six years. There is no time limit if your return is "false or fraudulent" or if no return is filed. Most IRS audits, however, are initiated within twenty

months of filing the return. So, if you haven't heard from them by then, you probably won't.

This chapter is full of vague words: "reasonable cause," "without intent to defraud," "intentional disregard of rules and regulations," "willful attempt to evade," "unusual" this and "unreasonable" that. Many people make their livings arguing over these and other godawful terms. As with so many other legal situations, the words often wind up meaning whatever the agent or the judge wants them to mean. This is not an area for amateurs. If you are caught up in an audit involving these issues, your philosophy and your finances will have to dictate your reactions. Good luck.

Failure to File a Tax Return

I would like to cover briefly an area about which I have received a surprisingly large number of questions over the years: what if someone has been in business a few years and never filed a tax return? It's rarely a case of intentional dishonesty. A typical example is a craftsperson who starts out with a hobby. At Christmas, he sells a couple hundred dollars worth of merchandise, and he never thinks of his craft as a business. But now, two or three years have passed, and he realizes that $5,000 or $10,000 a year is going through his bank account, and he's never filed a tax return. Now what?

Contrary to what many people think, the Internal Revenue Service is not all-powerful nor all-seeing. Their computers are not set up for Big Brother snooping—not yet, anyway. The IRS will not know you have earned money unless you or someone else reports it to them. For most Americans, this information comes to the IRS on a Form W-2, report of income of employees. All employers are required to prepare a W-2 for each employee each year. A self-employed person is most likely to be known to the IRS via something called a Form 1099, report of income paid an individual other than an employee. If you sell your services to another business (not goods, just services) and that business paid you $600 or more during one year, they are required to file a Form 1099, notifying the IRS that you have received this money. Also, if you are an independent sales agent and you purchase $5,000 or more in goods for resale (from one company in one year) that company will report the purchase to the IRS on a 1099 form. In both of the above situations, the business that files the 1099 must also send you a copy of the form.

If you receive a copy of Form 1099 or a W-2, the feds have your name. If the amounts paid exceed the minimum requirements for filing, you are likely to get a letter of inquiry or possibly even a tax bill from the IRS. On the other hand, if no one reports you, the IRS will probably not know of your existence. Probably. But you are breaking the law, and there is no statute of limitations on how many years later they can come after you.

The law says, and I recommend, that you file returns for all those prior years, pay the back taxes, interest and penalties. Some people will just go on their merry way and never file and never be found; we've all heard of someone with that kind of experience. Other delinquent folk may decide that this is the year to file their first return, and let the prior years lie, hopefully, unnoticed.

The penalty for failure to file an income tax return, as I mentioned above, depends on several factors including how long it's been, how much you owe and the reasons why you haven't filed. There is no penalty if you can show that failure to file was due to some reasonable cause and not to willful neglect.

If you find yourself summoned by the IRS to discuss those tax returns you never filed, I suggest you get some professional help. Maybe, get yourself a stiff drink first.

Federal Excise Tax

Most small businesses are not liable for federal excise taxes.

Regular excise taxes are imposed on manufacturers of trucks, truck trailers, truck parts, tires, inner tubes, fishing equipment, outboard motors, bows, arrows, firearms, ammunition, coal, gasoline, lubricating oils and cars that do not meet fuel economy standards; on businesses operating aircraft; on businesses using fuel in inland waterways; on retailers of heavy trucks and trailers; on retailers of diesel, noncommercial aviation and marine fuels.The excise tax is payable quarterly on Form #720, "Quarterly Federal Excise Tax Return." Excise taxes are also imposed on brewers; on wholesale and retail beer, wine and liquor dealers; on manufacturers of stills; and on importers and dealers in firearms. These excise taxes are paid on Form #11. For more information on the above taxes, ask the IRS for a free copy of Publication #510, "Excise Taxes."

A highway motor vehicle Federal Use Tax is imposed on owners of large highway trucks, truck trailers and buses. Form 2290 must be filed annually. For more information, see IRS publication #349, "Federal Highway Use Tax."

State Income Taxes

As of last year, every state had some form of income tax on resident businesses except Alaska, Connecticut, Florida, Nevada, New Hampshire, South Dakota, Tennessee, Texas, Wyoming and Washington, though New Hampshire and Washington have a "gross receipts tax" (more on that later). The states which do levy income taxes have procedures and rules similar to the federal ones. Most states simply compute state tax either as a percentage of your federal income tax or based on a percentage of the income shown on your federal return. Some of the more ambitious—maybe I should say ornery—states have their own separate set of income tax rules just different enough from the federal rules to require separate calculations. The Royal Pain In The Butt Award to Alabama, Arkansas, Mississippi, New Jersey, North Carolina, and Pennsylvania.

State income taxes, like federal income taxes, are based on your net income or net profit. Income less deductible expenses gives you net income. Generally, states allow businesses to deduct the same expenses as the feds allow with a few important exceptions: you may deduct state income tax on your federal return but not on your state return; you may not deduct federal income taxes on your federal tax return, but several states allow a deduction for federal income taxes; several states do not make allowances for Net Operating Loss carryback and carryforward; many states have varying numbers of years allowed for NOL carryback and carryforward; most states do not have an investment credit; self-employment tax is a federal tax only, although some states allow a deduction for it; and remember, not all states allow the same nontaxable retirement contributions the feds allow.

Most state income tax returns for calendar-year taxpayers are due April 15, the same due date as the federal returns. Six states have later due dates: Arkansas-May 15; Delaware—April 30; Hawaii—April 20; Iowa—April 30; Louisiana—May 15; Virginia—May 1.

The above state income tax information does not apply to corporations. Corporate income tax laws and filing dates vary considerably from state to state.

State Gross Receipts Taxes

Arizona, Arkansas, Delaware, Hawaii, Indiana, New Hampshire, New Mexico, Washington and West Virginia have what is commonly called a "gross receipts tax" on businesses. The gross receipts tax is in addition to the regular income tax except in New Hampshire and Washington which have no income tax. A gross receipts tax is a tax on total business receipts (sales, income) before any deductions for expenses. The tax varies from nominal amounts (a fraction of a percent) to as high as 3.75 percent in New Mexico, 4 percent in Arkansas and Hawaii, 5 percent in Arizona, and a whopping 8 percent in New Hampshire.

Michigan has a special state business income tax in addition to regular income taxes. Michigan's "Single Business Tax" is 2.35 percent of net though the state allows a credit against regular state income tax for businesses paying the Single Business Tax.

In addition to the above, here is a brief list of some more state taxes:

Chain stores: A tax per location, anywhere from $1 to $65 if you only have a few stores, is imposed by Alabama, Colorado, Delaware, Louisiana, Maryland, Montana, North Carolina, South Carolina and West Virginia.

Grain handlers are taxed in Iowa, Kansas and Ohio.

Hotel or meal taxes are imposed in Connecticut, Delaware, Illinois, Massachusetts, New Hampshire, Pennsylvania and Vermont.

Special state business licenses are required in Alabama, Alaska, Delaware, Missouri, West Virginia, D.C., and Washington.

And more: **The fishing industry** is taxed in Alaska and Washington. **Malt extract** is taxed in Kansas. **Cement** is taxed in Montana and Texas. **Salt production** is taxed in Louisiana, Kansas, Mississippi and Ohio.

Special Note: All state tax information is as of 1985 and is meant as a general guideline only. Tax information may change year to year. You should contact your state government for current information.

Other States Taxes

The list of state taxes on businesses is virtually endless. Many states tax either the manufacturers, wholesalers or retailers (and sometimes all three) of alcoholic beverages, fuel oils and gasolines, tobacco products, and motor vehicles and airplanes. Mining operations, financial institutions, utilities, insurance companies and real estate dealings are taxed in most states. Many states have an admissions tax on theatres, amusement parks, etc. Many states tax freight, express and private car companies. Several states tax logging, timber and forest land.

Inventory (Floor) Tax

Inventory or "floor" taxes are locally imposed property taxes on business inventory and/or equipment. Inventory taxes, where levied, are collected by the state or county government and are based on the market value of the taxable property. Many retail stores hold big sales just before tax time to bring their inventories down in order to reduce the tax.

Not all states and localities impose inventory taxes. You can contact your county offices to inquire about inventory taxes. Chances are, if such a tax is levied in your area, they'll contact you! Inventory taxes are deductible business expenses.

Section Five
APPENDIX

"Mercy!" Scrooge said. "Dreadful apparition, why do you trouble me?"

The same face; the very same. Marley in his pigtail, usual waistcoat, tights and boots. The chain he drew was clasped about his middle. It was long, and wound about him like a tail; and it was made of cashboxes, keys, padlocks, ledgers, deeds, and heavy purses wrought with steel. His body was transparent; so that Scrooge, observing him, and looking through his waistcoat, could see the two buttons on his coat behind.

"You are fettered," said Scrooge, trembling. "Tell me why?"

"I wear the chain I forged in life," replied the Ghost; "I made it link by link and yard by yard; I girded it on of my own free will, and of my own free will I wore it. Is its pattern strange to you?"

Scrooge trembled more and more. "But you were always a good man of business, Jacob," faltered Scrooge.

"Business!" cried the Ghost, wringing its hands again. "Mankind was my business. The common welfare was my business; charity, mercy, forbearance, and benevolence, were all my business. The dealing of my trade were but a drop of water in the comprehensive ocean of my business."

Excerpted from **A Christmas Carol**
by Charles Dickens

How to Balance a Bank Account

The balance on your bank statement will rarely agree with the balance in your checkbook. But you know that. What you probably don't know, if you've never balanced a bank account, is that the difference is almost always easy to locate and reconcile. The difference is due to one or more of the following:

1. Checks you have written but that have not yet cleared the bank; called "outstanding checks."

2. Deposits not yet posted by the bank; called "deposits in transit."

3. Interest earned or bank service charges you have not recorded in your checkbook and any return (bounced) checks that you still show as deposits; called "reconciling items."

4. Someone's error, usually yours; called "oops."

If you follow these procedures, balancing your bank account will take only a few minutes each month (hopefully):

1. Sort the cancelled checks returned with the bank statement into numerical order.

2. Match each cancelled check with the corresponding entry in your checkbook. Put a checkmark (✓) next to your checkbook entry so you'll know the check has been cancelled. It is also a good idea to compare the amount on the cancelled check with the amount you wrote in your checkbook. Too many of you speedy checkwriters will write a check for $15.16 and post it in your checkbook as $16.15. It is

known as "transposition" and is an occupational disease of even the best bookkeepers. There will most likely be several checks you have written that have not cleared the bank yet. Don't worry: people are often slow in cashing checks, or the checks may have to travel back and forth across the country, from bank to bank.

3. If the bank returns copies of your deposit slips with the statement, match these to the deposits in your checkbook. The banks, however, are getting lazier in their old age, and many will not return duplicate deposits slips to you. You will have to match your checkbook record of deposits with those recorded on the bank statement. Again, check off (✓) the deposits in your checkbook. And again beware of transposition errors. Unlike checks, deposits should clear the bank immediately. Mailed deposits should clear within a few days. Any real lag in a bank recording of deposits may mean a lost or misplaced deposit, which can be disastrous for you; contact the bank at once.

4. Look for any unusual items returned with the bank statement: notice of a bounced check or a check printing charge or some other bank charge. Also examine the statement itself for any bank charges or service fees. They will be listed along with the checks with a reference number or letter next to the amount. Somewhere on the statement is an explanation of what it means. By the way, if they hit you for a bank charge you don't think is proper, call the bank and complain. Quite often, the bank will cancel the charge. They would rather

CHECKS OUTSTANDING	
NUMBER	AMOUNT
TOTAL	$

THIS FORM IS PROVIDED TO HELP YOU BALANCE YOUR CHECKING ACCOUNT STATEMENT

HELPFUL HINTS

1. Compare the list of checks paid on this statement with your check record.
2. At left, list outstanding (unpaid) checks, including any from previous months.
3. Finish reconciling your account by entering figures in the appropriate spaces below.

ENTER
new checking balance as shown on this statement. . . . . $ _____

ADD
any deposits entered in your check record that are not shown on this statement. $ _____

TOTAL . . . . $ _____

SUBTRACT
checks outstanding. . . . . $ _____

BALANCE . . . . $ _____

Balance should agree with your checkbook balance after deducting any Automatic Transfers, loan payments, or other bank charges shown on this statement from your check record.

The back of your bank statement may include a form to help you balance your bank account.

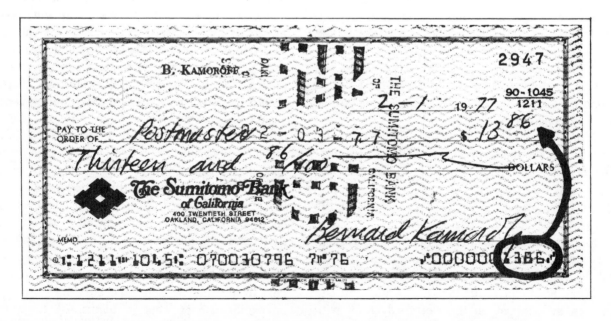

Another possible error if your bank account won't balance: compare the amount of the check to the computer-punched amount in the bottom right-hand corner of the cancelled check. They should be the same.

keep your business and your good will than get a $2 fee out of you. If your account pays interest, the amount is usually shown as the last item on your bank statement.

Now that you've checked off everything and marveled at all the little entries buried here and there on the bank statement, you are ready to reconcile. With pencil in hand and a blank piece of paper, or the back of the bank statement if there is enough room:

1. Write down your checkbook balance.

2. Total all the checks you have written that have *not* cleared the bank, the ones without a check (✓) next to them. These are your outstanding checks. *Add* this total to your checkbook balance.

3. *Subtract* from your balance any deposits you have recorded that have *not* cleared the bank. These are your deposits in transit.

4. *Subtract* from your balance any of those extra charges the bank included in the statement.

5. *Add* to your balance any interest paid.

6. If you made any errors recording check or deposit amounts adjust your balance.

The final figure you come up with should equal the bank balance on the statement. It doesn't? Damn. Let's try to isolate the problem.

Repeat the reconciliation, and check your addition. If you don't have an adding machine, this may be a good time to read the chapter on adding machines and calculators at the end of the bookkeeping section; at least it will be a good excuse to get away from these numbers for a little while. Still computes the same? When you checked off the cancelled checks and the deposits, did the amounts all agree? Are you sure?

At this point, the error is 99 percent certain to be in your running checkbook balance. Sometime during the month, you wrote a check and recorded the correct amount but subtracted it incorrectly from the balance. Go back and re-subtract each check from the balance, check by check. You are bound to find the error.

No luck? Did you lose one of the cancelled checks? Add up the number of cancelled checks and compare with the total number of checks listed on the bank statement.

Still can't find the difference? There *may* be a bank error but it's not very likely, unless you have your account in a small, non-computerized bank—the likelihood just increased. Examine the bank statement: the beginning balance should be the same as last month's ending balance. Was there

a reconciling item on last month's statement you forgot to post to your checkbook? Did you balance last month's bank statement? (I'm still trying.) Check the addition on the bank statement. If you do find something amiss on the statement, notify the bank.

I think that it is impossible to go through all these procedures and not locate the error. But if you've done the impossible, I'd suggest two more things: (1) Cool it for a few days. Just put it all away and forget it. Later, when you're in a better mood, repeat the procedures outlined here, from scratch: don't look at your old calculations; if they're wrong they will throw you off. *AND IF THAT DOES NOT WORK*, then (2) take your checkbook and the statement and the cancelled checks and all down to the bank and get them to help you.

The one solution I failed to mention is the easiest: forget it. Assume you've made a mistake somewhere, correct your balance to agree with the reconciliation, and forget it. But that's just not my nature, so...

Correcting Your Books

If you do have an error or if there are reconciling items such as bank charges, you must correct your books accordingly:

Error in addition: Adjust the most recent checkbook balance up or down to correct the error. Make a note in the checkbook as to exactly what you are doing.

Error in check or deposit amount: Adjust the most recent checkbook balance and write a note of explanation. If you recorded a check incorrectly, make sure you haven't made the same mistake on your expenditure ledger.

Bank charges: Record them on your checkbook the same way you record a check, reducing your bank balance accordingly. Remember also to post the charge to your expenditure ledger in Column Two—*Supplies, Postage, Etc.*

Balance Sheets

A balance sheet, also known as a "statement of assets and liabilities," is a listing of your assets, liabilities, and net worth or equity at any given point in time. Balance sheets are sometimes required on partnership and corporation income tax returns. Most banks will ask to see a balance sheet (as well as a statement of income and expense; see the "Financial Management" chapter in the bookkeeping section) when considering business loans. Audited corporate financial statements must include comparative (current year and prior year) balance sheets.

All balance sheets are made up of three sections: assets—the property you own; liabilities—money you owe; and equity—the net worth of your business, the difference between the assets and the liabilities.

Assets are broken down into two basic categories:

Current: Cash, and assets that will be used or sold in the normal course of business within a year. Current assets usually include accounts receivable—your customers' unpaid credit accounts—less an allowance for uncollectible bad debts; notes and loans receivable—money owed to you other than regular credit accounts—due within one year; inventory—finished goods, work in process and raw materials—valued at cost or market, whichever is less; prepaid expenses (beyond 12 months) such as next year's insurance. Current prepaid expenses such as rent or this year's insurance are not included.

Other Assets: Cost of depreciable fixed assets such as equipment, vehicles, furniture and buildings less the accumulated depreciation; cost of land; intangible long-term assets such as patents and capitalized incorporation fees; notes and loans receivable which will not be collected within one year.

Long term notes and loans receivable that are payable to you in installments over several years should be split between "current" and "other." The amount coming due within one year should be shown as "current"; the balance should be listed under "other assets."

Liabilities are also divided into similar categories:

Current: Notes and loans payable due within one year; unpaid taxes and tax penalties; unpaid wages.

Long-term: Any loans or other liabilities due after one year. Like long-term receivables, notes and long-term loans payable in installments over several years should be split between "current" for the amount due within twelve months and "long-term" for the balance.

You should also include under liabilities any "contingent" liabilities you know about. Contingent liabilities are crystal-ball suppositions about the

```
          BALANCE SHEET
        Bear Soft Pretzel Co.
         as of December 31

             ASSETS
Current Assets
  Cash                             $ 375
  Accounts Receivable     $140
    Less allowance for
    bad debts              (20)
                                     120
  Prepaid insurance                  150
  Inventory (at lower of cost
    or market):
    Pretzels--hot         $ 25
    Pretzels--stale          1
    Flour, sugar, salt      75
                                     101
Other Assets
  Equipment, at cost     $2,300
    Less accumulated
    depreciation          (450)
                                   1,850
  Total Assets                    $2,596
                                  ======

           LIABILITIES
Current Liabilities
  Accounts Payable                $ 120
  Loan payable, portion due
    within one year                 250
Long-Term Liabilities
  Balance of loan payable           750
  Total Liabilities              $1,120
NET WORTH (owner's equity)        1,476
                                  ------
                                 $2,596
                                 ======
```

future: liabilities which may or may not materialize. If the IRS is auditing you or you are being sued, for example, and there is a possibility you will owe money, some dollar estimate of the liability must be included on the balance sheet. Contingent liability estimates should be clearly labeled as such and should be explained fully.

Balance sheets can be simple or quite complicated. A balance sheet prepared for your bank when requesting a loan need not be elaborate. The audited financial statements required of corporations that sell stock to the public, however, include fully detailed and footnoted balance sheets. Any basic accounting textbook will include a chapter on balance sheets. The best way to learn about balance sheets, I have found, is to study the published financial statements that most corporations put out. You usually can get them free on request.

Seeking Professional Help: How to Locate a Good Accountant

This book should help you with most aspects of beginning and operating a small business and successfully steer you through the common obstacles without need of an accountant. But the time may come when your finances are getting a bit too complicated, or you may need help incorporating your business, or you may want tax help. Even I admit that business income tax returns can be complicated and difficult. So how do you find a good accountant?

Locating a good accountant is like trying to find a reliable doctor; you have to ask around. The best people to ask are those like you, in business for themselves. If you do not know an accountant and cannot get a reliable recommendation, here are a few suggestions to help in your search:

1. Picking a name at random from the telephone book is probably the biggest mistake you could make. There is no way to know what kind of person you will get or how qualified he or she may be.

2. Stay away from the storefront tax operations, the ones that open shop every January and promptly disappear April 15. Most of the people who work for these chains have little experience, brief training, and are usually familiar only with Mr. and Mrs. Nine-to-Five and their typical tax problems. These part-time accountants are not trained to handle complex problems nor do they take the time to delve into your business finances looking for tax savings.

3. Choose an experienced tax accountant, preferably one who specializes in small business. It's not necessary to hire a certified public accountant; CPA's are probably the best qualified, but most of them specialize in complex transactions and

big business. Expect to pay professional prices.

4. Talk to the accountant personally before you commit yourself. If he or she will not talk to you on the phone other than in vague generalities, call someone else. Does the accountant seem familiar with your situation and your problems? Is the man too "grey flannel suit" and big business oriented to relate to you? Most important, does he make sense to you? Beware of the accountant who talks Advanced Sanskrit or IRS code sections. You need an accountant to answer questions, not show off the glories of his trade.

Cash Method of Accounting

Under the cash method of accounting, income is recorded when the money is received and expenses are recorded when paid. This method is different from the accrual method, where income is recorded when earned and expenses recorded when incurred, whether paid or not. Businesses that buy and sell inventories must use the accrual method; and since this includes most businesses, the posting instructions in the bookkeeping section were given for the accrual method. (See the chapter "Cash Accounting Vs. Accrual" in the bookkeeping section.)

Businesses that have no inventory or parts can, and usually do, choose to use the cash method. The bookkeeping is somewhat easier both to understand and to perform. Remember, however, that under the cash method credit sales and purchases will not show on your ledgers until you receive or pay the cash. Once a method of accounting is selected, it cannot be changed without written approval from the Internal Revenue Service.

You will be able to use the ledgers in this book without alteration. Here are posting instructions for cash method accounting:

Income. Record in your income ledger only those sales for which you have received payment. Credit sales should still be recorded on your sales invoices and in your credit ledger but should *not* be posted to your income ledger until the money is received. A sales return should be posted to your income ledger only if the original sale is already paid for and posted to the ledger. Year-end procedures are the same as those for the accrual method.

Expenditures. The posting instructions for expenditures are the same as those for accrual accounting *except* for year-end procedures. At year-end, summarize your monthly expenditure totals (see Step One of "Year-End Procedures for Expenditures" in the bookkeeping section), calculate automobile expense (Step Four), and record depreciation (Step Five). Bad debts (Step Three) should include return checks but *not* unpaid and uncollectible credit sales. Skip Step Two of the year-end procedures: do *not* record any unpaid expenditures on the year-end summary, and do not mark unpaid bills "Accounts Payable." Ignore the procedures for accounts payable. That's it.

A Special Chapter for Farmers

Federal income tax rules for small time farmers are somewhat different from those for other small businesses. Some of the differences are outlined in this chapter but for complete information farmers should obtain a free copy of IRS publication #225, "Farmer's Tax Guide." It is revised annually.

Farmers do not report their profit or loss on schedule 1040C. Farmers should use schedule 1040F, "Farm Income and Expenses."

SCHEDULE F (Form 1040)
Department of the Treasury
Internal Revenue Service

Farm Income and Expenses

▶ Attach to Form 1040, Form 1041, or Form 1065.

▶ See Instructions for Schedule F (Form 1040).

OMB No. 1545-0074

1985
14

Name of proprietor(s)	Social security number (SSN)
Frank & Fay F. Jones	123 : 34 : 4566

A Agricultural Activity Code. (Write in the code that best describes your principal income-producing activity. The codes are listed on page 2 of this schedule.) ▶ 0250

B Principal Product. (Describe in one or two words your principal crop or output for the current tax year.) ▶ Poultry & eggs

If you disposed of commodities received under the payments-in-kind (PIK) program, check the box(es) that apply:

☐ Feed for livestock ☐ Sold and reported in income

Employer ID number (NOT SSN)
9 4 5 6 7 8 9 0

Part I Farm Income—Cash Method—Complete Parts I and II
(Accrual method taxpayers complete Parts II and III, and line 12 of Part I.)
Do not include sales of livestock held for draft, breeding, sport, or dairy purposes; report these sales on Form 4797.

1 Sales of livestock and other items you bought for resale	1	
2 Cost or other basis of livestock and other items you bought for resale	2	
3 Subtract line 2 from line 1	3	
4 Sales of livestock, produce, grains, and other products you raised	4	$7,526
5 a Total distributions received from cooperatives (from Form 1099-PATR) 5a		
b **Less:** Nonincome items 5b		
6 Net distributions. Subtract line 5b from line 5a	6	
7 Agricultural program payments:		
a Cash	7a	
b Materials and services	7b	
8 Commodity credit loans under election (or forfeited)	8	
9 Crop insurance proceeds	9	
10 Machine work	10	65
11 Other income, including Federal and state gasoline tax credit or refund (see instructions)	11	10
12 **Gross income.** Add amounts on lines 3, 4, 6, and 7a through 11. If accrual method taxpayer, enter the amount from Part III, line 52 ▶	12	$7,601

Part II Farm Deductions—Cash and Accrual Method

Do not include personal or living expenses (such as taxes, insurance, repairs, etc. on your home), which do not produce farm income. Reduce the amount of your farm deductions by any reimbursements before entering the deduction below.

13 Breeding fees		26 Mortgage interest paid to financial institutions (see instructions)	
14 Chemicals		27 Other interest	
15 Conservation expenses		28 Pension and profit-sharing plans	
16 Depreciation, and section 179 expense deduction (from Form 4562)	$ 872	29 Rent of farm, pasture	
17 Employee benefit programs other than on line 28		30 Repairs, maintenance	40
18 Feed purchased	482	31 Seeds, plants purchased	
19 Fertilizers and lime		32 Storage, warehousing	
20 Freight, trucking	40	33 Supplies purchased	221
21 Gasoline, fuel, oil	80	34 Taxes	38
22 Insurance		35 Utilities	100
23 a Labor hired 860		36 Veterinary fees, medicine	50
b Jobs credit 0		37 Other expenses (specify):	
c Balance (subtract line 23b from line 23a)	860	a _____	
		b _____	
24 Land clearing (see instructions)		c _____	
25 Machine hire	50	d _____	
		e	

38 **Total deductions from Part II**. Add amounts in columns for lines 13 through 37e ▶	38	$2,833
39 **Net farm profit or (loss)** (subtract line 38 from line 12). If a profit, enter on Form 1040, line 19, and on Schedule SE, Part I, line 1. If a loss, you **MUST** go on to line 40. (Fiduciaries and partnerships, see the instructions.)	39	$4,768

40 If you have a loss, you **MUST** answer this question:
"Do you have amounts for which you are not at risk in this farm (see instructions)?" ☐ Yes ☐ No
If "Yes," you **MUST** attach **Form 6198.** If "No," enter the loss on Form 1040, line 19, and on Schedule SE, Part I, line 1.

For Paperwork Reduction Act Notice, see Form 1040 Instructions.

Schedule F (Form 1040) 1985

Farmers, even those with inventories, can use either the cash or accrual method of accounting (any business other than farming *must* use the accrual method if there are inventories). Most farmers choose the cash method because the bookkeeping is substantially easier. Under the cash method, farmers need not account for any inventory and need not concern themselves with cost-of-goods-sold calculations. For more information on the cash method, see the chapter "Cash Accounting Vs. Accrual" in the bookkeeping section and the chapter "Cash Method of Accounting" here in the Appendix.

The cost of livestock purchased for eventual resale is not deducted on your tax return until the livestock is sold even if you are using the cash method of accounting. One exception to this rule: the cost of egg-laying stock—chicks, pullets and hens—can be written off to expense the year of purchase. Purchased breeding stock and dairy stock must be depreciated just like a tractor or a piece of machinery. Livestock born on your farm cannot be depreciated because there is no dollar cost to you.

The cost of feed, fertilizer, seeds and young plants (except cost of seeds and young plants for tree farms, orchards and timber operations) can generally be deducted the year of purchase even if they are purchased for future years' use.

The cost of clearing, leveling and conditioning land, purchasing and planting trees (other than certain young plants), building irrigation canals and ditches, laying irrigation pipes, constructing dams and building roads must, in most cases, be depreciated. Some land clearing expenditures, however, and some soil and water conservation expenditures (other than those for an almond or citrus grove) can, at your option, be deducted as expense the year incurred instead of being depreciated. The specific requirements and dollar limitations are explained in the IRS's *Farmer's Tax Guide.* All expenditures for citrus and almond grove development must be depreciated.

Farmers—and fishermen, too—do not have to make quarterly estimated tax payments if your gross income from farming is at least two-thirds of your total estimated gross income from all sources. One estimated tax payment for the entire prior year's taxes is required of farmers, due on January 15. And you don't have to make that estimated tax payment if you file your regular income tax return by the last day in February.

Farmers can use the ledgers in this book, but you will probably need to make some alterations.

Generally, most farm sales are not subject to sales tax, so you probably do not need a sales tax column in your income ledger. I suggest that you delete the headings on columns three, four, five and six in your income ledger and retitle them to suit your needs. Use a different column for each different type in income, such as livestock sales, produce sales, milk sales, patronage dividends, etc. The columns in the expenditure ledger can also be retitled to make them more useful to a farmer. Column One—*Merchandise and Materials* can certainly be deleted, probably Column Five—*Advertising*, and possibly one or two other columns. In their place, you may want columns for livestock purchases, repairs, feed, fertilizer, veterinary fees or other typical farm expenses.

A few words from the Internal Revenue Service to part-time and "weekend" farmers: "A farmer who operates a farm for profit may deduct all the ordinary and necessary expenses of carrying on the business of farming. The farm must be operated for profit. Whether a farm is being operated for profit must be determined from all the facts and circumstances in each case. However, you will not ordinarily be considered as operating a farm for profit if you raise crops or livestock mainly for use of your family, but derive some income from incidental sales."

Husband & Wife Partnerships

When a husband and wife operate a business together, the business may be a partnership or it may be a sole proprietorship. If the couple execute a written partnership agreement and run the business as partners, the business is definitely a general partnership. Beyond this one clear distinction, the law is not cut-and-dried. The IRS has ruled that, generally, if one spouse (let's say the wife) is the main operator of the business, the wife is a sole proprietor. The husband, with a lesser interest in the business, is an employee. Some criteria the IRS uses in determining the status of a husband-and-wife business are (1) does one spouse spend more time than the other operating the business? (2) are the business licenses in one spouse's name? (3) does one spouse have other employment? Generally, the IRS will assume that either the husband or wife (your choice) is operating a sole proprietorship unless the couple states otherwise, prepares a partnership agreement and files a partnership tax return.

A sole proprietorship is easier and less expensive to set up than a partnership. For starters, a husband-and-wife partnership will require a written partnership agreement. A partnership must also prepare a separate tax return in addition to the couple's 1040 return. Some partnership tax returns must include a balance sheet and a schedule of each partner's contributions and withdrawals (family farms and family-owned wholesale and retail stores are usually exempt from this requirement). Sole proprietorship tax returns do not include balance sheets or schedules of owner's draw.

In a sole proprietorship, the owner can hire his/her spouse as an employee and deduct the wage as a business expense. Of course, the wage paid the spouse is taxable income to the couple. Assuming the couple files a joint tax return, their income tax is the same whether the couple operate as a partnership or as employer-employee. There is, however, quite a difference in social security taxes.

You will recall that a sole proprietor or a partner in a partnership pays self-employment tax which is social security for the self-employed. Employees have social security deducted from their paychecks, and the employer pays an additional amount out of his own pocket towards employees' social security. A husband and wife who set up a partnership will each pay self-employment tax on his and her share of the profits. But when the sole proprietor hires her spouse as an employee, there is no social security tax (employer or employee) on the spouse's wages. The savings to the couple in social security and self-employment taxes can be substantial. The other side of the coin is that the employee spouse gets no social security credit in his own name. The only way for both spouses to get social security is to form a partnership. Like everything else in life, there is a trade off.

Let's try an example. A husband and wife set up a 50-50 partnership. The business earns a profit (before any draw or wage paid the partners) of $20,000 for the year. Each partner's share is $10,000. The partners file a joint return and pay income tax on the combined $20,000. Each partner is also subject to self-employment tax on $10,000; together they pay self-employment tax on $20,000. They hire their tax accountant to prepare two federal (and possibly two state) tax returns—a partnership return and a regular 1040 return.

Now we'll change the example. The same business is instead structured as a sole proprietorship with the wife as owner and the husband as employee. The husband is hired at a salary of $10,000 a year. The sole proprietorship also earned the wife a profit of $10,000 (after paying her husband his wages). The couple file a joint return and pay income taxes on the combined $20,000—the exact same amount of income tax paid on the above partnership. But the husband, being an employee, is exempt from social security tax. The wife pays self-employment tax on her $10,000 profit. So the couple involved in this sole proprietorship pays half as much self-employment tax as the same couple involved in the above partnership. The couple also files only one federal tax return, their 1040 (and takes a trip to Hawaii on the money they saved in accountant's fees).

Here is another consideration. Sole proprietors and partners are not eligible for company-paid fringe benefits such as health insurance. Employees *and their families* are eligible, and the employer is allowed a tax-deductible business expense for the cost of these fringe benefits. So if one spouse is employed by the other, the entire family (including the employer spouse) can get company-paid fringe benefits. If the company is structured as a partnership, neither spouse is eligible.

Regardless of whether the business is a sole proprietorship or a partnership, neither spouse is subject to unemployment taxes and neither is eligible for unemployment benefits. Both spouses can participate in a Keogh retirement plan and an IRA (Individual Retirement Account).

The IRS says you should determine whether you are a partnership or a sole proprietorship based on the facts, based on how the business is set up and operated, and not based on the tax consequences.

If you incorporate your husband-and-wife business, the rules are different. Both spouses as owner-employees of a corporation are subject to the same payroll taxes as regular employees. You are eligible for company-paid fringe benefits, and you can set up a corporate retirement plan for yourselves (which is different from a Keogh plan).

Filing Your Business Records

I read somewhere that 85 percent of all business papers which get stuck in the filing cabinet are never looked at again. From my own experience, I can believe it. But it is the other 15 percent of the paperwork that you want or need to locate, and it is the outside chance of an audit, or a lawsuit involving someone who worked for you eight years ago, that makes an organized filing system a necessity for all businesses.

Complete records and a good filing system are as important as a complete bookkeeping system.

Every business and financial transaction, every meeting, every action involving employees should be documented and kept for future reference or for proof if you get audited. If all documents—or groups of documents such as sales invoices for the month of March—have their own *labeled* file folder or their own *labeled* envelope, locating them at a later date will be an easy job.

Here is a list of documents you should keep:

1. Articles, by-laws, partnership agreements and other documents which establish and define the business. Keep as long as the business exists.

2. Names, addresses, social security numbers and other pertinent data for all owners and stockholders including date joined and date departed. Keep as long as the business exists.

3. Record of owners' contributions and withdrawals and all other financial transactions between owners and the business. Keep as long as the business exists.

4. Minutes of board meetings. Keep as long as the business exists. You'll find yourself going back to old minutes many times. If owners ever get in a dispute, old minutes will often provide ready answers.

5. Permits, licenses, insurance policies and leases. Keep as long as they are in force but, for IRS purposes, keep at least three years.

6. Loan papers. Keep as long as the loan is outstanding but, for IRS purposes, keep at least three years. Actually it's a good idea to keep loan papers for as long as the business exists. Though a loan may have been paid off several years ago, you may want to show a bank a record of the old loan when you apply for a new one.

7. Invoices, bills, sales receipts, cash receipts, credit memos and other day-to-day business documents. For IRS purposes, keep at least three years. If your sales documents include customers' names and addresses, you may want to keep them longer should you decide to do a mailing or other promotion.

8. Complete data on all current and past employees: names, addresses, social security numbers, date hired, wage rates and dates of raises, payroll withholding, W-4 exemptions, injuries and workers' compensation claims, evaluations, date employment ended and why. Keep as long as the business exists. It is rare but it does happen that some government agency or court will ask you to produce 15 year old employment records. If this happens, be sure you are legally required to produce the records and be sure you are not violating a law or an agreement of confidentiality by providing the records. Either get a written statement from the employee or else get some professional advice.

9. Bank deposits, cancelled checks and bank statements. For IRS purposes, keep at least three years.

10. Annual profit and loss and other annual financial statements. Keep as long as the business exists. Monthly, periodic or other sporadic financial statements probably should be kept two or three years. It is useful to compare monthly profit and loss statements for two or three consecutive years to see if there is a pattern—a cycle—of business activity.

11. Tax returns. Keep a copy of each year's income tax return for as long as the business exists. Assuming payroll tax information is also recorded on individual employee's permanent records, keep payroll tax returns at least three years for IRS purposes. Keep property tax returns for as long as the business exists. Keep all other tax returns, such as sales tax, excise tax, etc., at least three years.

12. Ledgers. Keep as long as the business exists.

I try to go through my files once a year. I admit I don't always succeed but when I do the results are always rewarding. I invariably find some old note or letter or inquiry or clipping which is immediately useful to me. I also invariably find a good part of

that 85 percent of the paperwork which can be thrown away—to make room for this year's 85 percent.

ACCESS

This is an encyclopedia/catalog/bibliography of useful books, pamphlets, periodicals, government agencies, organizations, supplies and miscellaneous tidbits. I have included publishers' addresses but left off prices—they change too fast.

Publishers take books out of print without any warning. A book that is no longer available from the publisher may be in your local library. You might also try writing the author, care of the publisher, and ask where you can obtain a copy of the book. The author may have a couple hundred copies sitting in the garage.

Access is fondly dedicated to the *Whole Earth Catalog* and its ongoing progeny, the *Whole Earth Review*. The ideas and the sources in them are excellent.

"The WHOLE EARTH CATALOG got started in a plane over Nebraska in March 1968. The sun had set ahead of the plane while I was reading *Spaceship Earth* by Barbara Ward. Between chapters I gazed out the window into dark nothing and slipped into a reverie about my friends who were starting their own civilization hither and yon in the sticks and how could I help. The L.L. Bean Catalog of outdoor stuff came to mind and I pondered upon Mr. Bean's service to humanity over the years. So many of the problems I could identify came down to a matter of access. Where to buy a windmill. Where to get good information on beekeeping. Where to lay hands on a computer without forfeiting freedom.

"Shortly I was fantasizing access service. A Truck Store, maybe, traveling around with information and samples of what was worth getting and information where to get it. A Catalog, too, continuously updated, in part by the users. A Catalog of goods that owed nothing to the suppliers and everything to the users. It would be something I could put some years into.

"Amid the fever I was in by this time, I remembered Fuller's admonition that you have about 10 minutes to act on an idea before it recedes back into dreamland. I started writing on the end papers of Barbara Ward's book (never did finish reading it).

"One of the main things that drove me into business was ignorance. A liberally educated young man, I hadn't the faintest idea how the world worked. Bargaining, distribution, mark-up, profit, bankruptcy, lease, invoice, fiscal year, inventory—it was all mystery to me, and usually depicted as sordid.

"I noticed that great lengths were gone to in order to prevent 'consumers' from knowing that part of purchase price went to the retailer. It seemed exquisitely insane to me. You sell deception and buy mistrust, to no advantage. The retailer in fact earns his 25-40 percent by tiresome work, but the prevailing attitude makes him out a clever crook. Ignorance institutionalized. Would you mind leaving the room, we're talking about money.

"As Fuller advises: Always promise less than you deliver, and let customers, business associates, staff come to their own conclusions about you. Small business is based on earned trust. Send cash-with-order in your first dealings with another firm. Pay bills scrupulously on time. Keep exact, open books on all your accounting. Small businessmen respond faster to honesty than any other kind of person: Most of them couldn't care less what you wear, smoke, or think if you're straight with them and don't care what they wear, smoke, or think.

"What you're trying to do is nourish and design an organism which can learn and stay alive while it's learning. Once that process has its stride, don't tinker with it; work for it, let it work for you. Make interesting demands on each other."

—Stewart Brand in the *Last Whole Earth Catalog*

101 BUSINESSES
(Choosing a Business)

If you've decided that being your own boss is what you want but you don't know what kind of business to start, there are lots of folks willing to sell you ideas. Dozens of books with titles like *184 Businesses Anyone Can Start & Make A Lot Of Money*, *300 Ways To Make Money In Your Spare Time*, *1001 Ways To Be Your Own Boss*, and *101 Businesses You Can Start & Run With Less Than $1000* (to name just a few I've seen) have been published over the years—and they continue to proliferate—yet I've never seen one worth recommending. Most of them are shallow, with one or two paragraph descriptions, and they lack any real detail.

The Small Business Administration publishes a **Starting Out Series** of one-page fact sheets describing financial and operating requirements for various manufacturing, retail and service businesses. The SBA also publishes **Small Business Bibliographies** which list reference sources for different types of businesses. Write the Small Business Administration, Box 30, Denver, CO 80201-0030 for a list.

Bank of America publishes **Business Profiles**, a series of well-written pamphlets about specific businesses. For a complete list, write Bank of America, Dept. 3120, P.O. Box 37000, San Francisco, CA 94137.

The Small Business Administration at one time published a well written "Starting and Managing" series of booklets. Each booklet dealt with a different small business. The series, I'm sorry to say, is out of print. Sterling Publishing Company (2 Park Avenue, New York, NY 10016) has reprinted several of the old SBA booklets in a book, **How to Start Your Own Small Business**. The businesses covered are beauty shops, children's wear shops, bowling alleys, dry cleaners, dress manufacturers, building services contracting, furniture stores, industrial launderers, machine shops, mobile catering, pet shops, photo studios, small restaurants, supermarkets and a few more.

"Unless a machine shop is large and located in an area where industry is diversified, its output tends to be specialized to serve one or two customers or a single industry. This leaves the machine shop operation overly dependent on customers over whom it has no control. This can result in seasonality of work, abrupt loss of work when a customer closes his plant or moves, loss of work if a particular industry is declining, and so on."

"The success of a beauty shop rests squarely on satisfying the perceived needs of the client. If a customer is satisfied with the service she receives, she will continue to frequent the establishment on a regular basis. Moreover, she will serve as the single most effective form of advertisement for the shop. ('Where did you get your hair done? It looks terrific!...'). On the other hand, if she is *not* satisfied with the services received, she will be certain to mention this to friends and associates. The negative consequences can be significant."

Finally, "cottage industry" home business ideas are a regular feature of **The Mother Earth News**, a fat, cheerful bimonthly magazine. Write "Mother" at P.O.Box 70, Hendersonville, NC 28739.

MANAGING YOUR BUSINESS

Volumes have been written on the subject of small business "management." I put the word in quotes because it is such an all-encompassing term. Just about anything you, the owner, do is labeled "management." And just about every study made on small business failures blames over 90 percent of those failures on "poor management."

"Poor management" refers to everything from sloppy bookkeeping to lousy business location. If you make or sell clothing, and the fashions suddenly change leaving you with unsalable merchandise, it's labelled "poor management": you should have been aware of the market trends and should have made advance preparations to anticipate them. If you expected your business to show a profit the first year, but you wound up with a loss and not enough reserve cash to keep things going, that's another situation they call "poor management."

Almost every library in the country has at least ten books on the subject of business management. Some of the books are excellent, some are shallow; almost all of them go unread. An interesting Small Business Administration study of eighty-one small businesses showed that only one owner in eighty-one read any management literature. Half of those eighty-one businesses failed. There are thousands of defunct businesses, gone belly-up because of the same management errors repeated over and over again. I guess it's just human nature to want to learn from your own mistakes.

Management is an organic part of your business, interwoven into every aspect of business. It isn't like Step One—get a business license, Step Two—manage, Step Three—post the ledgers, etc. Management is something you can learn only by doing, but a few evenings spent with some good management reading certainly won't do you any harm.

I've seen dozens of books on business management, ranging in price from less than $2 to over $30. I found: almost all of them are good; price is no indication of quality; the inexpensive publications put out by the Small Business Administration are consistently among the best.

Starting and Managing a Small Business of Your Own (Small Business Administration; available from the U.S. Government Printing Office, Washington, D.C. 20402).

This excellent booklet, offers good general information about getting started. It devotes a lot of attention to several before-you-even-start areas in more detail than does *Small Time Operator*: personality traits for success in business, potential return on investment, buying a going business and investing in a franchise. Full of checklists and rate-yourself score sheets. Highly recommended.

"Your decision to go into business may not depend entirely on financial rewards. The potential return on investment may be overshadowed by your desire for independence, the chance to do the type of work you would like to do, the opportunity to live in the part of the country or city your prefer, or the feeling that you can be more useful to the community than you would be if you continued working for someone else. Such intangible considerations must not be overlooked. Nevertheless, you cannot keep your own business open unless you receive a financial return on your investment.

Will the rate of return on the money you invest in your business be greater than the rate you could receive if you invested the money elsewhere? While your decision to go into business for yourself may not depend entirely upon this, it is one of the factors which will interest you. Too frequently a person has invested money in his own business under the misapprehension that the financial return will be far greater than the return he can expect from other investments. Some investigation of the average annual returns in the line of business in which you are interested is worthy of your time."

The Small Business Administration publishes a series of self-study booklets, called **Business Basics**, on the basics of day-to-day business management. Each booklet covers a different subject—cost control, marketing, buying, inventory control, credit, employees, sources of money, fixed assets, insurance—and each booklet includes test-yourself questions and exercises. For a free list of all the *Business Basics* booklets, write the SBA, Box 30, Denver, CO 80201-0030.

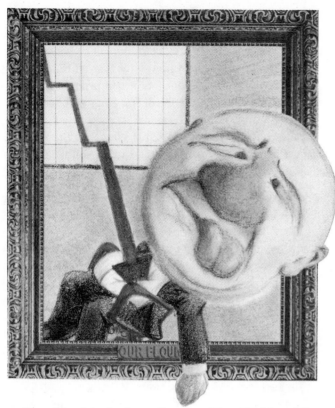

Guerilla Marketing; Secrets For Making Big Profits From Your Small Business, by Jay Conrad Levinson, 1984. Houghton Mifflin Company, 2 Park St., Boston, MA 02108.

I have a business friend who had an extremely successful product. Much of its success was due to its image. The packaging was bright, almost garnish, with a well-recognized illustration as its centerpiece. Well, after eight years, that illustration was getting *old*. It looked dated, out of place in the conservative eighties. Sales were as good as ever, but, he thought, how much longer? What's more, my friend was sick of looking at that illustration; he'd seen it a million times. So he spent a good amount of time, energy, and money redesigning the package. The result? Sales dropped off almost immediately.

My friend didn't read *Guerrilla Marketing*. Right there on page 14, Number Three of "The Three Most Important Secrets Of All" is *consistency:* "Don't change messages! Consistency equates with familiarity. Familiarity equates with confidence. And confidence equates with sales."

"Stick with one ad until it loses its pulling power. That's hard for most advertisers. In the beginning, most people will like your ad. Then, you'll become bored with it. Next, your friends and family will get tired of it. Soon your fellow workers and associates will feel ho-hum about it. And you'll be tempted to change the ad." (Does this man know my friend?).

"Don't do it!" (Too late).

Guerrilla Marketing is full of this sort of $5 wisdom, full of good ideas how to successfully promote your business, and without spending a lot of money either.

The Practice of Management, by Peter F. Drucker; 1954. Harper and Row, 10 East 53rd Street, New York, NY, 10022.

Peter Drucker is the high priest of business and management analysis, and this 404-page textbook is his treatise.

"It is almost an article of the American creed that in the small business there are no problems of spirit and morale, of organization structure or of communication. Unfortunately this belief is pure myth, a figment of the Jeffersonian nostalgia that is so marked in our national sentiment. The worst examples of poor spirit are usually found in a small business run by a one-man dictator who brooks no opposition and insists on making all the decisions himself. I know no poorer communications than those of the all too typical small business where the boss 'plays it close to the chest.' And the greatest disorganization can be found in small businesses where everybody has four jobs and no one quite knows what anyone is supposed to be doing."

Managing For Profits. Published by the Small Business Administration; available from U.S. Government Printing Office, Washington, D.C. 20402.

This is another useful SBA publication. It covers marketing, production, systems, financial management, credit and collections, purchasing, inventory management, and budgeting.

"The terms of credit extended by a small firm have significant effects on its cash needs. Special incentives offered to customers for early payment can be *very expensive*; in many instances, it may be wiser to offer normal trade terms and borrow funds that may be needed.

"An example of this is the experience of the Williams Machine Company. Jack Williams, the owner, found that in July and August of last year he was pressed for funds. So he offered his major customers an additional two percent discount during those months. When Jack changed accountants, the new accountant questioned this practice. After considerable discussion, a cash flow projection was developed for the critical two-month period. The new accountant also showed Jack that it was cheaper to use short-term bank loans than to offer his customers additional discounts. Jack's banker welcomed this opportunity to provide the necessary loans."

Honest Business. by Michael Phillips & Salli Rasberry. 1981. Random House, 201 E. 50th Street, New York, NY 10022.

"Business should be fun...going slow is fundamental to business...being honest is a superior way to do business...being open about business is important, beneficial and necessary...too much capital is like too much food, it makes people lethargic...love of business is vital: you *have* to love business to put up with the trials it brings you."

Michael (who wrote *The Seven Laws of Money*) and Salli don't just throw out these gems; they back them up with solid reasoning and real life examples. I agree with most everything they have to say, and I recommend this book highly.

Successful Small Business Management by David Seigel and Harold Goldman. 1982. Fairchild Publications, 7 East 12th Street, New York, NY 10003.

It is a fact that certain types of people are likely to succeed in a business while others will fail—in the same business. It has a lot to do with the owner's personality, ambition, temperament and other "human" traits. This excellent 340-page book identifies and discusses these human traits in a logical and well organized manner. It covers prestart up, getting started, different types of businesses, pricing, selling, advertising and even accounting from the personal perspective of the business owner. The authors emphasize that you need to understand the common-sense basics of operating a business (which they explain well) but you also need to offer a quality product or service, and you need to treat your customers honestly and with respect.

Straight Talk About Small Business by Kenneth J. Albert, 1981. McGraw Hill, 1221 Avenue of the Americas, New York, NY 10020.

This is a *very* good book, and one to be read before going into business. It discusses different ways to get a business off the ground, the different skills you will need and the problems you are likely to encounter. It is quite different from *Small Time Operator* because its emphasis is on the individual, the market, your ability to sell and other nontechnical subjects. It is a down to earth, personal, and well written book. I think the future business owner will get a lot out of it.

Your Manufacturing Company: How To Start It, How To Manage It, by Robert A. Crinkley, 1982. McGraw Hill, 1221 Avenue of the Americas, New York, NY 10020.

This 240-page book is written for both small beginning manufacturers and larger, growing businesses. It covers product lines, manufacturing processes, sales and marketing, inventory and financial controls. It is well written and appears to be thorough and quite useful.

A large retail trade organization, the National Retail Merchants Association, publishes numerous books on all aspects of retailing. One book I have seen, **Independent Retailing** (by Harold Shaffer and Herbert Greenwald, 1976) is a comprehensive guide to buying, inventory control, pricing, selling, advertising, employees and more. It is a well written, useful book. Write NRMA, 100 West 31st Street, New York, NY 10001, for a catalog of their publications.

Setting Up Shop by Randy Baca Smith. 1982. McGraw Hill, 1221 Avenue of the Americas, New York, NY 10020.

This book is delightful to read. It is clever and witty. The book covers nothing new (though there is some very useful information here), but it is one of the only business books I've ever actually enjoyed reading. Some of the chapters: Are You Sure You Want To Do This ("It never ceases to amaze me how many small business owners will decide what they are going to do and where they are going to do it without even a passing glance at the marketplace"); Everybody Wants To Run A Restaurant ("It ranks No. 5 in the 10 worst small business ventures according to a poll conducted by Money magazine"); Fancy Phones & Other Costly Mistakes ("If you are getting the feeling that most of the people who say that they want to help you are really trying to help themselves to a chunk of whatever working capital you may possess, you're right. High on the list of these helpful folks is your friendly Ma Bell service representative"); It's A Great Location But Don't Sign Anything Yet ("A good rule of thumb here is if the customer must find you, be easy to find."); and my favorite chapter title, KISS Record Keeping ("Keep It Simple, Stupid").

In Business For Yourself by Jerome Goldstein. 1982. Scribners, 597 Fifth Avenue, New York, NY 10017.

Jerome Goldstein is editor and publisher of *In Business* magazine (listed with the magazines in this section). This 169-page book is mostly reprinted from *In Business,* "capsule profiles" of actual small businesses. There is always a lot to be learned from others who have already gone down the small-business path. The book is easy, enjoyable reading.

"The new small business movement has nothing to do with national franchises in the fast food, car wash, dry cleaning, cosmetic, plastic dish or precious metal field. Forget about somebody else's get-rich-quick scheme and put yourself on a get-rich-slowly route that blends your talents, interests, and finances with the right market niche."

Freelance Forever by Marietta Whittlesey, 1982. Avon Books, 959 Eighth Avenue, New York, NY 10019.

This is a very unusual book. Its premise is, basically, that it's a tough life, and being a freelance artist is about the toughest life there is. If you are going to survive, you gotta learn (1) how to work around the system, and (2) how to make the system work for you—sometimes legally, sometimes not, sometimes ethically, sometimes not. Although the contents seems fairly typical—chapters include getting and using credit, suing people, work spaces, insurance, grants, collecting what's owed you, employees vs. non-employees, finding work, budgeting time, relationship problems ("work vs. love")—the author's viewpoint and her advice are anything but typical. More nitty-gritty, more from a poor person's standpoint, and (forgive me) more kind-of New York City. The author calls this book a "survival manual". That it is.

"It's important to note when people say to call back in two weeks, because if you bug them enough they will see you. They're putting you through a test: 'How many times can this person stick it out?' You don't want to be obnoxious, but you do have to be persistent."... "Computer Sabotage: An X-Acto knife is the perfect instrument for adding a few holes to computer punch cards. Your holes won't be noticed by humans, yet the computer will be confused, so your card will be spat back on the floor and have to be reprocessed by hand, which gives you a few days leeway."... "Credit cards are charge cards, but not in the way banks would have you believe. When you buy goods or services with a bank credit card, what you are actually doing is borrowing money from the bank—money which they pay to the merchant or purveyor of services. Unless you are able to pay off your bills at once, you should think of credit-card purchases as cash loans with interest. And since the banks are lending you depositors' money, they are far more interested about getting it back than corporations working with their own money. When you charge a purchase to an account with a merchant, if the merchandise proves shoddy you are in a better position to complain since your creditor is also the seller and you can withhold payment from him."

Several publishers have brought out series of small business management books, each book dealing with a specific area of business. John Wiley & Sons (650 Third Ave., New York, NY 10016) publishes a *Small Business Series* of reasonably priced paperback books, 110-120 pages each, and packed with good information. Amacom (American Management Association, 135 W. 50th St., New York, NY 10020) publishes dozens of hardback books on all aspects of business management.

Last, but a *long* way from least, is **The Small Business Sourcebook** (1983; published by Gale Research, Book Tower, Detroit, MI 48226), an amazingly comprehensive listing—796 pages, thousands of entries—of information resources for small business. Want to know the names, addresses and details about the trade associations, trade periodicals, trade shows, sources of supply, education programs and statistical studies for dry cleaning businesses? or hobby shops? or jewelry stores? or a hundred other businesses? Want resource information about over 300 federal, state and local government agencies? Want a state-by-state list of business consultants, educational institutions, venture capital firms? How about a run-down on 1,000 business books, directories and periodicals? It's all here. The book is expensive, but I know of no other single source with so much information.

Free and Almost-Free Management Assistance

The Small Business Administration publishes dozens of low cost publications. Several are reviewed in this section. Write the SBA, P.O. Box 30, Denver, CO 80201-0030 for their list of "Business Development Pamphlets." These lists are not complete, so if you are near an SBA office or a government bookstore, stop in and see what's available. Most of the SBA literature is well written and very useful.

I also mention several Bank of America publications in this section. If you would like a complete list of their small business publications, write Bank of America, Dept. 3120, Box 37000, San Francisco CA 94137. These publications are inexpensive and highly recommended.

The Federal Trade Commission publishes several free small business publications. For a list, write the FTC, Washington, DC 20580.

The U.S. Chamber of Commerce also puts out inexpensive small business publications. For their list, write Chamber of Commerce of the U.S., 1615 H Street NW, Washington, DC 20062.

Business and trade organizations are a valuable source of information and assistance. If you are unable to locate the organization for your particular business, you can get a copy of the **Directory of Business, Trade & Public Policy Organizations** from the Government Printing Office, Washington D.C. 20402.

Many states have small business assistance programs, offering free publications and counseling. Contact your state's Small Business Assistance Office or Small Business Development Center. If you cannot find the help you need, the Small Business Administration publishes a free directory of state offices and programs, **The States & Small Business: Programs & Activities.** Write SBA Office of Advocacy, 1726 I Street NW, Room 408, Washington, D.C. 20416.

The SBA also offers free one-on-one counseling to small businesses through their SCORE (Senior Corps of Retired Executives) and ACE (Active Corps of Executives) organizations. Contact any SBA office.

Help for women: The federal Interagency Commission on Women's Business Enterprise and the Small Business Administration's Office of Women in Business are both working to obtain more federal contracts for women-owned businesses, give women a larger share of SBA loans and provide education and counseling to women who are interested in starting their own businesses. Both agencies are located at the Office of Chief Counsel for Advocacy, U.S. Small Business Administration, Washington, D.C. 20416.

Help for minorities: The federal Minority Business Development Agency (MBDA) coordinates and oversees all federal efforts to assist minority business ventures. The MBDA, through its nationwide network of business assistance organizations, provides management and technical assistance to existing and potential new businesses owned or controlled by minorities. A directory of MBDA funded organizations is available from Minority Business Development Agency, U.S. Department of Commerce, Washington, D.C. 20230.

The very best advice you can get: Businessmen and businesswomen, I find, love to talk about business. Business is a large part of their lives, and they love to share their experiences and their ideas. You can't get better advice at any price; no accountant or lawyer or college professor knows half of what the person who's doing it every day knows. Strike up acquaintances, get to be friends with business people, find out about their local merchants organizations and attend their luncheons.

Lara Stonebraker, Cunningham's Coffee: "It's important to keep your merchandise rotating in the store, to constantly change the position of things. You'd be surprised how many people will say, 'Gee, you've got something new in,' when you know it's been sitting there for two years; you've just moved it from this shelf to that shelf. It has to be displayed in a coherent manner. You can't have pepper grinders next to coffee pots; you have to have all those things that are related together. And you have to give your customers an incredible selection of things. If you have espresso pots, you have to have them in nine sizes because people will not be inclined to buy if there is only a choice of two or three. Even if you stock only one of these odd-sized items that you know will not be selling, you still have to have it just to fill up your shelf, to give the impression that you have a huge variety. People will come to your store because they know you have a large selection. A lot of times I know that it's purely psychological, because I know that I will never sell a twelve-cup pot and I know that I will never sell a one-cup. But I have to have them there just for the comparison, just so that people will feel that this is a store that has everything, that has all the choices they can possibly get, that they don't need to go anywhere else for it. I've seen a lot of coffee stores make this mistake, having only two sizes of something. It just doesn't give you confidence in the store.

"I do rotating displays on the very expensive things every other week. I try to create the kind of display that will make customers stop and look, but not so much that the background will overpower the item. You can't have too many plants, you can't have something that will distract from your merchandise. And you can't have a no-don't-touch atmosphere. You don't want things looking too pretty because then people will be afraid to touch them, they'll feel inhibited. Most important of all, you can't have any bare walls. There was a place in San Francisco that opened and the woman just didn't have enough money to buy another cabinet, so she had one wall, the prime wall for display, just blank. Mr. Peet came in and said, 'Oh, that's a lovely wall; are you selling walls?' "

The best definition of an entrepreneur is someone who spends 16 hours a day working for himself so that he doesn't have to work 8 hours a day for someone else.

—Mark Stevens, "Profit Secrets For Small Business"

CRAFTS

Creative Cash: How To Sell Your Crafts, Needlework, Designs & Know-How by Barbara Brabec, 1979. Brabec Productions, P.O. Box 2137, Naperville, IL, 60566.

This 200-page book discusses many of the unique problems of and opportunities for selling crafts: selling through the mail; gift shop in the home; fairs; dealing with shops and galleries; specific markets for needlework; publicity; advertising and promotion; pricing; marketing; and a good deal more including an extensive crafts resource list.

Craft Resources is a free government publication that lists federal resources for crafts development, publications and national organizations that serve the crafts community. Copies are available from Agriculture Cooperative Service, Room 3405, Auditor's Building, 14th & Independence Avenues, SW, Washington, D.C. 20250.

HOME-BASED BUSINESSES

I'd guess that on every city block and on every rural road in the United States, someone is operating a business out of a home. Home-based businesses have their own unique problems and rewards. In addition to the publications listed below, several of the other books listed in this section discuss home businesses.

Home-Based Businesses by Beverly Neuer Feldman, 1983. Till Press, P.O. Box 27816, Los Angeles, CA 90027.

There is a little bit of everything in this chatty guide to starting and operating a business out of your home. Nothing is covered in depth, and the book sure could use some editing, but it is enjoyable to read and the first part of it is loaded with useful ideas, hints and valuable tips. More than one-third of the book, however, is a sometimes superficial list of ''new, exciting, creative business ideas''—including Closet Manager (''the closet manager decorates and organizes closets''), Sperm Donor, Surrogate Mother (''rent-a-womb'') and other sure-bet money makers. But I still like the book, and I think inexperienced people will find it worthwhile.

Entrepreneurial Mothers, by Phyllis Gillis, 1984. Rawson Associates, 597 Fifth Ave., NYC 10017.

Entrepreneurial Mothers is a rare book in that it skillfully combines ''you can do it'' inspiration with common sense. Mothers looking to start a business have more considerations and obstacles to deal with — kids, family, lack of encouragement — and these issues permeate the text. But women in general, and men, too, will benefit from the well-considered advice. The book wisely suggests that you have some experience in your chosen field; and that you conduct some do-it-yourself market research to determine (1) if your business is needed in the community, and (2) if you are the person to do it. The information on taxes and legalities is often misleading and at times totally incorrect (a problem with most business books written by non-accountants), but this encompasses only a small part of an otherwise worthwhile and well-written book.

Home-based businesses are the main topic of discussion in **Sidelines Business Newsletter** (Box 351, Emmaus, PA 18049), put out by the editors of *In Business* magazine. Another useful little newsletter is **Barbara Brabec's National Home Business Report** (P.O. Box 2137, Naperville, IL, 60566).

MAIL ORDER

If you want to make an honest living in mail order you must first have a solid knowledge of the mail order market in general. Certain products naturally sell well in mail order and others do not. You must know how to locate your specific market, how and where to advertise, how to write ad copy. Mail order is an expensive way to sell: advertising budgets of successful mail order operators are often 50% of their income. The high expense of mail order means that your product must also be expensive to make the effort profitable.

If you are considering mail order, don't do anything until you read **How to Start and Operate a Mail Order Business** by Julian L. Simon. 1981. McGraw Hill, 1221 Avenue of the Americas, New York, NY 10020.

This 462-page book is an in-depth study of mail order, very well written and highly recommended.

"Use direct mail only if you expect to get at least $10 out of the average customer, including all future purchases—$25 may be a more sensible figure."

"Most classified advertisements offer free information to develop inquiries. Direct sales are seldom made from the classified ad. The reason is obvious: It is rare that you can tell enough about a product in ten words or twenty words so that the potential customer (1) wants the products, (2) understands what it is, and (3) knows how much it costs and where to order."

Two other good books are **Mail Order Moonlighting** and **Mail Order Know-How,** both by Cecil C. Hoge, Sr. (both published by Ten Speed Press, Box 7123, Berkeley, CA 94707). The Small Business Administration publishes a **Selling By Mail Order** "Small Business Bibliography" and a **Selling By Mail Order** "Starting Out Series" fact sheet. Order both from the SBA, Box 30, Denver, CO 80201-0030.

How To Build A Multi-Million Dollar Catalog Mail-Order Business By Someone Who Did, by Lawson Traphagen Hill. 1984. Spectrum Books, Prentice Hall, 1230 Avenue of the Americas, New York, NY 10020.

This is far and away the most thorough book I've seen on putting together a mail order catalog. If people don't look at your catalog, they won't even get the chance to consider your merchandise. What inspires someone to look at one mail order catalog and yet throw away another after the first glance? What convinces someone to place an order? What inspires the customer to buy "add on" merchandise at the same time? A lot has to do with the catalog itself: cover design, choice of illustrations, typeface, wording, guarantees, order form. The list is almost endless, but it's all covered here in great detail; and once you read it, it all makes perfect sense. Mr. Hill appears to have thought of everything.

EXPORTING

Export assistance and advice is available free from the U.S. Department of Commerce and from the Small Business Administration.

The Department of Commerce has foreign trade specialists who can assist you with international contacts. Write U.S. Department of Commerce, Washington, D.C. 20233.

Export management companies offer a range of services including credit, licensing, shipping and

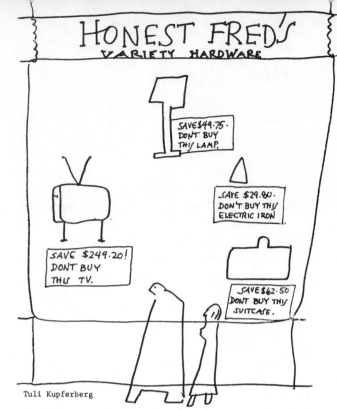

Tuli Kupferberg

advertising. For more information contact Agent/Distributor Service, Bureau of International Commerce, U.S. Department of Commerce, Washington, D.C. 20233.

Information about air and ocean transportation is available from the Federal Maritime Administration, Department of Commerce, Washington, D.C. 20230.

When overseas, contact the U.S. Embassy and Consular Officers who can provide you with reviews of local market conditions and leads to buyers. The Department of State publishes a booklet, **Key Offices of Foreign Service Posts.**

Export Marketing for Smaller Firms is an introductory guide put out by the SBA and available from the Government Printing Office, Washington, D.C. 20402. Another SBA pamphlet, **Market Overseas With U.S. Government Help,** is available from the Small Business Administration, P.O. Box 30, Denver, CO 80201-0030.

A Commerce Department publication, **Basic Guide to Exporting,** is available from the Government Printing Office, Washington, D.C. 20402.

The Department of Commerce publishes the **TOP Bulletin** (stands for Trade Opportunities Program), a weekly listing of up-to-date export trade leads developed and reported by over 200 U.S. embassies and counsular posts around the world. The Commerce Department claims that their bulletin is the best single source of export leads available. It's expensive but may be worth it if you're looking to expand your export market. For more information and a free sample copy, write U.S. Department of Commerce, Industry and Trade Administration, Trade Opportunities Program, Room 2323, Washington, D.C. 20230.

Manufacturers who import materials used to manufacture products that are later exported may be entitled to a refund of customs duties. For information, write the U.S. Customs Service, Washington, D.C. 20229.

FRANCHISE BUSINESS

A franchise is an individually owned business operated as though it was part of a large chain. Midas Muffler, Colonel Sanders, McDonalds and H&R Block are examples of well known national franchises. Under a franchise operation, services and products are standardized; trade marks, advertising and store appearance are uniform. Your own freedom and initiative are obviously limited. But a franchise gives you "instant recognition"—the goods and services of the franchisor are proven and well known.

For a fee, the supplier (the franchisor) gives you (the franchisee) the right to use the franchisor's name and sell his product or service. The franchise agreement may require you to purchase your supplies or equipment from the franchisor; you may have to pay the franchisor a percentage of your gross sales. Franchise agreements are usually lengthy and full of requirements you must adhere to.

Before signing any franchise agreement, investigate the franchise thoroughly. Have a lawyer review the contract with you and explain to you *exactly* what you're getting into.

The SBA's **Starting and Managing a Small Business of Your Own** (mentioned earlier) includes a brief but informative chapter on franchise businesses. The SBA also publishes a booklet called **Franchise Index/Profile**. It is a step-by-step evaluation process for franchise businesses. Both booklets can be purchased from the Superintendent of Documents, U.S. Government Printing Office, Washington, DC 20402.

Pilot Books, 103 Cooper Street, Babylon, NY 11702, publishes two excellent little books. **Franchise Investigation and Contract Negotiation,** by Harry Gross and Robert S. Levy, 1985, discusses contract provisions you may have to deal with: exclusive locations, bookkeeping stipulations, length and renewal of the franchise, pricing policy,

contributions towards advertising, purchasing and vendor restrictions on equipment and supplies and inventory. **Understanding Franchise Contracts,** by David C. Hjelmfelt, includes a sample franchise contract and disclosure statement.

There are several thick books that list names and addresses and detailed information for individual franchises. Some of these books are updated every year, so choose one that's current. Four that I have seen are **Franchise Opportunities Handbook**, published by the U.S. Department of Commerce and available from the U.S. Government Printing Office, Washington DC 20402; **Directory of Franchising Organizations,** published by Pilot Books, 103 Cooper Street, Babylon, NY 11702; **Franchise Opportunities,** published by Sterling Publishing, 2 Park Avenue, New York, NY 10016; **The Source Book of Franchise Opportunities,** by Robert E. Bond, published by Dow Jones Irwin, 1818 Ridge Road, Homewood, IL 60430.

If you want more information about a specific franchise — how reputable it is, how financially sound it is — write to the International Franchise Association, Inc., 1025 Connecticut Avenue, Washington, D.C. 20036. The IFA is a not-for-profit industry organization of franchisors; all members must subscribe to the Association's Code of Ethics and Ethical Advertising Code.

The Federal Trade Commission requires franchisors to give prospective franchisees—before any agreement is signed—detailed and accurate information on the earnings franchisees can reasonably expect, the costs they will incur, the company's history and financial standing and terms of the agreement. Gasoline companies and auto manufacturers are exempt from this law.

Other literature on the subject:

Franchise Business Opportunities. Federal Trade Commission, Washington, DC 20580.

Facts On Selecting A Franchise. National Better Business Bureau, 1515 Wilson Blvd., Arlington, VA 22209.

A lot of people sit in their living room and see something on TV and say, "I thought of that two years ago!" Well, thinking of it and doing it are two entirely different things.

—Dick Clark

MAGAZINES & PERIODICALS

Every general type of business has its own trade magazine, written for the business people in that particular trade. **Publishers Weekly, Womens Wear Daily, Advertising Age, National Fisherman, Whole Foods** are a few; the list is long. They are useful and, you'll probably find, essential publications. Columnist Nicholas Von Hoffman said, "Trade magazines can't lie because if they did, they'd be of no use to the trade." You can often locate your trade's magazine in a large library. If not, I again refer you to Gale Research's *The Small Business Sourcebook*, reviewed under "Managing Your Business".

Within the general category "business," there are hundreds of magazines and newsletters, fact sheets and tip sheets, bulletins and reports. Here is a guide to some of them:

Business Week (McGraw-Hill Building, 1221 Avenue of the Americas, New York, NY 10020) focuses mainly on the operations and the problems of large corporations, domestic and international: corporate mergers, executives moving from General Motors to Ford, conglomerates expanding and contracting, government's interaction with and regulation of the marketplace. Of all the big-business publications, I'd rank this one as the best.

If you want your business news five days a week, there is only one **Wall Street Journal** (Dow Jones & Co., 22 Cortlandt St., New York, NY 10007.) The inside of the paper is almost entirely big business, investment and stock market news. The front page has good feature articles about business and regular reports on taxes and government regulation. That much writing manages to cover most everything in business, sooner or later.

Forbes (60 Fifth Ave., New York, NY 10011) and **Fortune** (Time Inc., 541 N. Fairbanks Ct., Chicago, IL 60611) are both big-business feature magazines: gossip about famous executives and their famous corporations. Little or no nuts and bolts information here and absolutely nothing for small businesses.

In Business (Box 323, Emmaus, PA 18049) is a bimonthly magazine devoted entirely to small business. It includes feature articles and solid legal, tax, financial and management information. I write an occasional column for this magazine. It is my favorite of the small business magazines.

Inc. (38 Commercial Wharf, Boston, MA 02110) bills itself as the magazine for growing companies, which is an accurate description. It's slick and flashy but contains good, usable information for larger small businesses.

Venture: The Magazine for Entrepreneurs (35 West 45th Street, New York, NY 10036) is primarily a feature magazine. Most of its articles are about bold and speculative business ideas and about raising money, mostly via venture capital.

Commerce Clearing House (4025 W. Peterson Ave., Chicago, IL 60646) publishes a series of over 170 **Topical Law Reporters**: periodicals, most of them in loose leaf format, on federal and state taxes, insurance laws, labor relations and employment, pension planning, securities, and many other business and legal subjects. Most of these publications are technical, written for accountants and lawyers; but if you need detailed information on a specific area of business law, CCH is an excellent, reliable source. Write for a free copy of **A Handy CCH Checklist**, which lists all of their Law Reporters.

Prentice-Hall (Simon & Schuster, 1230 Avenue of the Americas, New York, NY 10020) is another respected publisher of loose leaf legal and business reports. One, **Executive Action Report,** is a non-technical newsletter for business owners and executives. Wide ranging, it covers management problems and employee relations as well as taxes and government regulations.

Be wary of the mail order business newsletters (and organizations) which promise—as most of them do—to (1) make you rich, (2) show you how to pay no taxes, (3) clue you in on the hottest new franchise, (4) tell you how you can pay half what everyone else has to pay for goods and sell them for twice what everyone else gets, or (5) all the above. These publications are for dreamers, more hype than help.

If any business periodical interests you, write for a sample copy. Most publishers will mail you a free issue on request.

FINANCES

The Seven Laws of Money by Michael Phillips. 1974. Random House/Word Wheel, 201 East 50th Street, New York, NY 10022

This classic book is over ten years old, yet it still sells a lot of copies. It is unique in its approach to finances. If money is a problem to you, if finances have got you down, *Seven Laws of Money* may just be the spark to pick you up.

"The First Law: Do It! Money Will Come When You Are Doing the Right Thing... The essential argument, plea, advice here is that if an idea is good enough, and the people involved want it badly enough, they'll begin to put their own personal energy and time into it, and the idea will soon be its own reward. Money itself cannot accomplish their goal; only the people themselves can accomplish it."

Six more laws: Money Has Its Own Rules; Money Is a Dream; Money Is a Nightmare; You Can Never Really Give Away Money; You Can Never Really Receive Money as a Gift; There Are Worlds Without Money.

"There are logical fallacies in all the Seven Laws. They cannot be arrived at by a 'logical' process. The Seven Laws deal with a part of man that is outside the realm of the typical body of Western thought."

Michael is not joking. The laws work. Bankers don't know everything.

Starting On A Shoestring: Building A Business Without a Bankroll by Arnold S. Goldstein. 1984. John Wiley & Sons, 605 Third Avenue, New York, NY 10158.

I've known for a long time that starting a business with little or no money is not only possible, it happens all the time. I started two businesses that way; many of my tax clients were small businesses whose start-up capital bordered on zero. This book spells out how it's done better than any other I've seen. The book is equally useful for people who have a lot of money to start a business. Business success really has little to do with how much money you do or don't have. It has more to do with common sense and "market research", which is just a fancy term for "look before you leap." Mr. Goldstein knows what he's talking about, and he covers his subject well, with humor and wisdom.

"Most people think money is the number one priority in selecting a business. Put it on the bottom of your list. The psychic rewards—enjoyment—head the list. When you enjoy your business the success and money are bound to follow, but it never quite works in reverse. And if you happen to make serious money in a business you don't enjoy, I'll guarantee you'd make twice the money in a business—any business—that does get your adrenalin flowing."

"If you don't have the experience in the type of business you have in mind, then don't try to open it just yet. Defer it until you can obtain valuable hands-on experience as an employee. You may have to moonlight to pick up the experience or sacrifice some income for a few months but it will be a much smaller loss than what you will sustain by operating a business you know nothing about."

AMACOM (135 West 50th Street, New York, NY 10020) publishes a good, 184-page book, **Financial Management for Small Business.**

Past Due: How To Collect Money by Norman King. 1983. Facts On File Publishing, 460 Park Avenue South, New York NY 10016.

Dealing with creditors who don't pay their bills is, for me, the most difficult aspect of business. If you read my "Credit Sales" chapter, you know that my only advice is "good luck". This little book, subtitled "An essential primer on the theory, psychology and practice of collecting what's owed you", offers a good deal of advice. It pigeonholes different types of creditors—the good, fair and poor risks; the "seasonal delinquents"; the "disaster victims"; etc.—and how to deal with each. It explains different ways to set up collections systems, including sample collection letters. If you have collection problems, this book is worth reading.

"Although the average creditor may think the primary purpose of a collection letter is specifically aimed at getting money owed, the *real* purpose is somewhat different. It is to collect the money, but at the same time to keep the customer's good will."
"The creditor should always remember that even a deadbeat is a human being. A courteous, tactful attitude will always collect more money than anger or intemperance—so long as the attitude is backed up with firmness and patience."
"Promptness and regularity are inseparable. A quick first reminder not followed up immediately in the allotted time with a second reminder, becomes meaningless. The debtor tends to forget a lone reminder. No customer minds being jogged every so often, particularly if the reminder is regular, prompt and courteous."

Bank of America (Dept. 3120, Box 37000, San Francisco, CA 94137) publishes two pamphlets, **Financing Small Business** and **Cash Flow/Cash Management**

Many states make loans to small businesses. Write your state's Small Business Assistance Office, Office of Business Services, Department of Economic Development, or whatever they call it. For a listing of all state programs, write for a copy of the SBA's **The States & Small Business: Programs & Activities** (SBA Office of Advocacy, 1725 I Street NW, Room 408, Washington DC 20416).

PARTNERSHIPS

A comprehensive book specifically about partnerships is **The Partnership Book** by Denis Clifford and Ralph Warner (1981. Nolo Press, 950 Parker Street, Berkeley, CA 94710). Clifford and Warner are attorneys, partners (not in the same business) and experienced authors, and they have included in their 290-page book just about everything there is to know about partnerships. The book covers partnership agreements in detail.

"A partnership cannot legally hold itself out to be a corporation. This means that you can't use Inc., Ltd., Corporation, Incorporated or Foundation after your name. However, terms that don't directly apply that you are incorporated, such as Company (Co.), Associates, Affiliates, Group and Organization are normally okay. As far as titles the partners take for themselves go, you are legally free to let your imagination run loose. You can call yourselves partners, managing partners, or Dukes or Barons for that matter. Denis's law firm has but three partners, all of whom are 'senior partners'."
"A partner can loan, lease or rent property to the partnership. Loaning (etc.) property to a partnership can be particularly appropriate where one partner possesses an item that the partnership wants to use, for example, a valuable set of antique restaurant furniture, but does not want to donate it to the partnership and it's too expensive for the partnership to buy."
"Outgoing partners remain personally liable for all debts of the partnership incurred up to the time they leave. An incoming partner may or may not assume personal responsibility for those debts. Either way, this doesn't release the leaving partner from potential liability to existing creditors. If all the partners (including the new one) are broke, creditors of the old partnership can still come after the departed partner."

Tax Information on Partnerships (Publication #541) is free from any IRS office.

LEGAL

Legal advice is expensive. Lawyers charge high fees to pass on the legal information they have researched, studied and assimilated.

If you have the time and inclination, you can do your own legal research. Law schools and county, state and federal courthouses usually have extensive law libraries that are open to the public. Public and university libraries and city courthouses also have basic if not complete sets of law books. Law firms (if you are friends with a lawyer who will let you sit there and read) have their own libraries of legal books; the larger the firm, the bigger the library.

A good book to read is **Legal Research: How to Find and Understand the Law** by Stephen Elias (1982. Nolo Press, 950 Parker Street, Berkeley, CA 94710).

The Small Business Legal Problem Solver by Arnold Goldstein. 270 pages, 1983. CBI Publishing, 7625 Empire Drive, Florence, KY 41042.

173 questions and answers on just about every aspect of business law: contracts, loan agreements, employment rules, leases, bank accounts, advertising, insurance, taxes, collections, bankruptcy, liability, franchises and quite a bit more:

What are the advantages of incorporating in Delaware? Should we buy the building in our own names or have it owned by our corporation? We own a fast food operation and plan on opening two additional units; do you suggest using the same corporation? What are the advantages and disadvantages of a factoring arrangement? What specific questions are illegal to ask on an employment application? What essential points should we consider for a sales agent agreement? Can we legally restrict our distributors from carrying a competitor's line? Are we legally obligated to continue buying supplies from our franchisor?

Every business owner probably has a slew of legal questions. I'd guess that, regardless of the business you are in, several of your questions are answered (or at least partially answered) in this book. The answers are brief, concise and easy to understand.

Anyone can make mistakes, and usually does.
—Parkinson's Law.

INCOME TAXES

Latest Revision For:

1040 Individual Income Tax Return
1985
Department of the Treasury—Internal Revenue Service

Income — Please attach Copy B of your Forms W–2 here.

Your social security number

1. How much money did you make last year? . . . . ▶

2. Send it in . . . . ▶

There are several well known, commercially prepared tax guides for individuals and small businesses. But the best all around tax guidebooks I have seen are the free ones put out by the Internal Revenue Service. **Tax Guide for Small Businesses,** IRS Publication No. 334, is a well written and comprehensive book covering every aspect of small business tax law. Sole proprietorships, partnerships and corporations are discussed; employment and excise taxes are also covered. The *Tax Guide* is revised every year and is available from any IRS office. Everybody in business should get a copy of this publication.

The IRS publishes dozens of other free tax books and pamphlets. For a complete list of IRS publications and other IRS help, request a copy of Publication No. 910, **Taxpayer's Guide to IRS Information and Assistance.**

A warning about IRS help: Although IRS publications are usually accurate and reliable, the same cannot always be said of tax information the IRS gives out over the phone or in person. The IRS people do, on occasion, give out totally incorrect information. Tax laws are vastly complicated and even the experts make mistakes. Do not rely on verbal information unless you can verify it. Ask the IRS person for a reference in their *Tax Guide* or in one of their other publications, and look it up.

Two useful tax newsletters I've seen (and used) are **Tax Update For Business Owners** (81 Montgomery Street, Scarsdale, NY 10583) and **Tax Hotline** (500 Fifth Avenue, New York, NY 10110). *Tax Update,* a monthly publication, runs about 16 pages and typically includes lengthy articles on Keogh plans, fighting the IRS, fringe benefits, family members as employees and other typical tax-saving strategies. Since tax laws don't change all that often, much of the "update" is often "rehash", clarifying or explaining laws already on the books. *Tax Hotline* runs about 8 pages each month. It covers much of the same territory as *Tax Update*, but its articles are usually brief, one or two paragraphs. Both newsletters are well written and easy to understand.

BUYING AND SELLING A BUSINESS

Buying a business is often a lot more difficult than starting one from scratch and can be fraught with tax and legal complications. In some ways, however, a person who buys a going business has an advantage over one who starts his own because he has more facts to work with—*if* he knows where to find them and how to use them.

Buying and Selling a Small Business. Published by the Small Business Administration. Available from the U.S. Government Printing Office, Washington, D.C. 20402.

Some of the information in this book is a rehash of general "getting started" information—though it never hurts to read it a second or even a third time—and some of the accounting and tax terminology is confusing and occasionally incorrect. Most of the book, however, is filled with good, practical buy-sell knowledge. Chapters include Sources of Market, Financial, and Legal Information; Determining the Value of a Business; Negotiating the Buy-Sell contract; Financing and Implementing the Transaction; Analyzing the Market Position of the Company; and more.

"There are two basic methods of determining the value of a business. The first is based on expectations of future profits and return on investment. This method is preferable by far. It forces the buyer and seller to give at least minimum attention to such factors as trends in sales and profits, capitalized value of the business, and expectancy of return on investment.

"The second method is based on the appraised value of the assets at the time of negotiation. It assumes that these assets will continue to be used in the business. This method gives little consideration to the future of the business. It determines asset values only as they relate to the present. It is the more commonly used, not because it is more reliable, but because it is easier. The projections needed to value the business on the basis of future profits are difficult to make."

How to Buy or Sell a Business is one of the Bank of America *Small Business Reporter* series. Write

Bank of America, Dept. 3120, Box 37000, San Francisco, CA 94137.

DO-IT-YOURSELF CORPORATIONS

Several books on the market tell you how to set up your own corporation, usually without a lawyer and very inexpensively. Most of these books suggest you incorporate in Delaware—even though you may be living and working in another state—because the Delaware corporation rules are easy to meet and the fees are minimal. What the books usually do not tell you is that every state has a different set of rules for corporations. Many states regulate and tax corporations doing business in the state regardless of where the businesses are "officially" incorporated. Generally, you will find it advantageous to incorporate in your own state.

The Small Business Administration publishes a leaflet, **Incorporating a Small Business.** For a copy, write the SBA, P.O. Box 30, Denver, CO 80201-0030.

Do-it-yourselfers in California, New York and Texas can obtain an excellent step-by-step book that will show you how to set up a small corporation yourself: **How To Form Your Own California (or New York, or Texas) Corporation,** by Anthony Mancuoso (Nolo Press, 950 Parker Street, Berkeley, CA 94710). Each book includes full instructions how to incorporate a new or already existing business. The books come complete with all tear-out forms necessary including articles, bylaws and stock certificates.

COMPUTERS

There are several *thousand* computer books on the market now. Among the most common are beginner's guides with general information applicable to all small computers. If you know nothing about computers, a good guide of this type is worthwhile reading. There are also books about specific computers, specific computer languages, specific programs, specific applications, and various combinations of all of these.

Computer books present a problem. Not all of them are good, not all of them are accurate. It is difficult to judge if a given book provides accurate, up to date and useful information unless you can test it thoroughly in a real computer application, which, for most of us, is impractical if not impossible. Here are a few guidelines:

1. Has the book been recommended by someone you know who actually uses it?

2. Who wrote it? Does the author own a small business, or is the author a small-business accountant? I wouldn't trust an author who does not have real experience in small business, no matter how great a computer expert he may be.

3. How old is the book? The technology is moving fast. A book that is a year or two old may be out of date. Check the copyright.

4. While you are checking the copyright, see what printing the book is in (the information is usually on the same page as the copyright). A book in its third or fourth printing is telling you not only that a lot of people buy this book, but that any typographical errors in the first printing are probably corrected. If the book includes specific programming instructions, typographical errors could be disasterous.

5. Regarding typographical errors, computer instructions that have been printed directly from a computer print-out (called a "dump") are much less likely to have typos than if the information has been typeset (copied from the computer printout by the typesetter). Some books will state that the computer instructions are a direct "dump". Sometimes you can tell by looking at the typeface.

Here is some help: Stewart Brand and friends, creators of the *Whole Earth Catalog*, publish the **Whole Earth Software Catalog** (27 Gate Five Road, Sausalito, CA 94965). This fat book critiques not just software but hardware and publications as well.

SUE THE BUM

Taking a nonpaying customer to court is often more expensive and more of hassle than it's worth. If the claim is small, however, it's fairly easy to handle the lawsuit yourself in Small Claims Court, a place where decisions are made cheaply, quickly and with the participation of the disputing parties.

Small claims procedures are established by state law, which means there are 50 sets of small claims rules (of course). For example, "small"—the maximum amount you can claim—is $600 in Michigan, $2,000 in Indiana, $10,000 in Tennessee. Some states require you to sue where the defendent lives; some allow you to sue where the contract was signed—important details if you're in New York and your deadbeat customer is in California.

Help is here. **Everybody's Guide to Small Claims Court** by Ralph Warner (Nolo Press, 950 Parker Street, Berkeley, CA 94710) is an excellent book, well written, and includes legal information for all fifty states.

"I ask all of you who are thinking of filing a Small Claims suit to focus on a very simple question—can you collect if you win? Collecting from many individuals or businesses isn't a problem as they are solvent and will routinely pay any judgements entered against them. But there are many ways for a debtor to protect himself. A creditor can't take the food from the debtor's table, or the T.V. from his living room, or even the car from his driveway. Substantial debtor protection laws exist everywhere."

"Corporations are legal people. This means that you can sue and enforce a judgement against a corporation itself. You should not sue the owners of the corporations or its officers or managers as individuals unless you have a personal claim against them that is separate from their role as part of the corporation. In most situations the real people who run or operate the corporation aren't themselves liable to pay for the corporation's debts."

And maybe you won't have to sue the bum. Two SBA pamphlets, **Credits and Collections** and **Outwitting Bad Check Passers**, are available from the Small Business Administration, P.O. Box 30, Denver, CO 80201-0030.

TRADEMARKS, PATENTS & COPYRIGHTS

A **trademark** is a word, a name, a symbol or logo, or some combination of these adopted and used by a business to identify its goods and distinguish them from goods manufactured or sold by others.

Your primary right to a trademark is acquired by creating and using it. That's the first step. Then, you can acquire exclusive legal rights to your trademark by registering it with the United States Patent and Trademark Office. To be eligible for federal registration, your trademark must be in use in interstate commerce: you must be doing business across state lines or your product must cross state lines in the normal course of business.

The federal government charges a basic fee of $175 to register a trademark. The initial registration remains in force for 20 years and may be renewed every 20 years.

For more details, request a copy of **General Information Concerning Trademarks** from the Patent & Trademark Office, U.S. Department of Commerce, Washington, D.C. 20231.

A **patent** is a grant issued by the federal government giving an inventor the exclusive right to make, use and sell her invention in the United States. A patent may be granted to the inventor or discoverer of any new and useful process, machine, design or composition of matter, or any new and useful improvement of such. A patent will not be granted on a useless device (the government's definition of useless, not mine), on printed matter, on a method of doing business, on an improvement in a device which would be obvious to a skilled person or on a machine that will not operate. The government says it never has and never will issue a patent on a perpetual motion machine.

A patent will not be granted if the invention was in public use or on sale in the country for more than a year prior to filing your patent application. Also, an inventor is not entitled to a patent if the invention has been described in a publication more than a year before the patent application was filed.

Applying for and obtaining a patent is a lengthy and highly complex proceeding and usually requires help from a patent attorney or agent. Only attorneys and agents registered with the Patent & Trademark Office may handle patent applications. The U.S. Government Printing Office (Washington, D.C. 20402) sells a booklet, **Attorneys and Agents Registered to Practice Before the U.S. Patent and Trademark Office**, which contains an alphabetical and geographical list of people on the Patent and Trademark Register.

Patents are expensive. The basic filing fee is $65. When the patent is granted, you must pay an additional "issue fee" of $100. The government may also charge fees for printing and claims work. The attorney's or agent's fees will run in the hundreds (and sometimes thousands) of dollars.

A patent is good for 17 years and may not be renewed or extended. Anyone has free right to use an invention covered by an expired patent.

Write the Patent & Trademark Office for copies of **Questions & Answers About Patents, General Information Concerning Patents** and **Patents & Inventions: An Information Aid for Inventors.**

A **copyright** protects the writings of an author, illustrator or composer against copying. Literary, dramatic, musical and artistic works can be protected by copyright. The owner of a copyright has exclusive rights to print, reprint and copy the work; to sell or distribute copies of the work; to dramatize, record or translate the work; and to perform the work publicly.

Writing and illustrations and tunes can be copyrighted. Ideas and concepts cannot, nor can names and titles, nor can *things*. A description of a machine could be copyrighted as a writing, but this would not prevent others from writing a description of their own or from making and using the machine.

In the United States, a copyright is first obtained by printing the copyright notice—the word "copyright," the year and your name—on the face or on the title page of the work. Publicly distributing your work without this copyright notice automatically puts the work in "public domain": you've permanently lost your exclusive rights to it. The next step is to register your work with the U.S. Copyright Office. You fill out a simple form, pay a $10 fee and send them two copies of the work. The copyright is good for your lifetime plus 50 years; it's not renewable.

For more copyright information, write the Register of Copyrights, Library of Congress, Washington, D.C. 20540.

LEDGERS

Once the ledger section in *Small Time Operator* is used up, messed up (told you not to use ink!) or discarded as too complicated/too simple, you'll find the selection of commercially available ledgers plentiful and diverse. All varieties of prepackaged bookkeeping systems are available in most stationery stores.

You can also purchase a loose leaf binder and pads of ledger paper in any stationery store and have yourself a very inexpensive set of books. Ledger sheets come in sizes from 8½ x 11 inches to as large as 14 x 34 inches and from 2 columns on up to 30 columns. The more well known brand names are Wilson Jones, Standard (Boorum and Pease) and Eye Ease (National Blank Book Co.)

Ledgers get a lot of use and abuse. The loose leaf ledgers do not hold up well, the pages tear out easily and the ledgers are often awkward to work with. If you can afford a higher quality ledger, purchase a heavy duty cam-lock post binder and heavy duty ledger sheets. By the way, thrift stores are great places to find old (and excellent quality) ledger binders. I found two in a Salvation Army store, complete with unused sheets, for $1.50 each.

SAVE YOUR BUSINESS

Business Turnaround Strategies by Arnold S. Goldstein. 1983. Enterprise Publishing, 725 Market Street, Wilmington DE 19801.

"Getting into business is relatively easy. Staying in business is another matter. It's not crime to fail in business, but too many people quit while there remains a good chance they could pull their companies out of a nosedive."

"These people aren't looking for their first million. They don't want inspirational pep talks about building castles in the air or how to magically go from rags to riches. They face the more mundane problems of the real business world, and they need concrete plans to fend off creditors, stop checks from bouncing, and survive in the twilight world of no cash, no credit, dwindling assets and skyrocketing debts."

If your business is in trouble, you just might be able to rescue yourself with the sound, practical advice in this book. If your business is doing just fine thank you, this book will help keep it that way. Even businesses just getting started will benefit from the book's easy-to-understand suggestions. Mr. Goldstein, an excellent writer with over a dozen small business books to his credit, is a bankruptcy attorney who specializes in bailing out floundering businesses. "Have you had any flashing thoughts lately of grabbing the first plane to Mexico and starting anew driving a cab?" Instead, try *Business Turnaround Strategies*.

CENSUS DATA

If you want to do some serious market research without spending a lot of money—where are the people you're trying to reach? What businesses are already out there and how are they doing? What is the most effective advertising?—you can get help from the United States Bureau of the Census. The Bureau of the Census gathers and publishes statistics about the population and the businesses in the U.S.

The **Census of Population** and the **Census of Housing** provide information about sex, race, number of persons in a household; number and types of rooms, water availability, method of house heating; availability of telephones, presence of clothes washer, dryer, television, radio, air conditioner; number of automobiles; and other items. The **Census of Business** presents data such as sales size of establishments, employment size of establishments, and sales by merchandise lines. In addition, the Bureau of the Census, for a fee, will tabulate special data to meet a company's individual needs.

THE SMALL TIME OPERATOR UPDATE SHEET

State and federal tax laws, Social Security rates, Federal Trade Commission regulations, federal requirements for employers, Small Business Administration loan information, and similar government rules change all the time. Most of the laws that do change, particularly tax laws, usually become effective January 1 of the new year.

Every January, I prepare a one-page **Update Sheet for *Small Time Operator***. The *Update Sheet* lists changes in tax laws and other government regulations, referenced to the corresponding pages in the book.

If you would like a copy of the *Update Sheet*, send a self-addressed, stamped No. 10 envelope and $1.00 to Bell Springs Publishing, Box 640, Laytonville, CA 95454.

With the *Update Sheet*, you can keep your edition of *Small Time Operator* up to date, year after year.

"Small-scale operations, no matter how numerous, are always less likely to be harmful to the natural environment than large-scale ones, simply because their individual force is small in relation to the recuperative forces of nature. There is wisdom in smallness if only on account of the smallness and patchiness of human knowledge, which relies on experiment far more than on understanding. The greatest danger invariably arises from the ruthless application, on a vast scale, of partial knowledge such as we are currently witnessing in the application of nuclear energy, of the new chemistry in agriculture, of transportation technology, and countless other things."

Every person starting a business should consider along with profits, percentages and mark-ups, whether his or her actions are going to help or to damage this precious dwindling resource called Earth. E.F. Schumacher's book **Small Is Beautiful**, subtitled "Economics as if People Mattered," is an excellent history of what our blind race towards technology has done and is still doing to the world and its inhabitants and how we, as business people, can reverse the destructive process. Schumacher's philosophy comes on like a spring breeze in a muggy world of gross national product and quantity-not-quality. *Small Is Beautiful* is beautiful.

"It is, moreover, obvious that men organized in small units will take better care of *their* bit of land or other natural resources than anonymous companies or megalomanic governments which pretend to themselves that the whole universe is their legitimate quarry."

Even in our shaky economy, with giant corporations getting more and more of the consumer's dollars and with chain stores driving independents out of business, small businesses can and do survive and thrive. Small businesses attentive to local and neighborhood needs and small businesses attentive to customers' personal needs will always have an edge over large, faceless corporations. This is particularly true of service businesses where "the personal touch" is still very important.

Small business owners themselves can help foster this environment by patronizing other small businesses. We can purchase our food from local farmers markets and co-ops instead of huge supermarkets. We can buy locally made clothing and toys and furniture. We can patronize locally owned restaurants instead of national chains. We can have a competent local mechanic rebuild our car and truck engines instead of buying the latest piece of junk from Detroit or Japan.

But we small business people, all of us, have a much greater problem. The future of small business is tied directly to the future of this planet and its inhabitants. If corporations continue to pollute the earth with toxic chemicals, if logging companies continue to clear-cut forests, if agribusiness continues its chemical and erosion destruction of our farmlands, if the nuclear industry continues its mad fumbling with a technology it obviously does not understand and cannot control, we may not have a future worth talking about. And unless we can stop the lunatics in Washington from building more nuclear bombs, we may not have any future at all.

When we try to pick out anything by itself, we find it hitched to everything else in the universe.

—John Muir

Section Six

THE LEDGERS

INCOME LEDGER Month of _____

1	2	3	4	5	6	7
DATE	SALES PERIOD	TAXABLE SALES	SALES TAX	NON-TAXABLE SALES		TOTAL SALES
1						
2						
3						
4						
5						
6						
7						
8						
9						
10						
11						
12						
13						
14						
15						
16						
17						
18						
19						
20						
21						
22						
23						
24						
25						
26						
27						
28						
29						
30						
31						
	TOTALS FOR MONTH					

INCOME LEDGER Month of ———————

1 DATE	2 SALES PERIOD	3 TAXABLE SALES	4 SALES TAX	5 NON-TAXABLE SALES	6	7 TOTAL SALES
1						
2						
3						
4						
5						
6						
7						
8						
9						
10						
11						
12						
13						
14						
15						
16						
17						
18						
19						
20						
21						
22						
23						
24						
25						
26						
27						
28						
29						
30						
31						
	TOTALS FOR MONTH					

INCOME LEDGER Month of _____

1	2	3	4	5	6	7
DATE	SALES PERIOD	TAXABLE SALES	SALES TAX	NON-TAXABLE SALES		TOTAL SALES
1						
2						
3						
4						
5						
6						
7						
8						
9						
10						
11						
12						
13						
14						
15						
16						
17						
18						
19						
20						
21						
22						
23						
24						
25						
26						
27						
28						
29						
30						
31						
	TOTALS FOR MONTH					

INCOME LEDGER Month of ———————————

1	2	3	4	5	6	7
DATE	SALES PERIOD	TAXABLE SALES	SALES TAX	NON-TAXABLE SALES		TOTAL SALES
1						
2						
3						
4						
5						
6						
7						
8						
9						
10						
11						
12						
13						
14						
15						
16						
17						
18						
19						
20						
21						
22						
23						
24						
25						
26						
27						
28						
29						
30						
31						
	TOTALS FOR MONTH					

INCOME LEDGER Month of _____

1	2	3	4	5	6	7
DATE	SALES PERIOD	TAXABLE SALES	SALES TAX	NON-TAXABLE SALES		TOTAL SALES
1						
2						
3						
4						
5						
6						
7						
8						
9						
10						
11						
12						
13						
14						
15						
16						
17						
18						
19						
20						
21						
22						
23						
24						
25						
26						
27						
28						
29						
30						
31						
	TOTALS FOR MONTH					

INCOME LEDGER Month of ——————

1 DATE	2 SALES PERIOD	3 TAXABLE SALES	4 SALES TAX	5 6 NON-TAXABLE SALES	7 TOTAL SALES
1					
2					
3					
4					
5					
6					
7					
8					
9					
10					
11					
12					
13					
14					
15					
16					
17					
18					
19					
20					
21					
22					
23					
24					
25					
26					
27					
28					
29					
30					
31					
	TOTALS FOR MONTH				

INCOME LEDGER Month of _____

1	2	3	4	5	6	7
DATE	SALES PERIOD	TAXABLE SALES	SALES TAX	NON-TAXABLE SALES		TOTAL SALES
1						
2						
3						
4						
5						
6						
7						
8						
9						
10						
11						
12						
13						
14						
15						
16						
17						
18						
19						
20						
21						
22						
23						
24						
25						
26						
27						
28						
29						
30						
31						
	TOTALS FOR MONTH					

INCOME LEDGER Month of ⎯⎯⎯⎯⎯⎯

1	2	3	4	5	6	7
DATE	SALES PERIOD	TAXABLE SALES	SALES TAX	NON-TAXABLE SALES		TOTAL SALES
1						
2						
3						
4						
5						
6						
7						
8						
9						
10						
11						
12						
13						
14						
15						
16						
17						
18						
19						
20						
21						
22						
23						
24						
25						
26						
27						
28						
29						
30						
31						
	TOTALS FOR MONTH					

INCOME LEDGER Month of ———————

1	2	3	4	5	6	7
DATE	SALES PERIOD	TAXABLE SALES	SALES TAX	NON-TAXABLE SALES		TOTAL SALES
1						
2						
3						
4						
5						
6						
7						
8						
9						
10						
11						
12						
13						
14						
15						
16						
17						
18						
19						
20						
21						
22						
23						
24						
25						
26						
27						
28						
29						
30						
31						
	TOTALS FOR MONTH					

INCOME LEDGER Month of _____

1 DATE	2 SALES PERIOD	3 TAXABLE SALES	4 SALES TAX	5 NON-TAXABLE SALES	6	7 TOTAL SALES
1						
2						
3						
4						
5						
6						
7						
8						
9						
10						
11						
12						
13						
14						
15						
16						
17						
18						
19						
20						
21						
22						
23						
24						
25						
26						
27						
28						
29						
30						
31						
	TOTALS FOR MONTH					

INCOME LEDGER Month of _____

1 DATE	2 SALES PERIOD	3 TAXABLE SALES	4 SALES TAX	5 NON-TAXABLE SALES	6	7 TOTAL SALES
1						
2						
3						
4						
5						
6						
7						
8						
9						
10						
11						
12						
13						
14						
15						
16						
17						
18						
19						
20						
21						
22						
23						
24						
25						
26						
27						
28						
29						
30						
31						
	TOTALS FOR MONTH					

INCOME LEDGER Month of _____

1 DATE	2 SALES PERIOD	3 TAXABLE SALES	4 SALES TAX	5 NON-TAXABLE SALES	6	7 TOTAL SALES
1						
2						
3						
4						
5						
6						
7						
8						
9						
10						
11						
12						
13						
14						
15						
16						
17						
18						
19						
20						
21						
22						
23						
24						
25						
26						
27						
28						
29						
30						
31						
	TOTALS FOR MONTH					

INCOME LEDGER — Year-End Summary

1	2	3	4	5	6	7
	TOTALS FOR MONTH OF	TAXABLE SALES	SALES TAX	NON-TAXABLE SALES		TOTAL SALES
	January					
	February					
	March					
	April					
	May					
	June					
	July					
	August					
	September					
	October					
	November					
	December					
	TOTAL FOR YEAR					

CREDIT LEDGER

1 SALE DATE	2 CUSTOMER	3 INV. NO.	4 TOTAL SALE AMOUNT	5 DATE PAID	6 MEMO

EXPENDITURE LEDGER

DATE	CHECK NO.	PAYEE	TOTAL	1 MDSE. & MAT'LS.	2 SUPPLIES, POSTAGE, ETC.	3 LABOR NON-EMPL.

4	5	6	7	8	9	10	11
EMPLOYEE PAYROLL	ADVERTISING	RENT	UTILITIES	TAXES & LICENSES		MISC.	NON-DEDUCT.

EXPENDITURE LEDGER

DATE	CHECK NO.	PAYEE	TOTAL	1 MDSE. & MAT'LS.	2 SUPPLIES, POSTAGE, ETC.	3 LABOR NON-EMPL.

4	5	6	7	8	9	10	11
EMPLOYEE PAYROLL	ADVERTISING	RENT	UTILITIES	TAXES & LICENSES		MISC.	NON-DEDUCT.

EXPENDITURE LEDGER

DATE	CHECK NO.	PAYEE	TOTAL	1 MDSE. & MAT'LS.	2 SUPPLIES, POSTAGE, ETC.	3 LABOR NON-EMPL.

4	5	6	7	8	9	10	11
EMPLOYEE PAYROLL	ADVERTISING	RENT	UTILITIES	TAXES & LICENSES		MISC.	NON-DEDUCT.

EXPENDITURE LEDGER

DATE	CHECK NO.	PAYEE	TOTAL	MDSE. & MAT'LS.	SUPPLIES, POSTAGE, ETC.	LABOR NON-EMPL.
				1	2	3

4	5	6	7	8	9	10	11
EMPLOYEE PAYROLL	ADVERTISING	RENT	UTILITIES	TAXES & LICENSES		MISC.	NON-DEDUCT.

EXPENDITURE LEDGER

DATE	CHECK NO.	PAYEE	TOTAL	1 MDSE. & MAT'LS.	2 SUPPLIES, POSTAGE, ETC.	3 LABOR NON-EMPL.

4	5	6	7	8	9	10	11
EMPLOYEE PAYROLL	ADVERTISING	RENT	UTILITIES	TAXES & LICENSES		MISC.	NON-DEDUCT.

EXPENDITURE LEDGER

DATE	CHECK NO.	PAYEE	TOTAL	1 MDSE. & MAT'LS.	2 SUPPLIES, POSTAGE, ETC.	3 LABOR NON-EMPL.

EXPENDITURE LEDGER

4	5	6	7	8	9	10	11
EMPLOYEE PAYROLL	ADVERTISING	RENT	UTILITIES	TAXES & LICENSES		MISC.	NON-DEDUCT.

EXPENDITURE LEDGER

DATE	CHECK NO.	PAYEE	TOTAL	1 MDSE. & MAT'LS.	2 SUPPLIES, POSTAGE, ETC.	3 LABOR NON-EMPL.

EXPENDITURE LEDGER

4	5	6	7	8	9	10	11
EMPLOYEE PAYROLL	ADVERTISING	RENT	UTILITIES	TAXES & LICENSES		MISC.	NON-DEDUCT.

EXPENDITURE LEDGER

DATE	CHECK NO.	PAYEE	TOTAL	1 MDSE. & MAT'LS.	2 SUPPLIES, POSTAGE, ETC.	3 LABOR NON-EMPL.

4	5	6	7	8	9	10	11
EMPLOYEE PAYROLL	ADVERTISING	RENT	UTILITIES	TAXES & LICENSES		MISC.	NON-DEDUCT.

EXPENDITURE LEDGER

DATE	CHECK NO.	PAYEE	TOTAL	1 MDSE. & MAT'LS.	2 SUPPLIES, POSTAGE, ETC.	3 LABOR NON-EMPL.

4	5	6	7	8	9	10	11
EMPLOYEE PAYROLL	ADVERTISING	RENT	UTILITIES	TAXES & LICENSES		MISC.	NON-DEDUCT.

EXPENDITURE LEDGER

DATE	CHECK NO.	PAYEE	TOTAL	MDSE. & MAT'LS. (1)	SUPPLIES, POSTAGE, ETC. (2)	LABOR NON-EMPL. (3)

4	5	6	7	8	9	10	11
EMPLOYEE PAYROLL	ADVERTISING	RENT	UTILITIES	TAXES & LICENSES		MISC.	NON-DEDUCT.

EXPENDITURE LEDGER

DATE	CHECK NO.	PAYEE	TOTAL	1 MDSE. & MAT'LS.	2 SUPPLIES, POSTAGE, ETC.	3 LABOR NON-EMPL.

4	5	6	7	8	9	10	11
EMPLOYEE PAYROLL	ADVERTISING	RENT	UTILITIES	TAXES & LICENSES		MISC.	NON-DEDUCT.

EXPENDITURE LEDGER

DATE	CHECK NO.	PAYEE	TOTAL	1 MDSE. & MAT'LS.	2 SUPPLIES, POSTAGE, ETC.	3 LABOR NON-EMPL.

4	5	6	7	8	9	10	11
EMPLOYEE PAYROLL	ADVERTISING	RENT	UTILITIES	TAXES & LICENSES		MISC.	NON-DEDUCT.

YEAR-END EXPENDITURE SUMMARY

			TOTAL	1 MDSE. & MAT'LS.	2 SUPPLIES, POSTAGE, ETC.	3 LABOR NON-EMPL.
		January total				
		February total				
		March total				
		April total				
		May total				
		June total				
		July total				
		August total				
		September total				
		October total				
		November total				
		December total				
		Unpaid bills (Acct's. Payable):				
		TOTALS FOR YEAR				
		ADDITIONAL EXPENSES:				
		Return Checks (from your "Bad Debts" folder)				
		Uncollectible Accounts (from your "Bad Debts" folder)				
		Auto expense (if you take the standard mileage rate) Mileage for year _____				
		Depreciation (from Depreciation Worksheet—Col 11, 13, 15 or 17)				

4	5	6	7	8	9	10	11
EMPLOYEE PAYROLL	ADVERTISING	RENT	UTILITIES	TAXES & LICENSES		MISC.	NON-DEDUCT.

EQUIPMENT LEDGER AND DEPRECIATION WORKSHEETS

1	2	3	4	5	6	7	8	9
DATE	DESCRIPTION	METH.	WRITE OFF PERIOD	NEW OR USED	%	COST	REDUCTION FOR INV. CREDIT	WRITE OFF

10	11	12	13	14	15	16	17	18
BAL. TO BE DEPR.	DEPR. 19___	BAL. TO BE DEPR.	DEPR. 19___	BAL. TO BE DEPR.	DEPR. 19___	BAL. TO BE DEPR.	DEPR. 19___	BAL. TO BE DEPR.

PAYROLL LEDGER

Name _____

Address _____

_____

_____

Social Security _____

Pay Rate _____

1	2	3	HOURS		6	7	8	9	OTHER WITHHOLDING			13
PAYCHECK DATE	CHECK NO.	PAY PERIOD	REG	O/T	GROSS	F.I.T.	F.I.C.A.	STATE INCOME	10	11	12	NET PAY
			4	5								